IRON FROM THE DEEP

IRON FROM THE DEEP

The Discovery and Recovery of the USS Monitor

Robert E. Sheridan

Naval Institute Press
Annapolis, Maryland

Naval Institute Press
291 Wood Road
Annapolis, MD 21402

Library of Congress Cataloging-in-Publication Data
Sheridan, Robert E., 1940–
Iron from the deep : the discovery and recovery of the USS Monitor / Robert E. Sheridan.
p. cm.
Includes bibliographical references and index.
ISBN 1-55750-413-X (alk. paper)
1. Monitor (Ironclad) 2. Shipwrecks—North Carolina—Hatteras, Cape. 3. Hatteras, Cape (N.C.)—Antiquities. 4. Underwater archaeology—North Carolina—Hatteras, Cape. 5. Excavations (Archaeology)—North Carolina—Hatteras, Cape. I. Title.
E595.M7S54 2003
973.7'58—dc21
2003013482

Printed in the United States of America on acid-free paper ♾

11 10 09 08 07 06 05 04 9 8 7 6 5 4 3 2

First printing

This book is dedicated to the late John Newton and his family. Without his leadership of the discovery cruise, and his invitation to me to join in the effort to discover the *Monitor* wreck, there would be little for me to write. His personal dedication and sacrifice in his founding of the Monitor Research and Recovery Foundation led to today's status in the recovery of the wreck's major artifacts.

This book is also dedicated to my wife, Karen, and our three children, Jennifer, David, and Steven, who put up with my absences for nearly six hundred days while I was at sea on research cruises, and for many more days of absence while I was away at professional meetings of one kind or another. I appreciate their love and support.

Contents

Preface and Acknowledgments

My own fascination with the *Monitor*, a unique warship, began more than fifty years ago. As a boy, I was always interested in the Civil War, partly because my parents reminded my brother and me that we qualified for membership in the Sons of the Union, an organization for descendants of Civil War veterans. My great grandfather, James Joseph Sheridan, had emigrated from County Meath, Ireland, shortly before he enlisted in the Union Army in 1861. He served in Company K of the Third New Jersey Infantry Regiment, under the command of Col. George W. Taylor. The Third Regiment was part of the New Jersey First Brigade under the command of Gen. Philip Kearny. My great grandfather lived with my father's family from 1880 until he died in 1893. Born in 1885, my father knew his grandfather and recalled many Civil War discussions. My father transmitted his awareness of the war to his own children on many occasions.

My interest in the Civil War, beginning at age eight or nine, was furthered by stories in "Battlefield" comic books, and eventually by history books. The Civil War was the first war to be extensively documented with photographs, and the pictures in history books fascinated me. It became clear, with the photographs of the increased armament and military innovations during the Civil War, that this war was the first "modern" war. One of the modern innovations happened to be the *Monitor*.

For some reason I was struck with the photographs of the *Monitor*. I was so fascinated that I constructed a number of toy Monitors out of cut plywood decks, using empty tuna fish cans that I glued onto the decks. I played for hours with my Monitors and my toy Civil War soldiers. I believed the *Monitor*-class ships were awesome and effective ships of war. Little did I realize that fifty years later I would be on the decks of the salvage ships recovering the *Monitor*'s iron from the deep.

This book describes my involvement in the discovery of the wreck and recovery of artifacts. By penning my eyewitness recollections and verifying facts from primary contemporary records, such as letters, memos, proposals, cruise reports, and published articles, I hope to provide the reader with a more complete history of the discovery and recovery of the *Monitor* than has yet been written. Conversations are paraphrased; the wording is based solely on my perceptions, best recollections, and awareness of how the individuals spoke.

By interspersing in the narrative my personal "sea stories" of struggles to carry out research in stormy seas, similar to those that sank the *Monitor*, readers will sense the challenge of ocean exploration. The vastness of the ocean makes the search for sunken objects extremely challenging. In the ocean, even an object the size of the *Monitor* is considered small. In fact, the *Monitor* is about the same size as the research vessels used during the search. Good maneuvering of the search vessel and good use of the available navigation tools were essential.

Even with the best use of state-of-the-art technology, and with the best efforts of skilled and trained scientists and crews, luck plays a role. Discovery of the *Monitor* defied all odds. The area off Cape Hatteras is called "The Graveyard of the Atlantic" because there are numerous sunken ships there. The search for the *Monitor* wreck was often likened to "searching for a needle in a haystack." Indeed, prior to our discovery, several misidentifications of other wrecks as the *Monitor* had occurred.

Cooperation between individual researchers, engineers, historians, archaeologists, and divers was essential. Many behind the scenes interactions with government agencies supervising the wreck site are recounted. Conducting research on and development of the *Monitor* site demonstrate classic cases of science by committee and government by bureaucracy. The work within the committee and bureaucracy structure resulted in personality clashes, schisms, and fissures between the participants, not unlike conflicts experienced in other areas of research, including scientific ocean exploration. During presentations on the *Monitor*, I was often asked, "Why has it taken so long to do something with the wreck?" This book will help to answer that question.

The status of the *Monitor* recovery efforts and plans for future recovery of parts of the wreck are discussed. Clearly, the government agencies involved with the *Monitor* now understand the need for urgent actions. The *Monitor* is a very important vessel in the history of the U.S. Navy. It deserves preservation for posterity.

I want to thank all the people who rendered valuable assistance to me while I was writing this book. Charlotte Holland of the Rutgers Department of Geological Sciences spent many hours at the word processor producing the various different drafts of the book. Delores Daley, the secretary of the Department of Geological Sciences, maintained the paper supplies and kept the photocopier going. James Browning of the Rutgers Department of Geological Sciences helped with the computer drafting. Bruce Kaplan and Alison Kaplan of Snapshots Photography in Clinton, New Jersey, assisted in converting my color slides into the black-and-white prints used in the book. My wife Karen, the librarian of the *Hunterdon County Democrat* newspaper, found some 1862 Civil War reports on the battle at Hampton Roads. She also provided me access to her great grandfather's Civil War diary, which includes the entry that describes when he saw the *Monitor.* Many who assisted me in the laboratory and at sea at the *Monitor* wreck site are named in the text. I sincerely apologize to any individuals whose names I forgot to mention. I am grateful to everyone who has contributed to the discovery and recovery of the *Monitor.* I know every reader of this book and every visitor to related websites or museums thanks you also. I greatly appreciate the editorial assistance of my wife Karen and Barbara Johnson.

IRON FROM THE DEEP

1

Ericsson's Struggles

No story about the Union ironclad ship, the *Monitor,* can be told without first discussing John Ericsson. Rather than being an inspirational conception, the *Monitor* evolved in Ericsson's mind from facts he amassed during his extensive career producing engineering innovations, including several military weapons and other types of ships. As in other scientific pursuits in the nineteenth century, the engineering knowledge base was limited. Scientists and engineers had broad interests and a great diversity of experience and skills. They were far removed from the narrow specialists typical in today's technical fields. Ericsson's interest in naval warships expanded as a natural part of his vocation as a professional engineer.

Born in Sweden in 1803 (Peterkin 1981a, 12; Mindell 2000, 33), Ericsson developed an early interest in technology. His father was involved in mine construction and encouraged his engineering drawing skills. Even as a teenager, Ericsson provided drawings for a major canal project in Sweden and worked on the project as a surveyor (Hoehling 1976, 16).

Ericsson entered military service, as did many young Swedish men. Considered a well respected professional pursuit in the nineteenth century, the military offered the opportunity for technical training not available elsewhere. First as a cadet in the mechanical corps of the Swedish navy, and later as an officer in the army artillery (Peterkin 1981a, 12; Mindell 2000, 34; Hoehling 1976, 16), Ericsson furthered his training and experience as an engineer. His interest in ships and propulsion stayed with him throughout his career. His artillery experience provided knowledge of the capabilities of cannons and ammunition.

When he was twenty-one, Ericsson took a leave from the Swedish army and moved to London (Hoehling 1976, 16; Peterkin 1981a, 12). He wished to expand his engineering experience and demonstrate the caloric hot-air engine that he had developed. Although his engine was unsuccessful, he began a productive ten year association with English engineer John Braithwaite.

After resigning from the Swedish army with the rank of captain in 1826 (Peterkin 1981a, 12), Ericsson continued his engineering career in England. He patented many mundane and pragmatic devices. His air compressors, condensers, refrigerators, steam fire engines, and pumps serviced towns, mines, breweries, and other growing businesses of the early nineteenth century (Hoehling 1976, 17).

The newest form of ground transportation, railroads, drew Ericsson's attention. The Liverpool and Manchester Railway offered a cash award for the best steam locomotive design in 1829. Although Ericsson's steam locomotive, the *Novelty*, reached speeds in excess of sixty miles per hour, an amazing feat for the time, Ericsson's locomotive was beaten in the competition by a slower but sturdier engine (Peterkin 1981a, 12). The *Novelty*'s high speed was a little frightening, and the public was still apprehensive about the new form of mechanical transportation that the railroads presented. Ericsson was ahead of his time with this invention, similar to his later work on the *Monitor*.

A few years later, Ericsson associated with two American entrepreneurs: Francis B. Ogden and a wealthy navy officer, Capt. Robert F. Stockton (Hoehling 1976, 18; Peterkin, 1981a, 12). Both men saw a future for marine steam propulsion. The steam propulsion of ships consisted of side wheel and stern paddle wheel systems. To Ericsson's military mind, and with his awareness of the increasing effectiveness of naval armaments and solid shots and explosive shells, the vulnerability of the side and stern wheeler steamers was clear. He realized that placing the propulsion system beneath the waterline would offer a great deal of protection from shot and shell, a concept he used later in his design of the *Monitor*.

Ericsson patented his rotary, or screw, propeller design in 1833. It provided ship's thrust below the water. He then built a twin-propeller steam tug for Ogden, named it the *Francis B. Ogden*, and used it to try and convince England's Royal Navy of the value of screw propellers (Peterkin 1981a, 12). Although he failed to win the approval of the Admiralty, he earned support from Stockton. Coming from a wealthy New Jersey family, Stockton was heavily involved in the development of canal and river transportation along the Delaware River and in the construction of New Jersey's railroads (Mindell 2000, 36). Stockton visualized the future use of propeller-driven steamers on rivers and, being a naval officer, appreciated the military applications of the screw propeller.

In 1838 Ericsson built for Stockton a small seventy foot, iron-hulled, twin-propeller ship called the *Robert F. Stockton* (Mindell 2000, 36; Hoehling 1976, 18). Within a year, the *Stockton* sailed from England to the United States. Transatlantic steamships were rare, so the publicity about the *Stockton*'s trip created an American awareness of Ericsson's prowess as a naval engineer. Business contacts and associations formed through Stockton drew Ericsson to the United States in 1839. Stockton's initial attempt to convince the U.S. Navy to build a large propeller-driven frigate of Ericsson's design was unsuccessful (Peterkin 1981a, 12). In 1840–41, Ericsson found employment at the Phoenix Iron Works in New York City, where years later the *Monitor* would be built.

Stockton finally succeeded in his proposals to the navy to build a large propeller-driven frigate. In 1841, through Stockton's sponsorship, the navy contracted Ericsson to build a steam warship called the *Princeton* (Mindell 2000, 36). This was Ericsson's major contribution to naval construction from 1841 to 1844. In a practice to be followed later in the rapid construction of the *Monitor*, Ericsson supervised the subcontractors' manufacturing of the parts for the *Princeton*. The hull was constructed in Philadelphia while the engine was built in New York City (Hoehling 1976, 20). Many aspects of the iron-hulled *Princeton* were later repeated in the *Monitor*, including a multiple-bladed screw propeller, a direct-drive engine, and engine room blowers. Many of Ericsson's innovations were submarine to protect these essential propulsion systems from shot and shell (Hoehling 1976, 20; Peterkin 1981a, 13).

The *Princeton*'s armament included two 12-inch cannons, which were the largest guns placed in naval vessels at that time (Hoehling 1976, 20). One of the 12-inch guns was designed by Ericsson and built in England. He called it the "Oregon," because of the early 1840s territorial question between the United States and England about ownership of the Oregon area (Mindell 2000, 36). Ericsson favored the United States in that dispute. A heavy cannon of wrought iron, the Oregon featured a breech reinforced with belts of iron rings that strengthened the gun against the lateral pressures on ignition (Hoehling 1976, 20). Shot from the cannon could penetrate four inches of iron plate or fifty-seven inches of oak (Peterkin 1981a, 13). A contractor, following Stockton's specifications, built the *Princeton*'s second 12-inch gun. Called the "Peacemaker," it did not have iron rings reinforcing the breech (Hoehling 1976, 20).

Ericsson and Stockton successfully demonstrated the screw propulsion system in the *Princeton*. In 1843, the *Princeton*'s maneuverability and speed were greater than the existing paddle wheelers (Peterkin 1981a, 13). Unfortunately, the Peacemaker damned the *Princeton* project when a demonstration of the *Princeton*'s capabilities to President John Tyler and his cabinet members led to disaster in 1844. The Peacemaker exploded, killing Secretary of State Abel P. Upshur and Secretary of the Navy Thomas W. Gilmer. President Tyler was providentially spared because he was below decks (Mindell 2000, 37).

Stockton was not held accountable for the accident, possibly because he was a naval officer and President Tyler's friend (Peterkin 1981a, 13). Ericsson felt the navy unfairly blamed him for the Peacemaker's failure. He was never paid the more than ten thousand dollars that the navy owed him for his work (Hoehling 1976, 21), and he received no more government contracts. Although Ericsson was naturally embittered toward the U.S. Navy and the U.S. government in general, he obviously was impressed enough with other aspects of the country to become a U.S. citizen in 1848 (Peterkin 1981a, 13).

In the 1850s Ericsson again worked productively with the Phoenix Iron Works in New York City. He built the *Ericsson*, a 260 foot ship, to demonstrate the marine use of his caloric engine in 1854 (Mindell 2000, 37). Unfortunately, it sank within the year in a storm off the New Jersey coast (Hoehling 1976, 21). During this time frame Ericsson communicated with potential investors about his idea of a "sub-aquatic" ship with a movable battery system, which had many features later used on the *Monitor* (Peterkin 1981a, 14). Ericsson submitted his concept to Emperor Napoleon III during France's war with Russia in 1854. Napoleon never responded to Ericsson about the sub-aquatic war vessel (Mindell 2000, 38). Later, no documentation was found to substantiate Ericsson's claim, so arguments arose during and after the U.S. Civil War about who actually invented the movable battery turret.

Unknown to Ericsson, another inventor, Theodore Ruggles Timby, had conceived of a rotating multiple-gun turret or castle for harbor defense in 1841. He filed a written notice, or caveat, to establish claim on his invention with the U.S. Patent Office. The caveat mentioned a revolving metallic turret for use on land or water, so naval use was included (Farr 1997, 34). Ericsson indicated that he had thought about his concept of what would eventually become the *Monitor* as early as 1826, which was prior to Timby's inspiration (Peterkin 1981a, 13). Ericsson's financial partners in building the *Monitor* were apparently aware of Timby's patent, because they reached a financial settlement with Timby for the *Monitor*-class ships they built. The U.S. Navy, however, never officially recognized Timby's claim and did not award him any financial compensation on later *Monitor*-class ships built by other companies. Ericsson's ego made him resist any sharing of the credit for inventing the *Monitor*, and his publicity after the war prevailed. As late as 1907, the Federal Court of Claims decided that Timby did not warrant financial compensation or credit for inventing the *Monitor* (Farr 1997, 36).

Ericsson continued his engineering pursuits in association with Harry Delamater of the Phoenix Iron Works until Civil War hostilities began in April 1861. On 7 August the Navy Department sent out requests for proposals for the construction of ironclad warships (Peterkin 1981a, 14). The U.S. Navy was poorly disposed, with less than one hundred vessels; less than one quarter of the fleet was steam powered (Mindell 2000, 26). No navy warships were ironclad. Moreover, the knowledge that the Confederates in Norfolk were constructing an ironclad warship from the hull of the sunken USS *Merrimack* gave much urgency to the call for Union ironclads.

Responding to the request for proposals, Ericsson dusted off his drawings and models of the sub-aquatic warship he had submitted to Napoleon III. On 29 August 1861 he sent a letter to President Abraham Lincoln outlining his proposal to construct a ship that later became the *Monitor*: "Please look carefully at the enclosed plans and you will see that the means I propose to employ are simple... and so efficient too.... I have planned upward of 100 marine engines and... mechanical and naval structures of various kinds.... I have received a military education and feel at home with the science of artillery.... These statements... prove that you may safely entrust me with the work I propose" (Hoehling 1976, 42–43).

Ericsson was still wary of the U.S. Navy's criticism of him after the *Princeton* disaster, and he was defensive about what he considered unjust condemnation. He also realized that the navy would be extra-critical of any ironclad proposals that he might submit. Consequently, he stressed his background and capabilities in his letter to President Lincoln, hoping to avoid any early negative reaction from the navy. Unfortunately, Ericsson's plea to President Lincoln never made it through the bureaucratic channels for the president's consideration (Hoehling 1976, 44).

According to Secretary of the Navy Gideon Welles, a board of navy officers was appointed on 8 August 1861 to receive and evaluate ironclad warship plans that had to be submitted in the next twenty-five days. Called the Ironclad Board, its members were Commo. Joseph Smith, chief of the Bureau of Yards and Docks; Commo. Hiram Paulding; and Capt. Charles H. Davis (Welles 1996, 18). Appointed chairman of the Ironclad Board, Smith was mechanically minded and experienced. Moreover, he was a close friend of Secretary Welles and had his complete confidence. Seventeen proposals for ironclad warships were received by the board, including Ericsson's *Monitor* design.

Consideration of Ericsson's proposal, however, was fortuitously and indirectly brought before the Ironclad Board after 3 September 1861, which was the twenty-five day deadline for submission. This turned out to be a stroke of good fortune for Ericsson. Cornelius S. Bushnell had been given the go-ahead by the Ironclad Board to construct an ironclad warship, the *Galena*. By chance, Bushnell visited Ericsson around September 9 to have him evaluate the *Galena*'s stability. During the visit Ericsson showed Bushnell a model of his version of the sub-aquatic battery (Peterkin 1981a, 15). Ericsson impressed Bushnell with his description of his model warship and its "simple" efficiency, and stressed his ability to build the *Monitor* relatively rapidly (Hoehling 1976, 45).

Bushnell was so impressed with Ericsson's ideas that he took the *Monitor* model directly to Secretary Welles, who was in Hartford, Connecticut, preparing for his move to Washington, D.C. (Welles 1996, 18). Welles was so excited by the *Monitor* proposal that he acted immediately, in spite of the deadline of 3 September being past. Welles wrote, "I directed Mr. Bushnell to proceed immediately to Washington, and submit the model to the Board for examination and report. But, deeming the subject of great importance, and fearing the Board would be restrained by the limit of twenty-five days, I immediately followed, and arrived in Washington almost as soon as Mr. Bushnell with the model" (Welles 1996, 19).

After arriving in Washington, Bushnell contacted his two partners, John F. Winslow of the Albany Iron Works and John A. Griswold of the Rensselaer Iron Works. These capitalists had contracts to supply the plates for Bushnell's *Galena* (Mindell 2000, 39). Better still, Winslow and Griswold were friends with Secretary of State William Seward. Through Seward, the three men obtained an audience with President Lincoln on the evening of September 11. Sufficiently impressed with the *Monitor* model and concept, Lincoln requested a meeting with the Ironclad Board the next morning (Peterkin 1981a, 15).

Bushnell, Winslow, Griswold, and President Lincoln met with the Ironclad Board on September 12. The *Monitor* model and concept were met with some surprise as well as ridicule. The novelty, however, of this unique vessel became intriguing to all the conferees. Lincoln himself expressed interest, stating, "All I have to say is what the girl said when she stuck her foot into the stocking. It strikes me there's something in it!" (Hoehling 1976, 45).

Board discussion on the *Monitor* continued the next day. Two members, Smith and Paulding, liked the idea of the *Monitor* and were favorable to its construction (Peterkin 1981a, 15). Davis, however, was not satisfied; he said, "Take the little thing home and worship it, as it would not be idolatry because it was made in the image of nothing in the heaven above or the earth below or the waters under the earth" (Mindell 2000, 39).

With this rejection, Bushnell felt his presentation was not equaled to what could have been made by Ericsson himself. He remembered Ericsson's enthusiasm when he first described his own creation. Bushnell returned to New York City and met with Ericsson the next day. Bushnell cleverly did not speak of Davis's rejection. He advised Ericsson of the more favorable reactions, claiming that the board had some remaining technical questions that only Ericsson could answer. Bushnell requested that Ericsson meet with the board in Washington so it could finalize its consideration (Hoehling 1976, 45).

With some trepidation because of his treatment by the navy after the *Princeton* affair, Ericsson appeared before the board on 15 September. Ericsson was dismayed when he realized the board had actually rejected his proposal for the *Monitor*. Controlling his emotions, Ericsson inquired about the reason for rejection. He was informed of Davis's concern about the *Monitor*'s stability. Ericsson launched a vigorous rebuttal. His vast knowledge of naval architecture and engineering allowed him to address all the board's questions on many aspects of the vessel. At the end of the day Secretary Welles gave Ericsson his verbal approval to go ahead with construction (Mindell 2000, 40; Peterkin 1981a, 15).

The contract for the *Monitor* was signed on 4 October 1861. It stipulated:

> that she should be complete in all her parts and appurtenances; should have a speed of eight knots per hour, with security or successful working of the turret and guns, with safety to the vessel and the men in the turrets, and "that said vessel and equipments, in all respects, shall be completed and ready for sea in one hundred days from the date of this indenture." It was agreed by the Navy Department, that the government should pay therefore $275,000, in payments of $50,000, with the usual reservation of 25 percent as the work progressed, and that the final payment should be made after tests, satisfactory to the Navy Department, but which tests should be within ninety days after she was turned over to the Government (Welles 1996, 19).

Bushnell, Winslow, and Griswold, who had formed a financial partnership with Ericsson, co-signed the contract. Ericsson understood the necessity for the others' involvement—from the initial political access they facilitated to delivery of the iron plates for construction. Without his partners' contributions the hundred day stipulation on the contract could not be met.

Additionally, the "Battery Associates" subcontracted much of the work. For example, they signed a subcontract for building the hull and mounting the turret and armaments with Thomas Fitch Rowland of the Continental Iron Works of Greenpoint, New York. At Greenpoint, Rowland constructed a huge "ship-house" to cover the hull during construction. This was only one of many subcontracts used by Ericsson to achieve construction of the *Monitor* so rapidly. Other subcontractors included Winslow's Albany Iron Works of Troy, New York; Delamater Iron Works, Novelty Iron Works, and Holdane and Company, all of New York City; Clute Brothers Ironworks of Schenectady, New York; Niagara Steam Forge Company of Buffalo, New York; and Abbott and Son of Baltimore, Maryland (Peterkin 1981a, 16).

The *Monitor*'s construction was one of the first examples of the U.S. military-industrial complex. Construction involved the completion of parts of the vessel in different locations, each company relying on Ericsson's accurate drawings and plans to ensure that the puzzle would fit together when assembled at Continental Iron Works. For example, Albany Iron Works made most of the plates, Delamater Iron Works constructed the engines, and Novelty Iron Works built the turret (Peterkin 1981a, 17). This enormous and rapid undertaking was successfully achieved, proving the industrial capabilities and resources of the North during the Civil War. Although the Confederate leaders were probably aware of the North's military-industrial approach and the capacity of the North, nevertheless the South foolishly began the rebellion.

Iron ore for the plates, guns, and engines was sufficiently available in the New York City area. Magnetite mines in the New Jersey Highlands Province had been productive since before the Revolutionary War. Magnetite mines in the New York Adirondack Mountains supplied the Troy works. After the Civil War and the fame garnered by the *Monitor*, many of the mines bragged about being the mines that yielded the ore for the great ironclad.

The local wood resources for the construction of the *Monitor* were, in fact, more limited than the iron. Considerable wood was incorporated in the upper hull as part of the deck and armor belt (Peterkin 1981b, 43). The wood deck, deck beams, and backing of the side armor belts provided the major longitudinal strength element of the upper hull and a great deal of the buoyancy of the vessel.

In the New York–New Jersey area, extensive deforestation had occurred by the middle 1840s. Wood had been used to produce the coke for blast furnaces in the ironworks. Wood was used for building construction and home heating. The lack of forests was one of the main reasons for the railroad expansion in the 1840s and 1850s. The railroads brought coal from Pennsylvania to the existing ironworks in the New York–New Jersey area. Coal became the major fuel for the iron industry, and eventually for home heating.

Large stands of tall oak trees were rare in the New York–New Jersey area during the *Monitor*'s construction. Ericsson was forced to modify his plans for the *Monitor* to substitute white pine for the scarce white oak (Peterkin 1981a, 16). He wisely used the pine where stress was less, reserving the stronger oak for where the most strength was needed. For example, on the deck, two inches of wrought iron plates were laid on seven inch thick white pine planks that ran the length of the ship. The pine planks were supported underneath by ten inch by ten inch white oak beams laid athwartship. In the armor belts, five inches of wrought iron plates were backed by horizontal stacks of ten inch by ten inch white oak beams that had been backed by several inches of white pine blocks set vertically. The wooden planks, blocks, and beams were held together by long spikes and bolts, and the iron plates were riveted together in overlapping fashion and bolted to the wood (Peterkin 1981b, 43).

Many of the ten inch by ten inch oak beams in the construction of the upper hull were at least forty feet long. To mill these beams, oak trees of seventy or more feet in height had to be used. Only a few such stands of large oaks existed in the nearby New York–New Jersey area. Local lore from the Binghamton, New York, vicinity suggests that the large oaks northwest of the city were the source of the oak for the *Monitor*. In a locale today called Oakdale there were during the Civil War a working lumber mill, called Biglers Mill, and a stand of oaks. Residents during the Civil War recalled the long beams of oak, perhaps fifty feet in length being taken from the mill in specially built long wagons. The oak beams were transported to the Chenango River Canal, then by barge to the Erie Canal system, then to the Hudson River to New York City (Smith 1993, 1, 6).

Many residents erroneously thought the oak beams were for the "keel" of the *Monitor*. There was no keel to the lower hull of the *Monitor*, however. It was constructed completely of iron and suspended from the upper hull by fifty-five riveted angle iron frames. The *Monitor* had a single-chine, flat-bottomed lower hull. Without the standard, beamlike keel, the longitudinal strength of the hull comes from the upper deck and thick wooden part of the armor belts (Peterkin 1981b, 43). The strong wooden armor belts were even able to support the overturned deck of the *Monitor* at the wreck site as it was suspended from the turret to the pilothouse (Muga 1983, 7).

Construction of the *Monitor* began in earnest in the fall. Smith, chairman of the Ironclad Board, was Ericsson's main contact with the navy (Mindell 2000, 40). Smith dutifully questioned Ericsson on many construction aspects. Ericsson's responses defended his engineering calculations. The navy had naysayers who feared the *Monitor* would be another *Princeton* failure. At each point in construction, Ericsson justified his decisions, but he also made last-minute changes to ensure against possible failure.

One of Smith's main concerns was the approaching one hundred day deadline of 12 January 1862 for the fulfillment of the contract. This was the first time Ericsson had built a vessel so rapidly. Never before had such a large subcontracting scheme to get everything done been attempted. In addition, the navy's withholding of the final 25 percent payment until after successful testing gave Ericsson and his financial partners a great incentive to complete the construction and tests as rapidly as possible (Welles 1996, 19). Ericsson persisted despite the overwhelming logistical and engineering challenges.

The *Monitor* slipped down the ways with Ericsson on its deck on 30 January 1862 (Hoehling 1976, 69). The *Monitor* floated on the East River to the dismay of its naysayers, who had been calling the ship "Ericsson's Folly" (Davis 1975, 45). Some thought the heavy iron cladding would drag it straight to the bottom of the East River upon launching. Ericsson had completed the first step in defying his critics.

But there was still much to be done to complete the *Monitor*. Sea trials and tests of the guns were required. Armament, coal, ammunition, and ballast had to be installed to complete the weight of the vessel. To Ericsson's delight, the deck's eighteen inch freeboard with the standard load worked just as he had calculated (Peterkin 1981a, 18).

Sea trials in the East River on 25 February proved the steering mechanism inadequate. With ineffective steering, the *Monitor* meandered across the river and eventually crashed into a dock. The steering rope block and sheave were ineffectively arranged. Ericsson used an easy solution; he added another snatch block and chain (Peterkin 1981a, 19). On 3 March, successful sea trials were completed. A six knot speed was achieved. Outfitting of the *Monitor* was then completed and it was submitted to the navy.

Secretary of the Navy Gideon Welles wrote, "Unfortunately for the design of the Navy Department, and, perhaps, for the country, there was delay on the part of the contractors. Instead of completing and delivering the vessel as stipulated in one hundred days, which would have been in January, she was not turned over to the Government until the third of March—forty days later than was agreed upon and expected. This delay of forty days defeated an arrangement which the Navy Department originally designed, if successful, should be a satisfactory test of the capabilities of this extraordinary vessel" (Welles 1996, 19).

After the end of the Civil War, Welles also wrote, "The capitalists who were associated with Mr. Ericsson in the contract for the 'Monitor,' even though delinquent as to time, are entitled to great credit for what they

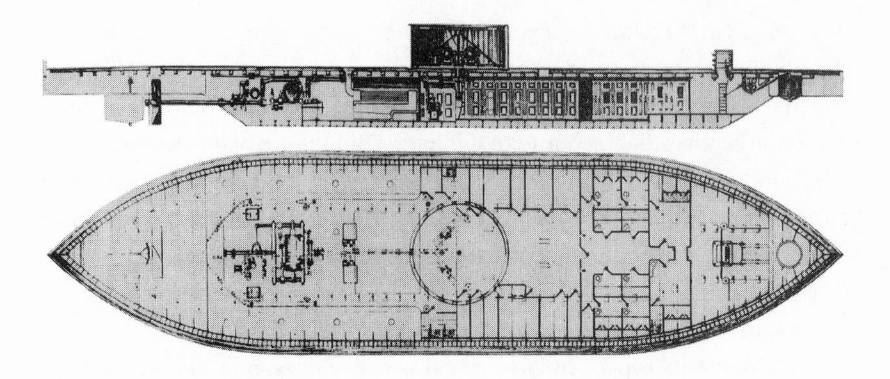

Transverse and plan views of the Union ironclad ship, the *Monitor*. These sketches, drawn in 1862 for Continental Iron Works of Greenpoint, New York, and on file with the New York Historical Society, are based on John Ericsson's 1862 builder plans.

Monitor National Marine Sanctuary. 1997. *Charting a New Course for the Monitor, Comprehensive, Long Range Preservation Plan with Options for Management, Stabilization, Preservation, Recovery, Conservation and Exhibition of Materials and Artifacts from the Monitor National Marine Sanctuary,* Draft. Newport News, Va.: U.S. Department of Commerce, National Oceanic and Atmospheric Administration, app., 46; NOAA Sanctuary and Reserves Division. 1992. *The Monitor National Marine Sanctuary Draft Revised Management Plan,* National Ocean Survey. Washington, D.C.: NOAA, Department of Commerce, 13; Watts, G. P. 1975. The Location and Identification of the Ironclad USS *Monitor, International Journal of Nautical Archaeology and Underwater Exploration* 4:302.

did, although, in addition to patriotic impulses, it was with them a business transaction, for which they claimed and received consideration in subsequent contracts" (Welles 1996, 20). He continued, "the 'Monitor' was one of the early, and, it may be said, one of the most prominent practical developments of what may be called the American idea evolved by our civil war, which has wrought a change in naval warfare" (Welles 1996, 20). Pride in Ericsson's immigrant Americanism was evident even then.

The *Monitor* was so unique in its design, so unlike the naval warships of the day—the classic wooden square-rigger ships-of-the-line with as many as fifty guns in fixed positions—that the *Monitor* was indeed a "change in naval warfare." It was 172 feet long and 42 feet wide. It had a flat ironclad deck mounted with a twenty-one foot diameter rotating turret armored with eight inches of iron plate and bearing two 11-inch caliber Dahlgren cannons. With a flat-bottomed, single-chine lower hull of only eleven foot draught, it was designed, as specified in the navy request for proposals, for blockade work in shallow estuaries and harbors. The upper hull overhung the lower hull by several feet, which gave the circular anchor well and the skeg, rudder, and propeller significant protection from shot, shell, and ramming. The five foot high pilothouse, heavily armored with five inches of iron plate over a wrought iron log casemate, was forward of the turret near the bow. A narrow eyeslit in the pilothouse gave the *Monitor*'s commander a view for steering the vessel. Innovations, like a horizontal side lever steam engine, removable smokestacks, forced-air ventilation, and indoor toilets, were marks of Ericsson's genius.

This novel fighting machine, this amazing new kind of warship, was not just another contract Ericsson was paid to fulfill. In his patriotism and love for his adopted country, he really wanted to produce the most effective warship possible to defeat the Confederate rebels who had dared to threaten the Union. Also, he wanted to warn and admonish potential interveners in the Civil War, such as England, by building an invincible craft. For this task of admonishing the Union's actual and potential enemies, Ericsson named his new vessel the *Monitor*, because he knew it would indeed monitor aggressive actions against the Union (Peterkin 1981a, 18).

2

Demise of Wooden Warships

The *Monitor* was one of the warships in the first battle between two ironclad ships on 9 March 1862 at the Battle of Hampton Roads. To better appreciate the significance of that battle, a short discussion of the *Monitor*'s opponent and the preceding day's actions is necessary.

Early in the Civil War it was clear to the Union that the Confederate ports must be blockaded. This strategy was important not only to prevent the flow of war matériel and arms to the Confederacy from foreign sources, but to prevent commerce and communication between the Confederacy and its potential allies.

The Confederates needed warships to break the blockade. Because of limited resources and limited industrial capabilities, the Confederates knew they had to build invulnerable ironclads to defeat the numerous Union wooden blockade ships (Still 1985, 10). As early as 1861, the Confederacy began funding the construction of ironclads.

Fortunately for the South, the hasty evacuation by Union forces from the Gosport Navy Yard in Norfolk, Virginia, on 21 April 1861 left the yard largely intact (Hoehling 1976, 35). Although scuttled and sunk at the dock, and burned to the waterline, there remained behind at Gosport the hull of the frigate USS *Merrimack*. Built in 1855, it was one of the Union's newest steam-powered ships-of-the-line. With the hull and engines still intact, the *Merrimack* offered the South an excellent opportunity to convert the hull into an ironclad warship. The hull was quickly pumped and refloated. By May the ship was at Gosport's dry-dock facility.

Secretary of the Confederate Navy Stephen R. Mallory was eager to take full advantage of the *Merrimack*'s hull and engines. Resources were committed to build what became a formidable ironclad warship. Conceived to be the major naval weapon of the South, the ironcladding and armament would make the ship invulnerable to enemy fire. Also, the ship would be able to destroy even the largest and newest Union ships-of-the-line.

Designed by Confederate naval engineer John M. Brooke, a barn-like ironclad superstructure, with sloping sides, was mounted on the *Merrimack*'s wooden hull. Sloping would make the glancing blows of enemy shot less effective (Miller 1981, 24; Wood 1956, 99). Consequently, the iron plating did not have to be as thick, an important consideration because the Confederates had limited foundry capacity. This barn-like superstructure became the standard design of all subsequent Confederate ironclads (Still 1985, 93). By July 1861 Mallory had approved Brooke's design and construction began (Hoehling 1976, 40).

Lt. John Taylor Wood, who served aboard the rebuilt *Merrimack*, described the construction in detail:

> On the midship section, 170 feet in length, was built at an angle of 45 degrees a roof of pitch-pine and oak 24 inches thick, extending from the waterline to a height over the gun-deck of 7 feet. Both ends of the shield were rounded so that the pivot-guns could be used as bow and stern chasers or quartering. Over the gun-deck was a light grating, making a promenade about twenty feet wide. The wood backing was covered with iron plates, rolled at Tredegar Works, two inches thick and eight wide. The first tier was put on horizontally, the second up and down—in all to the thickness of four inches, bolted through the wood-work and clinched. The prow was of cast iron, projecting four feet, and badly secured, as events proved. The rudder and propeller were entirely unprotected. The pilot house was forward of the smoke-stack, and covered with the same thickness of iron as the sides (Wood 1956, 98–99).

The armament on the rebuilt *Merrimack* consisted of a total of ten guns, including bow and stern pivot guns (two 7-inch rifles), two 6-inch rifles in fixed positions on each side, and six 9-inch smooth bores in fixed broadside positions, three on each side (Wood 1956, 99). With the ironcladding, the ram prow, and the guns, the *Merrimack* was a powerful new type of naval weapon, as was demonstrated on the first day of the Battle of Hampton Roads.

After construction, the rebuilt warship was commissioned the CSS *Virginia* on 17 February 1862 (Miller 1981, 26). However, the Northern press, Union naval officials, and, indeed, almost everyone in the North referred to this vessel as the *Merrimac.* The first battle between two ironclad ships at the Battle of Hampton Roads, therefore, has usually been described as the battle between the *Monitor* and the *Merrimac.* Use of the name *Merrimac,* instead of *Virginia,* appeared on everything from naval dispatches and *Harper's Weekly* magazine reports to Currier and Ives lithographs. While technically incorrect, the name *Merrimac* is used here as the name of the rebel ironclad.

Although the *Merrimac* was a powerful ship in terms of its armor and armaments, it was deficient in other areas. The original recovered engines were poor; they could not propel the heavy ship at a speed greater than five knots. Similar to the 1855 Union frigates *Minnesota* and *Roanoke, Merrimac*'s draught was twenty-two to twenty-three feet. Therefore, the *Merrimac* could navigate only in the deeper channels of Hampton Roads. With its rudder and engines, the *Merrimac* was as "unmanageable as a water-logged vessel" (Wood 1956, 100), and it took about thirty minutes to turn it full length (Miller 1981, 27), so maneuverability was limited. These deficiencies played a key role in the battle with the *Monitor.*

Despite these known deficiencies the *Merrimac,* under the command of Flag Officer Franklin Buchanan, departed Norfolk on Saturday morning 8 March 1862 and sailed into Hampton Roads to attack the wooden blockade fleet (Hoehling 1976, 95). The Union ships were stationed on the northern side of Hampton Roads from Newport News on the northwest to Fort Monroe on the southeast. The Union blockade line from the northwest to southeast included the *Cumberland* with thirty guns, the fifty-gun *Congress,* the frigates *Minnesota* and *Roanoke,* and the *St. Lawrence* (Miller 1981, 27, 31). The senior officer of the fleet at the time was Capt. John Marston on the *Roanoke.* According to Marston's report of the battle, "at 10 o'clock one of the lookout vessels reported by signal that the enemy was coming out. . . . The *Merrimac* went up and immediately attacked the *Congress* and the *Cumberland,* but particularly the latter ship" (Marston 1862, 1).

At about 1:40 P.M. in passing the *Congress* to get at the *Cumberland,* the *Merrimac* exchanged broadsides with the *Congress* (Wood 1956, 101). This very first action foretold the demise of wooden warships. The *Merrimac*'s broadside tore into the *Congress*'s gun deck, tearing it to shreds. Exploding metal, shrapnel, and large wooden splinter-stakes flew throughout the Union gunners, killing many and injuring more. It was devastating. In contrast, the *Congress*'s shots just glanced off the *Merrimac*'s ironclad casemate without causing any damage (Miller 1981, 27). The *Merrimac* proceeded past the *Congress* to attack the *Cumberland*.

At about three o'clock, the *Merrimac* steamed directly into the starboard side of the *Cumberland*. Its cast iron prow pierced through the wooden hull below the waterline. Immediately, the *Cumberland* began to sink. The *Merrimac* reversed engines to withdraw before being pulled down by its bow. During the withdrawal, the poorly secured cast iron prow ram was ripped off the *Merrimac*. The gunners on the sinking decks of the *Cumberland* fired broadside. This close-range fire shattered two of the 9-inch smoothbore cannons on the *Merrimac*, killing two gunners and riddling the *Merrimac*'s smokestack (Miller 1981, 28). The *Cumberland* listed to port, taking on water, and sank rapidly. "She went down with a roar, the colors still flying" (Wood 1956, 101). Casualties aboard the *Cumberland* included 121 dead and many wounded. Thus, the score of iron against wood was more than fifty-fold lopsided.

The *Merrimac* then turned on the *Congress*, which had grounded. For nearly an hour at a close range of 150 yards, the *Merrimac* poured shot and shell into the *Congress*, whose men fought valiantly but to no avail. Marston reported, "At ten minutes before four o'clock we had the mortification of seeing her [the *Congress*] haul down her flag" (Marston 1862, 1).

After the *Congress* surrendered, Buchanan climbed on the *Merrimac*'s promenade deck and ordered the smaller boats to take prisoners off the surrendered vessel. Union shore batteries and snipers began firing on the *Merrimac* and the smaller Confederate boats. Buchanan was wounded by a shot to his groin (Hoehling 1976, 123). Infuriated, Buchanan ordered the small Confederate boats away from the *Congress* and set the surrendered ship afire with hot shot. More than 125 hands from the *Congress* died.

At about 5 P.M. the *Merrimac* then began to attack the 50-gun *Minnesota*, which was also aground. Because of his wound, Buchanan transferred command of the *Merrimac* to Lt. Catsby Rogers Jones (Miller 1981, 28). For about an hour and a half, the *Merrimac* fired on the *Minnesota*, inflicting considerable damage. Fortunately for the *Minnesota*, Jones decided to withdraw to Norfolk because the tide was falling, he had little remaining shot and powder, and two of *Merrimac*'s guns had been destroyed. *Merrimac* had two dead and twenty-one wounded. The first day of the Battle of Hampton Roads thus ended.

Telegraph messages sped from Fortress Monroe to Washington, D.C. The results of the battle caused the expected reactions: sheer fear and panic. President Lincoln called an emergency cabinet meeting and demanded an appraisal from Secretary of the Navy Welles (Welles 1996, 23). The Union leaders feared that the next day the *Merrimac* would finish demolishing the remaining wooden Union blockade ships just as easily as it had destroyed the *Cumberland* and the *Congress*. Lincoln's cabinet even called the *Merrimac* a "monster." Secretary of War Edwin M. Stanton wanted to sink small boats, "Stanton's Navy," across the Potomac River to prevent the *Merrimac* from steaming up to Washington and destroying the Capitol. Welles assured the president that the *Merrimac*'s draught was too deep to reach Washington. He also was adamant that no blockage of the Potomac should be allowed because doing so would hinder troop movements. Lincoln accepted Welles's advice. Lincoln ordered that shore fortifications be prepared to protect Washington from the monster *Merrimac*, and New York City was notified to be prepared for an attack. The *Merrimac* was such an awesome naval weapon that the Union's major cities felt their safety was actually threatened (Welles 1996, 24–25).

Providentially, the *Monitor* had left New York City on 6 March 1862 under the tow of the tug *Seth Low* (Greene 1956, 112). After a storm-tossed voyage southward, the *Monitor* finally entered Hampton Roads on the evening of 8 March 1862, just missing the first day's battle action (Greene 1956, 113). The volunteer crew of the *Monitor* consisted of forty-seven enlisted men and ten officers under the command of Lt. John L. Worden (Hoehling 1975, 67; Miller 1981, 26). Worden had orders to leave New York and proceed up the Potomac to protect Washington from the expected attack by the *Merrimac* sometime in the near future. The events of 8 March, however, had altered all future plans for the *Monitor*.

Marston, aboard the *Roanoke* and in command of the Union blockade fleet at Hampton Roads, noted: "At 8 o'clock I heard that the *Monitor* had arrived and soon after [9 o'clock] Lieutenant Commanding Worden came aboard, and I immediately ordered him to go up to the *Minnesota* hoping she would be able to keep off an attack on the *Minnesota* till we had got him afloat again" (Marston 1862, 1). Later events proved that Marston acted correctly when he negated *Monitor*'s orders to proceed to Washington.

With little rest, the *Monitor*'s crew moved the ironclad to anchor beside the *Minnesota* at about 1:00 a.m. on Sunday 9 March (Miller 1981, 29). While aside the *Minnesota* an hour or so later, the crew of the *Monitor* heard an enormous explosion and saw the bright light of fireworks as the fires aboard the *Congress* finally reached the ship's magazines (Greene 1956, 113).

The next morning, as expected, the *Merrimac* came out at first light to finish off the *Minnesota*, which was still hard aground. At 8:00 A.M. firing on the approaching *Merrimac* began. The *Monitor* got under way with its commander, Lieutenant Worden, in the armored pilothouse and Lt. S. Dana Greene in command of the guns in the turret (Greene 1956, 114). With eight gunners working each of the two 11-inch Dahlgren cannons, and two others to work the stoppers, there were nineteen men in the turret. A pilot and helmsman were in the pilothouse with Worden. All other officers and crew were sub-aquatic, as Ericsson had planned when he designed the ship, and safe from shot and shell.

Worden steered directly toward the *Merrimac* in hopes of engaging the ironclad as far from the grounded *Minnesota* as possible (Greene 1956, 114). Marston's eyewitness report described the action:

> When within about a mile the ball was opened by the *Monitor* firing a shot, which struck the side of the iron-hided monster, the *Merrimac* at the same time slackening her speed. . . . [T]he *Monitor* began to move toward her antagonist, delivering her fire deliberately and with precision. The *Merrimac*, six times her size and with her armament equally out of proportion, awaited her at rest. At a distance of a quarter of a mile or less, both opened their terrible batteries—the *Merrimac* firing much the oftenness of course (Marston 1862, 1).

The presence of the *Monitor* was a rude awakening for the *Merrimac*'s crew, especially after the easy victories the day before. Firing was intense. "The *Monitor* was firing every seven or eight minutes, and nearly every shot struck" (Wood 1956, 102). The effect of the shots from the larger 11-inch Dahlgren cannons of the *Monitor* began to take their toll on the

Often reproduced lithograph of a drawing by artist J. O. Davidson depicting the battle between the *Monitor* and the *Merrimac* at the Battle of Hampton Roads on 9 March 1862. Note the vulnerable position of the pilothouse in the crossfire between the guns.

Greene, S. D. 1956. In the "Monitor" Turret, in *Battles and Leaders of the Civil War* (selections from original 1887–88 edition of R. U. Johnson and C. C. Buel), ed. N. Bradford. New York: New American Library, 111; Hoehling, A. A. 1976. *Thunder at Hampton Roads*. Englewood Cliffs, N.J.: Prentice Hall, Inc., 139; Newton, J. G. 1975. How We Found the *Monitor*, *National Geographic Magazine*, 60.

Merrimac; its plates dented inward and the smokestack was demolished. The little *Monitor* was more maneuverable. The deep-draught *Merrimac* began to run aground.

There were also difficulties aboard the *Monitor*. The turret's rotation was difficult to control. Greene tried to get a relative bearing on the *Merrimac*. He timed the opening of the gun ports and firing the guns even while the turret was rotating to reduce the length of time with opened gun ports and better protect the gunners. Greene also had to be careful to avoid firing into his own ship's pilothouse (Greene 1956, 115). On all later *Monitor*-class ships, the pilothouses were placed in a less vulnerable position atop the turrets.

"The two iron-clad combatants seemed to touch, fighting at close quarters, delivering their shots seemingly into the muzzles of each other's guns. . . . The *Monitor* moved around her, planting her shots where she could. . . . The contest was so hot that for a time the smoke obscured both the *Monitor* and the *Merrimac*." Marston's eyewitness report continued, "for more than an hour the battle was kept up without either side showing damage, when at about 11 A.M., the *Monitor* retired beyond the *Minnesota* to allow her guns to cool" and to bring more ammunition from below up to the turret. "The contest now raged between the *Merrimac* and the *Minnesota* and the gunboats. . . . The solid shots glanced in every direction from the *Merrimac*" (Marston 1862, 1).

When the *Monitor* returned to attack the *Merrimac* at close range the Southern crew was frustrated at its inability to inflict damage. The crew decided to concentrate on the pilothouse, taking deliberate aim (Wood 1956, 103). The shot from the *Merrimac* struck the pilothouse at close range and hit near the eye-slit shortly after the noon hour. The wrought iron log casemate splintered; dust and debris temporarily blinded Worden (Greene 1956, 116). Declaring himself badly wounded, Worden turned command of the ship over to Greene. The *Monitor* withdrew to shallow water to regroup and to allow Greene to take command in the pilothouse. The bloodied Worden was treated in his stateroom until about 2 P.M. (Greene 1956, 117).

The deep-draught *Merrimac* could not follow the *Monitor* into the shallower water, so the Southerners could only wait. After a while the *Merrimac*, with some sailors with minor wounds and low on powder and shot, was steered on a course toward Norfolk (Wood 1956, 103). As Greene returned to the fight, he steered the *Monitor* after the *Merrimac*. Greene explained, "I saw that she was in retreat. A few shots were fired at the retiring vessel, and she continued on to Norfolk" (Greene 1956, 117). Rather than pursue the *Merrimac* and destroy it, the *Monitor* followed its orders and returned to the wooden *Minnesota*'s side. The first battle between two ironclad ships ended.

To many the battle was considered a draw, but in reality there were three major victories for the *Monitor*. The first victory was on a strategic level. The *Monitor* prevented the *Merrimac* from destroying the Union blockade fleet and breaking the blockade at Hampton Roads. The *Merrimac* was actually defeated, because it returned to Norfolk before it achieved its mission to destroy the blockade fleet. Greene emphatically stated, "[I]t has never been denied that the object of the *Merrimac* on the 9th of March was to complete the destruction of the Union fleet in

Hampton Roads; and that she was completely foiled and driven off by the *Monitor*" (Greene 1956, 117). President Lincoln and naval leaders were convinced that the blockade strategy could be effective with more *Monitor*-class ships.

The second victory was for John Ericsson. Ericsson's Folly was totally vindicated (Davis 1975, 45). Marston's evaluation of the *Monitor* succinctly states, "Her performance was perfectly satisfactory" (Marston 1862, 1). In particular, the effectiveness of the rotating gun turret was tremendously demonstrated. A small ship, with two guns in a rotating turret and a crew of approximately fifty, defeated a much larger ship with ten guns in fixed positions and a crew of about three hundred. Ever since, all navy warships have used rotating gun turrets of various types.

The third victory was for iron. The battle between the *Monitor* and *Merrimac* had a profound effect on existing Civil War–era naval technology and architecture. Wood wrote, "It revolutionized the navies of the world. Line-of-battle ships, those huge, overgrown craft, carrying from eighty to one hundred and twenty guns and from five hundred to twelve hundred men, which, from the destruction of the Spanish Armada to our time, had done most of the fighting, deciding the fate of empires, were at once universally condemned as out of date" (Wood 1956, 97–98). Truly, the battle between the *Monitor* and the *Merrimac* led to the demise of wooden warships.

It has always intrigued me how this chance encounter between the *Monitor* and *Merrimac*, which led to the fantastic results discussed above, was just an accident of timing. It defies all odds that the *Monitor* was able to leave New York on 6 March 1862, that the ship was not further delayed by the storms encountered en route south, and that the ship arrived in Hampton Roads just in time to save the Union blockade fleet. Such favorable coincidences are impossible to explain. As will be seen in later chapters, discovery of the *Monitor* wreck also defied all odds. As a religious individual I have been able to accept many similarly unexplainable occurrences as God's will. This seems to be the case for the timing that allowed the battle between the *Monitor* and the *Merrimac*.

3

Disaster off Cape Hatteras

The "Graveyard of the Atlantic" title for the continental shelf off Cape Hatteras is well earned (Stick 1978, 75). Hundreds of wrecks litter the sea floor (National Geographic Society 1970, 1). Some wrecks, such as the German submarines U-352 and U-85 (Ewing et al. 1967, 32) sunk in World War II, were the result of battle action. Most of the other wrecks succumbed to the violent weather and seas common off Hatteras.

Personally, I can attest to those horrendous sea conditions based on my many cruises through the area, my first occurring in 1962. As a young twenty-one-year-old Columbia University graduate student, I helped tend a seismic recording station off Cape Hatteras for an onshore-offshore seismic experiment. The Columbia scientists and I, the only graduate student, were listening for refracting waves from two-ton shots of surplus navy TNT being exploded on the continental shelf. Under the leadership of chief scientist John Ewing, I was being introduced to sea duty aboard the research vessel *Crawford* out of Woods Hole Oceanographic Institution. And what an introduction it was! Looking back, I am glad we encountered such rough seas during our cruise on the *Crawford*, a relatively small ship. Converted from a World War II coast guard cutter whose deck was very close to the water, the *Crawford*'s crew used to joke that "she took on water at the dock." Immune to seasickness my entire seagoing career, I just thought rough seas were normal for the ocean.

I remember climbing the *Crawford*'s mast to fill hydrophone tubes tied as high as we could get them. The small ship would roll so much that I looked down directly over the passing blue ocean and white wake foam.

During one gale I had to cross the fantail deck to secure some gear. I could not believe we were trying to collect seismic data in such seas, especially with explosives. I heard stories of armed charges being flung by ocean waves back on deck where they exploded. Luckily that did not happen on my *Crawford* cruise. Unluckily, when I was crossing the fantail, the *Crawford* lurched and rolled and I left my feet to go sliding across the tilted deck. White water washed me downward toward the partially submerged deck rail chains, which I grabbed. I held fast. It all happened in an instant and I reacted instinctively, but I was scared. I then made my way back to the lab using "one hand for the ship" all the way. Believe me, the seas off Hatteras are often rough. These seas sealed the fate of many a ship, including the *Monitor*.

In December 1862 the *Monitor* was scheduled to be included in the "Monitor Squadron" that was being assembled to attack Charleston harbor. The squadron would consist of up to nine *Monitor*-class ironclads, modeled after the original USS *Monitor* (Hayes 1969, 5). With the Battle of Hampton Roads as evidence, it was clear to Union naval leaders that the Monitors were the best design for Civil War fighting vessels. This held consistently true throughout the war. When *Monitor*-class vessels battled Confederate ironclads, modeled after the barn-like *Merrimac* (Still 1985, 93), the *Monitor*-class vessels were victorious (Mindell 2000, 116).

A strategy was developed to use the Monitor Squadron, under the command of Rear Adm. Samuel Dupont, to capture the Atlantic ports from Hampton Roads southward (Hayes 1969, 5). Adm. David Farragut had captured New Orleans in 1862, and he would command a fleet to capture the Gulf of Mexico ports. The pincer movement to complete the blockade of the Confederacy was called the "Anaconda Plan" (Mindell 2000, 25), and the *Monitor* was to be part of the campaign. The attack on Charleston, South Carolina, occurred on 7 April 1863. The Monitor Squadron played a key role in the attack, but without the USS *Monitor*. The *Monitor* never made it to Charleston, because it had sunk off Cape Hatteras on 31 December 1862.

The shortcomings of *Monitor*-class ships became evident at Charleston and a scandal ensued. Before Charleston, the success of the Monitors against Confederate ironclads was real. The Union had good reasons to exalt the invulnerability of the Monitors. It was critical to expound on the superiority of the Monitors so European leaders would respect the U.S. Navy's power and not intervene in the war. Against fortifications on higher ground, however, the Monitors were unsuccessful, as was proved during the Monitor Squadron's assault on Charleston harbor (Hayes 1969, 6). Every *Monitor*-class ship was unable to elevate its cannons against the higher forts. Another major flaw was that, with only two or four cannons on each ship, the rate of fire was low. The assault on forts required a heavy rate of fire to destroy a fort's barricades and guns quickly and to keep return fire at a minimum. Without a rapid fire rate, return fire could eventually destroy the vessels despite ironcladding. Indeed, the deck armor was not as thick as the turret armor. While the thinner deck armor was effective against glancing shot in a battle with another ship, it was less resistant to more vertical shots, as was fired from mortars at higher ground. At Charleston the Monitor Squadron was hammered by coordinated fire from the forts and had to withdraw.

The scandal developed when the navy, in its desire to preserve the image of the *Monitor*-class ships as invulnerable, blamed the Charleston withdrawal on Dupont's weakness and lack of confidence (Hayes 1969, 110). He was relieved of command and fought for his reputation throughout the war. Later, naval historians vindicated Dupont. His decision to withdraw was the correct military action. Charleston was only captured in 1865 after withstanding the invasion of a large fleet coupled with the landing of thousands of infantry soldiers and sailors who attacked the shore emplacements. Finally, Charleston was evacuated with the approach of Gen. William Tecumseh Sherman's forces from the south.

The USS *Monitor* did experience failure in attacking shore emplacements shortly after its battle with the *Merrimac* at Hampton Roads. The *Monitor* kept the *Merrimac* at bay through March and April 1862, so the blockade held. In the meantime the Union army had crossed Hampton Roads and captured Norfolk and the coastal areas of northern North Carolina. This significant achievement established a "beach head" in the South. From this area Gen. George B. McClellan launched his "Peninsular Campaign" in early May 1862.

After Norfolk was captured, the *Merrimac* could not use it as a port. While attempting to flee up the James River toward Richmond, the *Merrimac*'s twenty-three foot draught was a detriment. Even after lightening the load and gaining a three foot shallower draught, nature conspired against the *Merrimac*. A falling tide and a northwest wind prevented further progress upstream. Comdr. Josiah Tatnall ordered the *Merrimac* scuttled on 11 May 1862. Within a few hours, the crew transfer ashore was complete and the ship fires reached the explosives, blowing the *Merrimac* to bits (Wood 1956, 107).

Without the *Merrimac* to threaten them, Union ships including the *Monitor* steamed up the James River to attack Richmond a few days later. They reached within ten miles of Richmond before being stopped by the shore emplacements at Fort Darling on Drewry's Bluff. Ironically, the *Merrimac*'s gun crews were manning the heavy cannons on the bluff; the ship's crew had prepared the emplacements in expectation of an attack by the *Monitor*.

On 15 May 1862 the exchange of fire was decisive. The *Monitor* could not raise its guns high enough and the guns had a slow rate of fire. The accompanying Union vessels included the USS *Galena*, a ship with an ironcladded conventional hull. While the *Monitor* was struck with steel shot and only suffered dents, some crew members were killed on the *Galena*. The ineffective Union ships withdrew. The *Merrimac* gun crews had saved Richmond.

Lt. John Taylor Wood described the role of the *Merrimac*'s crew in the battle of Drewry's Bluff:

> It only remains now to speak of our last meeting with the *Monitor*. Arriving at Richmond, we heard that the enemy's fleet was ascending the James River, and the result was great alarm; for, relying on the *Virginia* not a gun had been mounted to protect the city from a water attack. We were hurried to Drewry's Bluff, the first high ground below the city, seven miles distant.... We had only succeeded in getting into position three thirty-twos and two sixty-fours (shell guns) and were without sufficient supply of ammunition, when on the 15th of May the iron-clad *Galena*, Commander John Rodgers, followed the *Monitor* and three others, hove in sight (Wood 1956, 108).

Wood commented further on their victory over the *Monitor* and the *Galena:* "Had Commander Rodgers been supported by a few brigades, landed at City Point or above on the south side, Richmond would have been evacuated. The *Virginia*'s crew alone barred his way to Richmond" (Wood 1956, 108).

The battle at Drewry's Bluff was also described in one Harper and Brothers publication:

Four days after the destruction of the *Virginia* the *Monitor* engaged in her second and last action. The James River was now open for operations, and Commander John Ro[d]gers was sent up the river with five vessels, among which were the *Monitor* and *Galena*. It was hoped that they could reach Richmond and compel the surrender of the city. The expedition met with no serious obstacles until it reached within eight miles of Richmond. The river here makes a sharp turn, with high banks on either side. On the western side is Drewry's Bluff about 200 feet high, upon which the construction of a fort, since known as Fort Darling, had been hastily commenced.

The three wooden vessels anchored 1300 yards below the fort. The *Galena* ran up to within 600 yards, swung across the river, and was at once exposed to the full fire from the fort. The *Monitor* went still nearer, but found that her guns could not be elevated sufficiently to reach the battery, and fell farther down to a point from which her guns could be brought to bear.

The *Galena* suffered severely. Thirteen shot and shell penetrated her side.... The light armor of this vessel was of no practical use when opposed to heavy guns. The *Monitor* was hit squarely three times, once on the turret and twice on the side armor, but received no damage beyond a slight bending of the armor-plates. ... Having expended nearly all her ammunition, the *Galena* withdrew, followed by the *Monitor*. The *Galena* lost thirteen killed and eleven wounded....

This action was at the time of far greater importance than is indicated by the loss suffered or inflicted. It was considered by both sides as proving that earth-works could not be reduced by gunboats. "The action," said [Lt. William N.] Jeffers, who now commanded the *Monitor*, "was most gallantly fought against great odds, and with the usual effect against earth-works. So long as our vessels kept up a rapid fire, the enemy rarely fired in return; but the moment our fire slackened, they remanned their guns. It was impossible to reduce such works except with the aid of a land force" (Guernsey and Alden 1866, 257).

During June, July, and August 1862, the *Monitor* settled into boring, uneventful, blockade duty along the James River. Minor exchanges of fire with Confederate infantry on shore occurred as the *Monitor* supported McClellan's futile Peninsular Campaign against Richmond. The *Monitor's* crew had its real battle against heat inside the ironclad, and against boredom. Naval historian Adolph A. Hoehling quoted Acting Master Louis N. Stodder of the *Monitor*: "It was hell, being 170° in the fire room, and on the berth deck it was 95°" (Hoehling 1976, 186). Consequently, most activities were done on deck unless there was sniper fire from shore. Lt. S. Dana Greene, executive officer of the *Monitor*, lamented the living conditions on the vessel: "Probably no ship was ever devised which was so uncomfortable for her crew, and certainly no sailor ever led a more disagreeable life than we did on the James River, suffocated with heat and bad air if we remained below, and a target of sharp-shooters if we came on deck" (Greene 1956, 118).

In need of repair and an overhaul, especially a cleaning of the fouling on the lower hull, the *Monitor* was moved to the Washington Navy Yard in early fall 1862. While in Washington, dignitaries and visitors, including women and children, boarded the *Monitor* for tours. Stodder commented, "They went through the ship like a flock of magpies, prying loose as souvenirs anything removable. When we came to clean up at night there was not a key, doorknob, escutcheon—there wasn't a thing that hadn't been carried away" (Hoehling 1976, 188).

In early November, *Monitor* was back on its station off Newport News as part of the blockade fleet, remaining there through December 1862. The blockade was perfected in the Hampton Roads area by the arrival in late December of two new *Monitor*-class ships, the USS *Passaic* and the USS *Montauk* (Midshipmen 1974, 417). On this station off Newport News my wife's great grandfather, Sgt. James Joseph McCauley, saw the *Monitor*. He was on a troop ferry crossing from Newport News to Norfolk en route to Suffolk, Virginia. He served with company H of the 177th Pennsylvania Drafted Militia. On 9 December 1862 McCauley noted in his diary: "Passed Hampton Roads a small town the Rebbels [*sic*] had burned a short time previous. We passed the wreck of the *Cumberland* that the Rebels boat *Merrimac* had sunk a short time before. Passed several large iron clad gunboats. Also, the little *Monitor*. She is quite a curiosity" (McCauley 1869, 4).

The success of the naval blockade at Hampton Roads and the occupation of coastal Virginia and North Carolina were dampened by the great army losses in field battles in fall 1862 at Second Manassas, Antietam, and Fredericksburg. These Union losses fostered the need for another great naval success, thus the campaign to attack Charleston with the Monitor Squadron in spring 1863 was conceived.

The *Monitor* was made ready to be towed to North Carolina by the side-wheeler frigate USS *Rhode Island.* In 1862 the Monitors were underpowered and all needed assistance from tow ships on the open sea. The *Monitor*'s departure began on 29 December 1862. It was to be joined by the USS *Passaic,* towed by the USS *State of Georgia* (Midshipmen 1974, 418).

Complete coverage of the *Monitor*'s last voyage is compiled in volume two of a three volume research manuscript entitled *Project Cheesebox: A Journey into History* (Midshipmen 1974, 401). Information from ships' logs, crew members' letters, and formal reports from the commanders of the involved vessels form the primary references. Details of the remembrances of eyewitnesses Comdr. John P. Bankhead in command of the *Monitor;* Comdr. Stephen D. Trenchard of the *Rhode Island,* Assistant Surgeon Grenville M. Weeks, Acting Paymaster William F. Keeler, and Seaman Francis B. Butts of the *Monitor* are incorporated in the *Project Cheesebox* narrative.

Preparing the *Monitor* for sea was a familiar routine, similar to making any ship ready for sea. Some preparations began in early December. A new chest-high rifle shield of iron plate had been installed around the turret top to protect against shore-based snipers, as had been encountered along the James River. The *Monitor*'s small boats were taken off and put aboard the tow ship *Rhode Island.* The *Monitor* was left with only one inflatable Indian rubber raft (Midshipmen 1974, 416). On the morning of 29 December 1862 loose gear was stowed, coal was loaded on board, and stores were checked. Making preparations had enlivened the crew and ended the boredom of the last few months on blockade duty.

In the afternoon the *Monitor* and the *Rhode Island* cruised by Fortress Monroe at Hampton Roads and made a course out of the entrance of Chesapeake Bay. Earlier in the day the *Passaic,* towed by the *State of Georgia,* had left the Chesapeake. The ships maintained more than four miles distance from the *Monitor* and the *Rhode Island* on this voyage south.

The weather on the evening of 29 December was mild with light, warm, southerly breezes. Ship speeds of five to six knots were made and the *Monitor* rode well at tow. The crew and officers went about their daily routines. They enjoyed a good meal and a colorful sunset. The only complaints were about the stuffy conditions below and the heat from the coal fires. Sealing the *Monitor* for the ocean voyage had limited air circulation. Some crew members were unable to sleep, suffering from either the stuffiness or sea motion.

Keeler described conditions below decks on the *Monitor* in letters to his wife. His comments on the ventilation indicate that there was some reliance on air intake through the pilothouse and deck lights. Therefore, when these were sealed for the voyage south, the stuffiness below decks was understandable. Keeler wrote, "A large blower, driven by an engine attached, is placed partly above and partly below this deck, which draws the air down through the pilot house and through the deck lights (when open) in the ward room and our state rooms and forces it into the engine room to aid the draft of the furnaces" (Midshipmen 1974, 407).

On 30 December, the *Monitor* was making good headway along the North Carolina coast, heading for Cape Hatteras. As the day proceeded, there was a marked increase in wind speed, registering up to ten knots from the south, and an increasing swell and waves up to five feet in height, recorded on the *Rhode Island* as a Beaufort scale 3 (Midshipmen 1974, 420–21). The waves broke over the low deck of the *Monitor* as it was bearing into the sea. The sky was clear, although clouds were appearing to the south. The crew could no longer stand on the deck without getting wet by the breaking waves. They gathered on top of the turret behind the rifle shield to get the air.

At 6:30 the temperature increased to more than 70°F, reflecting the influence of the warm Gulf Stream (Midshipmen 1974, 429). As the *Monitor* entered this strong current, headway over the ground would be thwarted. I have spent much time in the Gulf Stream in my forty-plus seagoing years, off Florida, North Carolina, and Virginia. In all cases the current presents both interesting oceanographic phenomena as well as technical difficulties for our geophysical equipment. The northwest "wall" of the Gulf Stream is extremely sharp. Over a short distance of a few tens of feet, the colder waters of the southerly flowing Labrador current shear past the warmer water of the northerly flowing Gulf Stream. Temperature contrasts can be between thirty to forty degrees Fahrenheit. The cold Labrador current waters are green and brown, contrasting spectacularly with the clearer blue waters of the Gulf Stream. The *Monitor* crew took note of the color change as the ship crossed into the Gulf Stream (Midshipmen 1974, 429).

In my first cruise off Cape Hatteras aboard the *Crawford* in 1962, we were trying to detect seismic waves by lowering hydrophones on the outer side of the Gulf Stream. The warmer waters of the Gulf Stream have higher sound velocities, and thus refract the sound waves downward. This complication required us to lower the hydrophones to extraordinary depths to correct for the refraction.

As a Columbia University graduate student, I participated in measuring the structure of the western wall of the Gulf Stream during a 1966 cruise aboard the research vessel *Eastward*. Under the leadership of one of my former professors, Bruce Heezen, our closely spaced bathythermograph readings showed the temperature contrast between the Gulf Stream and the Labrador current. The wall is indeed sharp. The Gulf Stream behaves like a "river" in the ocean, flowing as a coherent body of water that meanders and eddies along its western wall. I noticed the change in color from the clear, blue, warm Gulf Stream to the murky, green, cold Labrador current. Our bathythermograph transect was made as *Eastward* was en route to its home port of Beaufort, North Carolina.

On another cruise in 1990 off Virginia on the seismic survey ship *Geco Searcher*, we ran into another Gulf Stream problem. We were towing a nearly twenty thousand foot long hydrophone array and we could not tow it faster than four and a half knots through the water or it would tear apart. We got into an eddy of the Gulf Stream that was flowing against us at four and a half knots. So we were not progressing over the ground at all. To terminate the survey we tried to haul in the long hydrophone streamer in the middle of the night. Needless to say, the Gulf Stream current wound the hydrophone array around the ship twice and we nearly cut it in two with the ship's propellers. Worse things have happened. Hydrophones have tangled in the screws, disabling ships. Care must be exercised vigilantly when towing objects in the Gulf Stream.

The *Monitor* ran into its own towing problem in the Gulf Stream. After rounding Cape Hatteras at about 7:30 P.M. on 30 December, the starboard tow hawser broke after the pounding into the waves and current chaffed the rope against the *Monitor*'s iron (Midshipmen 1974, 431–33). The *Monitor*'s progress through the water became unstable, with more yawing on the remaining tow rope. Compounding this problem, the wind picked up to fifteen knots, Beaufort scale 4, and the waves increased to eight feet in height. Waves broke over and submerged the *Monitor*'s pilothouse and pounded the turret. Rain began in squalls coming from the south. An eyewitness to the growing sea state, Weeks described the scene:

> Those of us new to the sea, and not appreciating our peril, hurrahed for the largest wave; but the captain and one or two others, old sailors, knowing its power, grew momentarily more and more anxious, feeling with dread instructive to the sailor that, in case of extremity, no wreck yet known to ocean could be so hopeless as this. Solid iron from keelson to turret-top, clinging to anything for safety, if the *Monitor* should go down, would only insure a share in her fate. No mast, no spar, no floating thing, to meet the outstretched hand in the last moment (Midshipmen 1974, 436).

Water was entering the *Monitor* at a fast pace despite the bilge pumps working at maximum capacity. The oakum seal around the base of the turret began giving way. However, the rate at which water was entering indicated leaks from other sources. The pounding of the seas may even have caused cracks where the main deck joined the hull. Sea state increased to Beaufort scale 6 with wind speeds of up to twenty-seven knots and wave heights of fifteen feet. Huge waves broke over the turret and the water level inside the *Monitor* began to rise (Midshipmen 1974, 443).

At 9:00 P.M. Commander Bankhead, in charge of the *Monitor*, signaled the *Rhode Island* to stop the tow ship's engines in hopes that the *Monitor* might ride better without banging into the sea and Gulf Stream current. Immediately, the *Monitor* "turned into the trough" with the waves from the southwest breaking over its beam. The ironclad began to roll violently, as all ships do in the trough (Midshipmen 1974, 443).

My experience with a trough situation occurred in 1968 off Antarctica while I was aboard the two hundred foot USNS *Eltanin*. Antarctic seas are routinely Beaufort states 4 and 5, and often reach state 6. One night I was working on the aft port quarterdeck where our seismic gear was towed. The captain was doing his usual deck inspection; if we left any tools out on deck he would take them and hide them to teach us a lesson. While the captain was standing beside me and chatting, I noticed my seismic gear tow lines go slack and behave strangely. A two month cruise, I had come to expect everything to be the same each day, and I routinely checked our tow lines. Also, I knew that if the gear went slack, our seismic equipment could possibly foul the *Eltanin*'s props and disable the ship. Everyone was always prepared to cut our tow lines with an axe to prevent any mishap. Consequently, I was more sensitive to this change in tow rope behavior than was the captain.

I yelled to the captain that we had lost power and were stopping. He shouted "Hell," and ran for the bridge. Within seconds the *Eltanin,* which was bigger than the *Monitor,* rolled off into the trough. The heavy seas rolled the ship like a bathtub toy. If the *Eltanin* remained in the trough it would eventually roll over and capsize. Being in the Antarctic with subfreezing water and three thousand miles from the nearest ships, we were facing a very dangerous situation. Fortunately, the captain got the engines going again and the *Eltanin* headed into the sea to stabilize its motion.

The *Monitor* faced similar danger in the Cape Hatteras storm. The *Rhode Island* quickly went slow speed ahead into the sea to turn the *Monitor* out of the trough against the heavy sea and Gulf Stream. The *Rhode Island* and the *Monitor* were barely making headway even with the *Rhode Island* now proceeding at a speed of three knots through the water. The heavy rain sprayed the seaman on deck and waves broke entirely over the *Monitor.* The water level continued to rise inside the ironclad.

At 10:30 P.M., Bankhead ordered the raising of a red signal lantern, which the *Rhode Island* officers knew was the signal to abandon ship on the *Monitor* (Midshipmen 1974, 448). Small boats, manned by volunteers, were lowered from the *Rhode Island* and began to cross the violent seas to rescue the *Monitor*'s crew. Meanwhile, Bankhead asked for volunteers to cut the remaining tow hawser that was pulling *Monitor*'s bow under the breaking waves. Two of *Monitor*'s crew members were swept overboard in the attempt, but Acting Master Louis N. Stodder succeeded in cutting the tow hawser with many blows from a hatchet.

About 11:00 P.M. or shortly thereafter, while the *Rhode Island* crew were getting the long boats lowered, Bankhead ordered the engines stopped, and used all the available steam to run the bilge pumps. Again the *Monitor* turned into the trough and rolled badly. Bankhead then ordered the anchor lowered with all the chain put out. As the anchor took hold, the *Monitor*'s bow turned partly into the sea (Midshipmen 1974, 455). This helped a little, but the water inside the ironclad continued to rise.

While panic ensued below the *Monitor*'s deck, and the crew struggled to the top of the turret to await rescue, the *Rhode Island* had its own problems. Unfortunately, the loose tow hawser cut free from the *Monitor* had tangled in one of the *Rhode Island*'s paddle wheels. Without headway momentarily, while the hawser was cleared with an axe, the *Rhode Island* was being blown down on top of the *Monitor*. One of the long boats from the *Rhode Island* was caught between the two ships. The *Rhode Island* was so close that a few crew members from the *Monitor* climbed ropes to safety on the Rhode Island; others tried and failed. Fortunately, the *Rhode Island* scraped by the *Monitor* and drifted away down current. The long boat luckily survived with only a few splinters and scratches. Sixteen of the *Monitor*'s crew were rescued in that long boat.

As the water inside the *Monitor* rose high enough to put out the fires, the engines and pumps became useless. Sinking was inevitable. All the crew members climbed to the turret and Bankhead ordered abandon ship. It was now every man for himself. A second boat from the *Rhode Island* approached, and struggled to stay next to the *Monitor*. Some crew members were washed away as they crossed the deck. Seaman Francis Butts described the horrific events, "As I reached the top of the turret I saw a boat made fast on the weather quarter filled with men. Three others were standing on deck trying to get on board. One man was floating leeward shouting in vain for help; another, who hurriedly passed me and jumped down from the turret, was swept off by a breaking wave and never rose" (Midshipmen 1974, 484).

Crew members who had successfully boarded the second rescue boat felt safe. But their safety was only momentary. In the storm-tossed sea the two rescue boats collided. The boat leaving the *Monitor* was hit by the first boat, which was returning from the *Rhode Island*. Weeks attempted to push the boats apart; his fingers got crushed and he dislocated his shoulder. Weeks's heroic attempts, however, helped to avoid disaster compounded on disaster. Three of his fingers were later amputated aboard the *Rhode Island*. Weeks later wrote, "An arm was a small price to pay for life" (Davis 1975, 164).

At about 12:15 A.M. on 31 December the first group of the *Monitor* crew members had been hoisted aboard the *Rhode Island* from the first long boat. Some more sailors were lost as they attempted to scramble up on the paddle wheeler. A third long boat was launched and the boat's crew steered toward the *Monitor*'s red light. Bankhead was rescued, but the boat became full; some of the *Monitor*'s crew members were still clinging to the turret. The boat made for the *Rhode Island* and again some sailors were lost boarding the *Rhode Island* (Midshipmen 1974, 490).

A final attempt to get a rescue boat to the *Monitor* was made at approximately 1:30 to 2:00 A.M. on 31 December. The rescue boat's crew steered toward the *Monitor*'s red lantern, by that time estimated to be about a mile away. This was the last sighting of the *Monitor*. When the rescue boat arrived at where the *Monitor* should have been, all the crew saw was an eddy, which may have been the result of the ship's sinking (Midshipmen 1974, 492).

Commenting on the sinking of the *Monitor*, Greene wrote, "The *Monitor* went down in a gale, a few miles south of Cape Hatteras. Four officers and twelve men were drowned, forty-nine people being saved by the boats of the steamer. It was impossible to keep the vessel free of water, and we presumed that the upper and lower hulls thumped themselves apart" (Greene 1956, 118). First-Class Fireman George Geer mentioned what he thought was the problem in a letter to his brother: "Around and under the Tower the Captain had Oakum put, but did not put any pitch over it and the sea soon washed the Oakum out and the water came under the tower and down on the Berth deck in torrents" (Geer et al. 2000, 235). Technology historian David Mindell indicated that Ericsson himself thought the *Monitor* officers erred in placing oakum under the turret (Mindell 2000, 140).

The last rescue boat became separated from the *Rhode Island* by the stormy seas and the darkness. Trenchard, the *Rhode Island*'s captain, presumed the boat had sunk and the crew had drowned, so he headed toward Beaufort, North Carolina, which was occupied by Union forces. The next day, the wayward rescue boat was rescued by a passing steamer, and the crew returned to the *Rhode Island* at Beaufort several days later (Midshipmen 1974, 506). Trenchard greeted the rescue boat crew as long lost prodigal sons; they were "lost but had been found."

With the *Monitor*'s disappearance, one of the great mysteries of the sea began: Where exactly had the *Monitor* sunk and where was the *Monitor* wreck? Everyone knew that it was somewhere off Cape Hatteras. For the remainder of the nineteenth century and the first half of the twentieth century, however, people only speculated about the location. Although technology existed in the nineteenth century to find and recover parts of sunken warships, especially the cannons, no documented attempts to

Harper's Weekly engraving shows the horrific events of the foundering and sinking of the USS *Monitor*. Rescue boats from the tow ship, the side wheeler frigate USS *Rhode Island*, cross the storm-tossed sea off Cape Hatteras in the darkness of night to take off most of the *Monitor*'s crew.

Harper's Weekly, 24 January 1863, 60

find the *Monitor* have been unearthed. Diving bells and hard-hat diving were used for salvage of other sunken vessels. Obviously, the prospect of diving in search of the *Monitor* in the rough open Atlantic was not of prime importance during the Civil War or even later when U.S. arms and warship production was prolific. There was no desperate need for the *Monitor*'s armament. Practically, diving searches were usually only conducted when the location of the wreck was precisely known, and this was not the case for the *Monitor* wreck.

Remote searching techniques using sonar and underwater photography, much more efficient to explore for wrecks, were developed for exploring continental shelf depths during World War II. My former professor of geophysics at Columbia University, Dr. Maurice Ewing, worked on a U.S. Navy program during 1941–44 to photograph sunken wrecks on the continental shelf off the eastern United States (Ewing et al. 1967, 27). For intelligence purposes, the U.S. Navy wanted to identify sunken tankers that were reported missing after leaving U.S. ports. Where were they being torpedoed? Were there patterns? Also, were there any sunken German submarines and where were they?

Ewing and his associates perfected underwater photography and sonar techniques and successfully identified sunken tankers and German submarines. Indeed, the German submarines U-352 and U-85 were photographed by Ewing and his colleagues near Cape Hatteras (Ewing et al. 1967, 32). Many submarines were sunk close to shore, thus proving the intensity of the German submarine warfare. During 1942 so many tankers were sunk that the New Jersey beaches were black with oil. Tankers were being attacked on the New Jersey shelf almost as soon as they departed the Philadelphia and Elizabeth refineries. By 1943 the U.S. destroyer fleet was increased and antisubmarine warfare was perfected, so sinkings did not occur as frequently as they had in 1942.

In 1950 the U.S. Navy first reported a sighting of a possible *Monitor* wreck. The navy intentionally searched for the *Monitor* as an evaluation of a newly developed underwater object locator (UOL) (Midshipmen 1974, 621; Newton 1973, 1). Starting at the historically reported position of the *Monitor*'s sinking, 34°50' N latitude, 75°30' W longitude, the navy used UOL to search a large area. The only large object detected was located at 34°55.5' N latitude, 75°24.5' W longitude in fifty fathoms of water. The UOL data indicated a 140 foot long, 25 to 40 foot wide wreck. Because of the strong current, no diver was sent down to the depth required. Photographs were attempted but none proved useful.

Interestingly, this wreck discovered by the navy UOL in 1950 is at the identical location of the first wreck we discovered on the research vessel *Eastward* during its search for the *Monitor* in August 1973 (Newton et al. 1974, 11). I was the watch leader that initially evaluated the side-scan sonar contact of this first wreck and it was indeed a clear *Monitor*-looking target. We photographed this wreck from the *Eastward* and we now have proof that it is not the *Monitor*. The *Eastward* cruise is discussed in detail in the next chapter. But it is certain that the 1950 navy report of discovery of the *Monitor* is erroneous.

Another erroneous report of the discovery of the *Monitor* wreck occurred in 1955. Robert Marx, a wreck diver, based his findings on a story that had circulated after the *Monitor* sank. Reportedly, two days after the sinking of the *Monitor* some Union soldiers found the bodies of five of its crew washed ashore near Cape Hatteras Lighthouse (Marx 1967, 57).

The bodies were supposedly buried on a high knoll one half mile behind the lighthouse. This story provided possible evidence that the *Monitor* may have remained afloat in the Gulf Stream and drifted north of the tip of Cape Hatteras before sinking. Marx described seeing portions of the *Monitor*'s turret sticking out of the sand in forty-five foot water depth when diving on a sonar target. The target was first identified from a small plane on a particularly clear water day. Triangulation based on bearings to several shore towers placed the position of the *Monitor* about two miles northeast of the tip of Cape Hatteras and about two miles offshore of Hatteras Lighthouse. When Marx tried to return to the wreck nearly a month later, the wreck could not be found. The water depth at the site appeared to be several feet shallower and Marx concluded that waves had shifted the sands and buried the wreck completely (Marx 1967, 68–70). This ended Marx's search for the *Monitor*.

Further attempts to find the *Monitor* were not reported until the early 1970s. One effort by U.S. Naval Academy midshipmen in 1973 was part of their Project Cheesebox research. They concentrated their search in the area of Marx's discovery (Midshipmen 1974, 701). Given the enthusiasm with which Marx had reported and publicized his finding of the *Monitor*, and his certitude about the description of the partially buried turret, it was not surprising that the Naval Academy effort followed his lead. No confirmation was reported by diving studies in the nearshore areas just north of Cape Hatteras. However, the Naval Academy analysis of the U.S. Navy's Project Magnet aeromagnetic surveys showed four possible anomalies in the area of Marx's discovery. The anomalies were discussed in Project Cheesebox as likely sites for the *Monitor* and one as the "most probable site" (Midshipmen 1974, 714). No follow up, such as by surface-towed magnetometer studies, sonar, photography, or diving, was done on these anomalies.

As of 1973, then, it was the best opinion of *Monitor* experts, such as Marx and the Naval Academy, that the *Monitor* had remained afloat and drifted to a few miles north of Cape Hatteras before sinking on that fateful night of 30–31 December 1862. According to this theory, the *Monitor* had to have broken off its anchor chain and remained afloat to within a few miles from shore. The *Monitor*'s crew would have been within sight of the Cape Hatteras Lighthouse and the desperate sailors clinging to the turret would have had a chance of survival. They could have swum or used the *Monitor*'s inflatable Indian rubber raft to cross the last few miles to shore. The lighthouse would have beckoned them in the dark and given them hope. By whatever means, the crew would have moved toward the safety of the shore. Based on the story of finding five sailors' bodies washed ashore at Cape Hatteras Light, apparently luck was not with them.

4

The Search

While the search for the *Monitor* in shallow water north of Cape Hatteras occupied the interest of some groups in the early 1970s (Midshipmen 1974, 689; Miller 1978a, 96–97), there were others who considered a search in the deeper water areas offshore. As mentioned in the previous chapter, the use of sonar systems and underwater photography to remotely identify wrecks in continental shelf depths, many of them off Cape Hatteras, had been done during World War II. In fact, in the 1940s Dr. Maurice Ewing and his associates photographed the wreck of the *Venore* at 35°05' N, 75°24' W, which was within about five miles of the *Monitor* wreck (Ewing et al. 1967, 32). Therefore, the thought of using modern state-of-the-art marine geophysical technology to search for the *Monitor* wreck in continental shelf depths was logical. All that was required was the imagination, interest, and curiosity of some experienced marine researchers. One such marine researcher was John Newton.

In the early 1970s Newton was the marine superintendent of the Duke University Marine Laboratory (DUML) based in Beaufort, North Carolina. He organized the research vessel *Eastward*'s schedule and logistics, and was responsible for maintaining the vessel. Much of the time, the *Eastward* was used by the National Science Foundation's Cooperative Oceanographic Program; professors and students from other universities sailed on the *Eastward* to conduct research. One goal of the research was the education of future marine scientists. As a young assistant professor of geology and geophysics at the University of Delaware, I was a frequent participant in the *Eastward*'s Cooperative Oceanographic Program and became acquainted with Newton.

I had been introduced to the *Eastward* program initially as a Columbia University graduate student. My first cruise on the *Eastward* was in 1966 under the leadership of Professor Bruce Heezen of Columbia University's Lamont-Doherty Geological Observatory. We researched the Blake Plateau and the Blake Outer Ridge. Heezen's approach was to record data every minute of the cruise. This led to an ancillary study of the western Gulf Stream wall. We used bathythermograph measurements at close spacings along the *Eastward*'s track across the North Carolina shelf and slope to and from Beaufort. When plotting the bathythermograph data, the sharp nature of the western boundary of the Gulf Stream was apparent to me. Temperature contrasts from the warm Gulf Stream to the colder Labrador current were significant, between 30 and 40 degrees Fahrenheit.

An assistant professor at the University of Delaware from 1968 to 1973, I used the *Eastward* each year on research cruises in the Blake Plateau area, and in studying the Delaware continental shelf. I was one of the first investigators on the *Eastward* to use seismic reflection profiling. As a result of this research, I was promoted to associate professor in 1973. During the 1969–71 research, we brought along our own portable Bolt high-pressure air gun reflection profiling system. Our success using this system on the *Eastward* led Newton and DUML to add a geophysical laboratory to the *Eastward* in 1972. The *Eastward* had always been well equipped for sea-floor photography and for geological sampling that was done using piston cores and dredges. The new geophysical laboratory added seismic reflection profiling capabilities, with recorders, a single-channel hydrophone, air guns, and compressors. Also in the geophysical laboratory were the recorders for a new Varian proton-precession magnetometer. Newton was responsible for acquiring the improvements in the *Eastward*'s capabilities.

As a marine geologist, Newton's interest in the *Monitor* search project stemmed from his own research. Prior to his position as marine superintendent at DUML, he had worked for Western Electric Company, doing seafloor analyses for submarine telegraph and telephone cables. He was familiar with submarine sediments, topography, and current technologies used to study these subjects.

In an early 1970s research project, Newton compiled the numerous echo-sounding records made on the research vessel *Eastward*'s crossing of the North Carolina shelf and slope. His research appeared in "An Oceanographic Atlas of the Carolina Continental Margin," which was printed by the North Carolina Board of Science and Technology (Newton et al. 1974, 4). Notable topographic features included the Pamlico canyon and its headwaters, which dissect the continental slope near the *Monitor* wreck location, and a northeast trending ridge and swale feature on the North Carolina shelf off Ocracoke Island.

Newton also included a map that showed the numerous wrecks detected on the *Eastward*'s echo-sounding records. Hundreds of wrecks litter the North Carolina shelf in what is called the "Graveyard of the Atlantic" (Ewing et al. 1967, 32; Stick 1978, 75). Working on his wreck map, Newton was aware of the local lore about the sinking of the *Monitor* off Cape Hatteras and he had a natural curiosity about its possible location. He was also aware of what wrecks looked like on echo-sounding records, and he realized the effectiveness of using sonar to search for wrecks.

Newton also had a sincere interest in Civil War history. Coming from an old Southern family, his great grandfather had served in the Confederate army. Newton told me stories of his ancestor, about how he had served throughout the war, been wounded, been captured, and had escaped to return to the fight. Newton's great grandfather was heroic. I remember telling Newton how this contrasted with my great grandfather's case. My ancestor had been a three year volunteer in the New Jersey Third Infantry Regiment and was discharged after a year and a half with an injured knee disability. Another contrast with Newton's great grandfather was my wife's great grandfather; he served nine months in the Pennsylvania Drafted Militia and the worst injury he suffered was a bee sting! I believe these contrasts are examples of the differences between the manpower resources of the North and the South during the Civil War. The Union had sufficient manpower resources to discharge more men before the end of hostilities than the Confederates had under arms in the entire war.

In October 1972, Newton discussed the possibility of using the research vessel *Eastward* for shipwreck location and identification with Gordon Watts, a marine archaeologist with the North Carolina Division of Archives and History (Watts 1975, 301). The *Eastward* had the required equipment, such as hull-mounted vertical and side-scan sonar, seismic profilers, a magnetometer, and a deep sea camera, to effectively find and identify wrecks, using similar techniques as those used since World War II (Ewing et al. 1967, 27). Also, the *Eastward* was a well laid-out, multipurpose research vessel capable of launching and towing many other kinds of equipment as needed. While only 117 feet long, the *Eastward* was wide abeam and had ample space. It could accommodate up to eighteen scientists. The *Eastward* was well known for its good maneuverability and station keeping. It was only a matter of proposing a worthwhile project to use the *Eastward* to search for wrecks. Newton and Watts agreed that off Cape Hatteras, the wreck of most historical significance was the USS *Monitor* (Watts 1975, 301).

Newton knew what kind of cruise proposals would be accepted for the *Eastward* Cooperative Oceanographic Program. Generally, endurance was limited by fuel and food needs as well as crew workload. The *Eastward* cruises operated out of Beaufort, North Carolina, and concentrated on the east coast of the United States from Delaware to the Bahamas. Cruises usually lasted two to three weeks. To maximize logistical efficiency and involve professors and students from more than one institution on a cruise, there were commonly multiobjective cruises. This was especially true if the multiple objectives could use similar oceanographic equipment and were geographically compatible along the cruise track. For example, in 1971 Professor Don Swift from Old Dominion University and I combined a cruise on the *Eastward* from Delaware to Beaufort. We both had interests in the origins of the ridge and swale topography so common on the Atlantic inner continental shelf. There were excellent examples of this topography off Delaware that I had studied seismically, and off Virginia, where Swift had studied. Further analysis of those ridges and swales required vibracoring that Swift and I did on a combined cruise on the *Eastward.*

This joint project with Swift was the first cruise on the *Eastward* to do vibracoring. Vibracoring uses a heavier core than the piston core available on the *Eastward.* In vibracoring, the core is vibrated into the coarse sand and gravel of the continental shelf. The piston core relies exclusively on gravity and the free fall of the ton weight of the core to penetrate the sediments. Often on the continental shelf, the coarse sand and gravel prevented penetration by piston cores. The active pounding by the ton weight vibrator on the vibracore succeeded in penetrating these shelf

The research vessel *Eastward* of the Duke University Marine Laboratory Cooperative Oceanographic Program was the vessel used to discover the wreck of the *Monitor* in August 1973 during cruise E-12-73.

Duke University Marine Laboratory

sediments. Newton was impressed with the successful use of the vibracore on the *Eastward* on the continental shelf off Delaware. His logistical supervision on that *Eastward* cruise was vital to our success.

With his knowledge of the benefits of joint, multiobjective cruises on the *Eastward*, Newton saw an opportunity to complete two worthy studies on the North Carolina shelf that stemmed from his atlas research. One was the study of the origins of the ridge and swale topography, and the other was to search for the wreck of the *Monitor*. To develop a cruise proposal and to carry out the research on these two topics, Newton gathered together a group of coinvestigators.

Newton invited me to participate because he was aware of my scientific interest in the origins of continental shelf ridge and swale topography. He also knew of my frequent use of the *Eastward* and, thus, my familiarity with the ship itself and the geophysical equipment on board. Newton also invited the participation of Professor Harold Edgerton from the Massachusetts Institute of Technology (MIT). Known as "Doc," Edgerton was a world-renown electrical engineer. He developed and used strobe light technology in time-lapse photography. He also used the strobe light to develop deep-sea cameras that his company, Edgerton, Germeshausen, and Grier (EG&G), built and sold. One EG&G camera was used on the *Eastward.* To give us archaeological expertise, Watts was invited to participate. He used discovery data on the *Monitor* wreck as the basis for his master's thesis at East Carolina University under naval historian Professor William Still.

I was delighted when Newton invited me to participate. Documenting the origin of another ridge and swale topography on the Atlantic continental shelf would be a valuable supplement to my own research off Delaware. As a marine geophysicist I was intrigued by the possibilities of using geophysical equipment to search for wrecks. The relatively small targets that wrecks represent, compared to the normal geological targets I was used to surveying, presented an unusual geophysical challenge. Not many marine geophysicists had surveyed wrecks. As a Civil War buff, I was thrilled to be able to participate in the search for the USS *Monitor.*

The proposal request was submitted in February 1973 and approved in March.

> A ship-use proposal for the research vessel *Eastward* was submitted on February 28, 1973 to the Cooperative Oceanographic Program of Duke University Marine Laboratory. Co-investigators in this ship time request were Dr. Harold Edgerton, Dr. Robert Sheridan, Mr. Gordon Watts, and Mr. John Newton. The request was reviewed and approved by a panel devised by the National Science Foundation. This approval for ship use was confirmed by letter on March 13, 1973 (Newton et al. 1974, 2).

The ship time award was for fourteen days aboard the *Eastward.* Both Newton and Edgerton approached the National Geographic Society for financial support; more than ten thousand dollars was obtained by mid-May 1973. With National Geographic Society involvement, the expedition gained the interest and participation of the society's historian, Dorothy Nicholson. She accompanied our investigative group on the *Eastward* cruise and proudly flew the National Geographic Society flag from the ship's rigging.

Fourteen days of ship time was not much time to accomplish the multiple missions proposed. Newton realized this and used his logistical organization expertise and his personal awareness of local North Carolina resources to garner further support. "[L]etters requesting Army Reserve support were sent to Captain Larry Hardy of the 824th Transportation Company (Heavy Boat) and Captain Wallace of the 650th Transportation Company. With General Thomas Thorne's concurrence, formal approval for use of a landing craft utility (LCU), J boat and twenty-ton crane was received in late July" (Newton et al. 1974, 3). These resources would allow the vibracoring part of the geological study of the ridge and swale topography to be done from the LCU-1488 rather than from the *Eastward.* The *Eastward* would now have time to do the seismic reflection, side-scan sonar, and photographic studies of the topography. Hardy and his army reservists were enthusiastic about the project (Editorial 1976a, 17).

As much as a day of ship time has to be consumed in mobilizing the vibracoring equipment on board the ship. By using the LSU-1488 for vibracoring, mobilization could be done while the *Eastward* was completing the seismic reflection and sonar surveys of the ridge and swale topography. This was a great advantage. With the LSU's logistical support in place, the vibracoring equipment and a vibracoring technician were contracted with the Alpine Geophysical Associates of Norwood, New Jersey. I have worked on five successful coring projects with Alpine over the years and Alpine always efficiently completed its contracts.

The *Eastward* cruise, designated E-12-73, was scheduled for 17–31 August 1973 (Newton et al. 1974, 2). This time frame offered the best weather window to work off Cape Hatteras; winds and waves were usually manageable. It also is just the beginning of the hurricane season in the Cape Hatteras area, so the odds were low that one would occur. The weather was very critical. Only good sea states, below sea state 2, would allow the launching of the ton weight vibracoring equipment from the LCU. Also, the seismic reflection and sonar systems work best in acoustically quiet seas, and holding station position with the *Eastward* for submarine photography is best below sea state 3.

Preparations for the cruise included the setup of shore-based navigational aids. Newton arranged for the free use of a Del Norte microwave navigation system. Two transponders were mounted on high positions on Cape Hatteras Lighthouse and on Diamond Shoals Light Tower (Newton et al. 1974, 16; Newton 1975, 58). Another preparation was the use of a Western Electric Company low-light-level deep-sea television camera and video recorder. Newton arranged for this free use through his contacts with his former employer. Edgerton brought along an EG&G dual-channel side-scan sonar, and I brought along a surfboard-mounted Raytheon 7 kiloHertz sub-bottom profiler.

The *Eastward* cruise got under way as planned on 17 August 1973. I immediately set up the seismic reflection and side-scan sonar equipment for the survey of the ridge and swale topography while cruising from Beaufort to Cape Lookout, and up the coast to off Ocracoke Island. At *Eastward*'s speed of ten knots, I had about eight hours to accomplish this. Once off Ocracoke Island, a zigzag grid, with most of the lines perpendicular to the axes of the northeast trending topography, was made 18–20 August. We set up the scientific party to simultaneously run a one cubic inch Bolt air gun, the Raytheon 7 kiloHertz sub-bottom profiler, the *Eastward*'s own hull-mounted 3.5 kiloHertz profiler, and the EG&G dual-channel side-scan sonar.

Profiles were analyzed and interpreted as they were collected. We could see sub-bottom reflections on our equipment that were fifty to sixty feet beneath the sea floor. The swale seemed to be underlain by an ancestral river drainage that developed into an estuary, similar to present-day Pamlico Sound. The ridges looked like many I had seen seismically off Virginia and Delaware; they result from the bottom current buildup of sand over the more ancient stratigraphic reflectors. Using the preliminary analysis of the seismic data, core sites were determined for the vibracoring that would be done from the LSU.

On 20 August, via the J boat, my geological assistants, Art Johnson, Joe Tuminello and Bob Brown, and I transferred to the LCU-1488 for the vibracoring. Meanwhile on the *Eastward* a photographic study of the sea floor was carried out in the ridge and swale topography area. The EG&G side-scan records showed ribbons of differing acoustic reflectivity, which show up as light (low reflectivity) and dark (high reflectivity) patches. Photographs showed that the dark areas had coarse sand and shell as bottom sediments, while the light areas were composed of well-sorted fine sand. The strong bottom currents form complex helical patterns that locally winnow the sediments into the ribbons.

I also transferred the Raytheon sub-bottom profiler to the LCU-1488 for recording the reflections directly at the core sites. The Alpine Geophysical Associates coring technician, Al Stockel, had done an excellent job installing the vibracoring device on the LCU-1488. The large, heavy rig would sit vertically on the sea floor and vibrate a twenty foot core barrel into the sediments with a vibrating ton weight core head. On the LSU-1488, the vibracoring device sat vertically on the floor of the ship where army tanks and other army vehicles usually sat. The large twenty ton crane on tracks was on the same floor; the crane had a large tower so the vibracoring device could be lifted directly over the LCU's high gunnels. If sea states exceeded sea state 2, there would be too much swing to do this safely. Consequently, we carried out the coring operation as quickly as possible while we had fair weather.

Eleven vibracores from key localities were successfully collected. These cores verified the seismic interpretations. One core recovered a tell-tale peat of the ancient marsh surface of the ancestral estuarine Pamlico Sound (Newton et al. 1974, 8–9; Editorial 1976a, 16). The peat was dated by radio-carbon techniques; it had been formed approximately thirteen thousand years ago. The ancient outer banks that bounded the ancestral Pamlico Sound had been more than twelve miles seaward of their present location when the sea level had been about one hundred feet lower than it is today.

On 23 August Johnson, Tuminello, Brown, and I transferred again via the J boat from the LCU-1488 to the *Eastward* to begin our next mission of the search for the *Monitor*. Newton and the others greeted us as if we were heroes because we had so rapidly completed the geological mission. "Credit for the efficiency of this coring program, which was completed in a record time of thirty-seven hours, is due largely to the prior assembly and check-out of the vibracore system by Mr. Stockel and the efforts exerted by him, the crew of the LCU and men of Dr. Sheridan's group, whose round-the-clock labors proved to be crucial in the success of the expedition" (Newton et al. 1974, 6).

The search for the wreck quickly commenced. The plan was to tow the EG&G dual-channel side-scan sonar and the Varian magnetometer, and to run the hull-mounted vertical sonar, on a close grid pattern over the predetermined search area (Newton et al., 1974, 11–12). After the ship time award was obtained on 13 March 1973, historical research on the *Monitor* was carried out by Watts and Nicholson (Watts 1975, 311). From the deck logs of the tow ships, the USS *Rhode Island* and the USS *State of Georgia*, the navigational sightings of onshore structures such as the Cape Hatteras Lighthouse were obtained. By plotting these fixes on an 1857 version of the U.S. Coast and Geodetic Survey chart of the area, the geographic locations of the tow ships were determined (Watts 1975, 311–12). These locations were then transferred to a contemporary National Oceanic and Atmospheric Administration (NOAA) navigational chart. Capt. Eric Nelson of DUML carried out a similar procedure to use "a dead reckoning track and weather information to provide a 'set and drift' probable location area based on the information now available" (Newton 1973, 1). The resulting target search area was a rectangular zone striking northeast-southwest with an approximately five mile by fifteen mile area (Newton 1973, 4; Newton et al. 1974, 11; Newton 1975, 56; Watts 1975, 313). The submarine topography of the search area was a smooth, gently sloping part of the outer continental shelf with water depths ranging from 25 fathoms (150 feet) to 60 fathoms (360 feet). These depths are within the range of the *Monitor*'s anchor chain length that was lowered during the foundering (Midshipmen 1974, 455).

As the search began, a problem immediately arose. One of the Del Norte navigators, the one on Cape Hatteras Lighthouse, was not transponding with the recorder on the *Eastward.* We assumed the twelve volt battery powering the transponder was dead. Only the Del Norte navigator on Diamond Shoals Light was working. This was a serious setback. The Del Norte system was based on radio microwave transmission that permitted location of the *Eastward* to a plus-or-minus ten foot accuracy. Two stations are needed to triangulate the location. With only the Diamond Shoals Light navigator working, we had a good plus-or-minus ten foot accurate range of the *Eastward* from Diamond Shoal Light, but we could be anywhere on that range circle.

Fortunately, the available accurate Del Norte range circles were oriented northwest-southeast in the search rectangle, nearly perpendicular to the gently sloping sea-floor isobaths that trended northeast-southwest as a near-parallel set of lines. Using basic marine geological techniques, we decided to use the bathymetry to navigate. Bathymetric maps, if reasonably accurate with respect to location of the submarine topography, are useful and can locate a ship. I did this once in 1968 while I was on board the USNS *Eltanin* off Antarctica. This was before the availability of a continuous satellite navigation system, such as the global positioning system (GPS) that is commonly used today. We were looking for a cluster of previously surveyed sea mounts; we planned to piston core the top sediments on one of them. As we approached the sea mount target, I

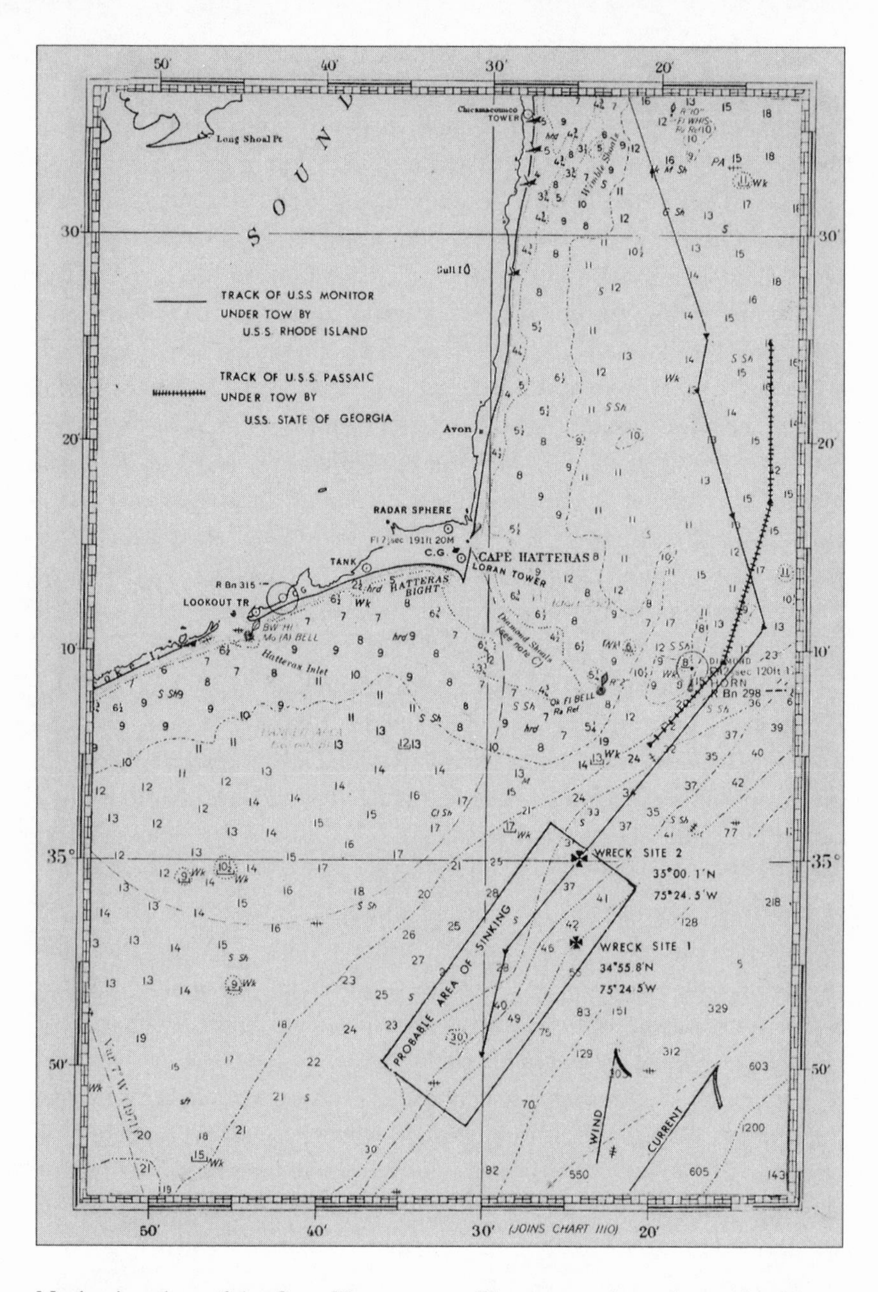

Navigation chart of the Cape Hatteras area. The proposed search area for the *Monitor* was based on the last sighting and location of the tow ship USS *Rhode Island*, taking account of the wind and current direction at the time. Wreck #1 and Wreck #2 were identified by the *Eastward* in August 1973. Wreck #2 turned out to be the *Monitor*. Depths are in fathoms.

Newton, J. G., H. E. Edgerton, R. E. Sheridan, and G. P. Watts. 1974. *Final Expedition Report: Cruise E-12-73*. Beaufort, N.C.: Duke University Marine Laboratory, 11.

watched our seismic reflection profiler in the geophysics lab. The bridge officer called for us to haul in our seismic gear and magnetometer in preparation for stopping on the coring station. I watched the profiler, anticipating the appearance of the sea mount, but it did not appear. I called the bridge officer and asked if he was sure of our position. He said yes, he was sure. But I was not.

I went directly to the *Eltanin*'s bridge and talked to the watch's third officer. Well qualified, his eyes were going bad so he had given up the first officer position. He discovered the error. South of the Antarctic Circle the longitudes are so close together that our easterly course dictated that plotting charts be changed every 15 minutes of longitude. During the last change, the previous bridge officer had inadvertently mislabeled the longitude as 15 minutes farther east than we actually were. The target sea mount was another three hours along our course. I returned to the geophysics lab and continued to watch the profiler. Sure enough, in three hours the sea mount appeared just as the bridge officer called to haul in our gear for the coring station.

The next day I was surprised when the *Eltanin*'s captain visited the geophysics lab, something he rarely did. He walked around with his hands in his pockets, and, as always, wearing his gold braided navy commander's hat. Finally he stopped in front of the seismic reflection profile recorder. He looked at it and asked, "Is this the machine that tells you where we are?" Obviously, he had received a report from the third officer on the bridge about the navigation error made the night before and he was curious about how I knew that we were not at the proper coring location. It's impossible to know how many nongeophysicist scientists without profilers might have been told by the bridge that they were on station when the target was actually many miles away.

In our search for the *Monitor* we were grateful for the smooth, gently sloping sea floor in the search rectangle. The depth contours, or isobaths, formed a near-constant spacing of northeast-southwest grid lines. By maintaining our depth at a constant value, we followed an isobath on our northeasterly and southwesterly tracks as we completed our search grid. The Del Norte single fixes gave us our accurate position along the isobath. Thus, we could complete a sweep on a northeast course on one isobath, then reverse to a southwest course and follow the next shallower isobath. In this way we had an overlapping scan of the sea floor and we did not duplicate the search sweep. Given the historical record of the length, about 400 feet, of the anchor chain let out during the sinking of the *Monitor*, and assuming that the anchor took hold (Midshipmen 1974, 455), we concentrated our search between the 360 foot (60 fathom) and 180 foot (30 fathom) isobaths.

On the bridge of the *Eastward* the bridge officers recorded measurements taken from a standard Loran A navigator. Running fixes on a Loran A were accurate to plus-or-minus one half mile, so they were not useful in a fine-scale search. The Del Norte navigator was in the geophysical lab near the vertical sonar recorder. Measurements could be read as we plotted our own navigation in the lab. The vertical sonar recorder was accurate to plus-or-minus one fathom (six feet). Given the gentle slope of the sea floor in the search grid of approximately seven fathoms per mile, the vertical sonar resolution of the depth gave an accurate northwest-southeast location of one seventh of a mile, or plus-or-minus approximately eight hundred feet. This was more accurate than the Loran system, whose accuracy was only about plus-or-minus three thousand feet.

Newton, as chief scientist on the cruise, organized the search work into three standard ship watches; each person's watch was four hours on, followed by eight hours off. Edgerton, Watts, and I were the watch chiefs for the last seven days of the cruise. Newton took a floating schedule to achieve overall supervision. As the watch chief with the most experience in utilizing the *Eastward*'s capabilities and its geophysical equipment, I took the 0000–4000 midnight watch, meaning my day's first duty began at midnight and I was relieved from duty at 4:00 A.M. I was responsible for the observations and interpretations of the sonar and magnetometer recorders. I supervised the watch standers who recorded times and dates on the recorders. Several watch standers were students who faithfully kept accurate records but were just learning to interpret geophysical data. Among the group of students was Cathryn, John Newton's sixteen-year-old daughter; she was a geology major at Duke University.

We had to react quickly to sonar and magnetometer contacts to effectively use our limited search time. There was no way we could completely sweep the search area in the allotted time. We had only enough time to check out some wrecks before we returned to Beaufort on 31 August. We had to make quick interpretations of the data and react rapidly. "The watch chief was often called upon to exercise critical judgements concerning which bit of data was most significant, how best to use the available ship time—specifically, whether or not a target or a method was worth pursuing" (Newton et al. 1974, 13).

As the search for the *Monitor* began on 23 August, Newton showed the watch chiefs the marker buoys being constructed on the fore deck of the *Eastward.* The buoys consisted of Danforth and sandbag anchors, with about fifty pounds of sand, anchor lines of four to five hundred feet of polypropylene line, eight foot long poles mounted through Styrofoam floats, and radar reflectors on the tops of the pole staffs. Details of the procedure follow. One of the marker buoys would be launched from the fantail of the *Eastward* when we crossed a wreck contact with the vertical sonar, after we had zeroed-in on the contact using the side-scan sonar. Immediately after launching the marker buoy, we would call the bridge on the geophysics lab squawkbox and order the bridge mate to hove-to. The *Eastward* would then slowly be maneuvered back to the marker buoy to reestablish vertical sonar contact and we would note the location relative to the marker buoy. The *Eastward* next would be moved upstream in the Gulf Stream to drop its bow anchor. Slowly the *Eastward* would drift downstream on its anchor chain to once again be positioned by the vertical sonar over the wreck. From this position, we would be ready to launch still and television cameras to photograph the wrecks.

The primary search tool was the EG&G dual-channel side-scan sonar. With a 105 kiloHertz sound source transducer, the unit provided a fine-scale resolution of the contacts. The power of the unit gave it an effective range of approximately one thousand feet in each direction from the side of the *Eastward.* The next important tool was the Varian magnetometer. The magnetic anomaly from iron ships about the size of the *Monitor* would extend only about two hundred feet from the center of a wreck, so the search vessel would have to be that close to a wreck to detect an anomaly. Finally, an Edo 12 kiloHertz vertical sonar recorded on a Raytheon precision depth recorder (PDR) would show a contact only if the *Eastward* passed directly over a wreck. When I was on watch, I planned to first identify a contact on the side-scan sonar. Next, I would do an increasingly close grid survey on that target until a magnetic anomaly was detected and a vertical sonar crossing was made. Then I would give the order for the marker buoy to be launched. As discussed in the next chapter, things did not always work exactly as planned.

5

The Wreck Is Discovered

I got some rest on 23 August 1973 after the intense work on the vibracoring. That night, a few minutes before midnight, just before I was due to take over the watch, I went to the *Eastward*'s geophysics lab. I inspected the records from the primary search tool, the EG&G dual-channel side-scan sonar. The watch stander had made some notes about what he thought were contacts. Most of the contacts had weak amplitudes and were of low relief. Sound, when reflected from the side of the contact, leaves a nonreflective shadow behind the object; the size of the shadow on the record is dependent on the contact's height above the sea floor, commonly referred to as its relief.

One contact, however, stood out with a strong, crisp reflection and shadow. I made note of the time the contact was made, its occurrence on the port-side channel, and its approximate slant range from the track of the *Eastward*. Shortly after midnight, I called Tom Stout, the mate on the bridge, and advised him of the location of this promising contact. I ordered him to return along the *Eastward*'s track to the closest Loran fix as possible. Stout, the third deck officer, was very competent at steering and navigating the ship, and he immediately began maneuvering the ship. A superb officer, Stout was on loan to DUML for this cruise from the University of Rhode Island School of Oceanography program, which ran the research vessel *Trident*.

While Stout was bringing the *Eastward* to the nearby Loran fix, I began preparing an enlarged grid for relative navigation and a maneuvering board. One axis of the grid was the plus-or-minus ten foot accurate

Del Norte lines from Diamond Shoal Light Tower, and the other axis of the grid was the water depth isobaths around forty to sixty fathoms. By reading the Del Norte range and water depth from the PDR, I could tell where the *Eastward* was on the relative navigation and maneuvering board. Using the rough location of the side-scan sonar contact relative to the Loran fix, I could place the contact on the enlarged grid. I then began a fine-scale grid search by giving Stout course directions over the geophysics lab squawkbox. I thus "conned" Stout to put the *Eastward* directly over the possible wreck (Newton et al. 1974, 12).

This was my first experience trying to locate wrecks with remote geophysical techniques, so my calculations and plotting required some time. I worked on the grid search for hours. It took a great deal of concentration to plot where the *Eastward* was and where it had been, and then to decide on the next course change to get closer to the wreck. As the grid tightened, the time on any one leg of the grid shortened and the right-angle turns became more frequent. Later, members of the search team said they knew something was up because the frequent turns were causing the *Eastward* to roll and their sleep was disturbed.

Finally, at about 3:30 A.M. on 24 August, the watch stander on the vertical sonar PDR saw the contact of the wreck. I went from the maneuvering board navigation plot station to the PDR station located a few feet away. And there it was—a great vertical crossing of the wreck. It seemed about the right height for the *Monitor*. I immediately crossed to the Varian magnetometer recorder a few feet away, just in time to see the nice magnetic anomaly typical of an iron ship emerge. We definitely had an iron wreck about the size of the *Monitor*.

I immediately called Stout and told him to mark the Loran fix at the time we crossed the wreck on vertical sonar, and to hove-to and maintain position as close to that fix as possible. This he did. I also recorded the Del Norte range and PDR depth of fifty fathoms.

At approximately 3:45, Doc Edgerton arrived at the geophysical lab to prepare for his 0400–0800 watch. After showing him the vertical sonar crossing and the magnetic anomaly, I told him we had located the wreck of an iron ship about the size of the *Monitor*. Edgerton was all smiles when he looked at the data. He said, "Alright, let's maintain this position until 0800, then have a strategy meeting with the search team after a good breakfast. We can decide then how best to approach the wreck."

I thought this was a strange plan. Coming from the Lamont-Doherty

Geological Observatory's school of thought, my mentors, Dr. Maurice Ewing and Dr. Bruce Heezen, always had used every bit of available ship time to collect data. To go to sleep for four hours and just let the *Eastward* sit would have been unheard of! Because Edgerton had seniority, however, and was the watch chief from 0400 to 0800 hours, I accepted his plan.

After breakfast on 24 August the search team met in the *Eastward*'s lounge to discuss how to approach the wreck for photography. I briefed the group on the geophysical sonar and magnetic data, and gave them an estimate of where the wreck was relative to the *Eastward*. I think there was some surprise when I told the group it might take as long as four hours to get over the wreck. Given my experience from the night before, and the fact that we were trying to maintain position in the strong Gulf Stream, I was trying to be as realistic as possible. John Newton outlined the procedure to drop the marker buoy, go upstream to drop the *Eastward*'s anchor, then drift back on the anchor chain to settle the *Eastward* directly over the wreck with an assist from the *Eastward*'s propeller and rudder working against the anchor chain. This plan worked well. Gordon Watts showed the team some of the photographs of the *Monitor* taken by the photographer James Gibson in July 1862 (Peterkin 1981c, 47–49). He pointed out key features that we should look for in the pictures we took. Watts also reviewed the *Monitor*'s architectural drawings and plans, some of which showed detailed construction features.

After the meeting we began our attempts to maneuver the *Eastward* over the wreck. By noon we were taking photographs of the wreck. Fred Kelly, the DUML liaison officer, and I ran the camera winch on the 01 deck. His role on the *Eastward* was to act as a go-between for the scientific party and the *Eastward*'s officers and crew. He was familiar with all the oceanographic equipment on the *Eastward* and responsible for the equipment's operation and repair. Kelly also loaded film in the camera and developed the film in the *Eastward*'s darkroom. I had worked with Kelly on many *Eastward* cruises and I appreciated his competency and efficiency. On this search cruise he continued to do his excellent work.

Lowering the EG&G still camera near the bottom, we had to be very careful. The camera had a trigger weight suspended below it that would make contact with the wreck. The release of tension on the trigger wire caused the camera's strobe light to flash and a picture to be taken. Only the release of tension on the camera wire at the 01 deck winch would indicate a contact. By watching the wire out depth indicator, we could anticipate when contact was made. To ensure against snagging the camera in the wreck, we watched for contact indicators carefully. After a contact, we would quickly raise the camera about thirty feet to ensure that we had cleared the wreck. Then we would slowly lower the camera again for the next picture. This raising and lowering of the camera for each picture had to be done gingerly. Often, we would take only six or seven pictures, rather than the full sixteen, to be sure to get some pictures and to be sure not to snag the camera in the wreck.

To improve the contact camera approach, we attached a down-wire sonar pinger just above the camera. This pinger could be "seen" on the vertical sonar echo-sounder PDR. The pinger's depth, and thus the depth of the camera below the pinger, could be measured precisely on the PDR. And, more important, the pinger's output ping also reflected from the wreck, so the distance from the pinger to the wreck, and thus the camera to the wreck distance, was precisely measurable. At the precise time when the camera was just above the wreck the winch operator would lower the camera and trigger a picture. By raising the camera quickly, the down-wire pinger would indicate that the camera was clear of the wreck.

The television camera equipment gave us less difficulty. With its real-time monitor/recorder in the *Eastward*'s wet lab, we watched what the camera viewed. When the camera was just above the wreck we could see the wreck on the monitor, and hold the camera winch steady at that amount of wire out. Because of the strong Gulf Stream current, the loose wire suspensions of both the still and television cameras were problematic, however. The varying strength of the current at varying depths caused unknown configurations of the catenaries of the flexible camera wires. During any lowering of the cameras, wires dangling in the current made maneuvering the cameras to any precise part of the wreck difficult to control. By working the *Eastward*'s propeller and rudder against its anchor chain, the cameras could be swung so we could at least get pictures of the wreck, but it was impossible to predict where exactly on the wreck the cameras would be focused. Consequently, during any camera lowering the scientists viewing the camera's pinger record and television monitor had to communicate with the mates on the bridge to ask them to change the *Eastward*'s propeller and rudder conditions. In this way, different photographs and views of the wreck were achieved.

For three days and three nights, 24–26 August, we photographed the first wreck we had found, and designated it Wreck #1 from that point forward (Newton et al. 1974, 11, 13). One feature we kept photographing was circular in nature, with about the same dimensions as the *Monitor*'s twenty-one foot diameter turret. Its appearance, however, did not seem exactly correct. Although encouraged, we remained confused. We had no idea how more than one hundred years on the ocean floor would have modified the turret. Other features of Wreck #1 were hard to relate to the *Monitor*. On the deck forward of the turret-like object was an encrusted upright structure that could have been some kind of boom crane or possibly a mounted 2-inch or 3-inch gun. Finally, on 26 August the image captured by the television camera showed what was clearly a gypsy-head capstan (Newton et al. 1974, 13). When I saw the capstan I immediately concluded that this wreck was not the *Monitor;* it was a twentieth century trawler. I sketched a deck diagram for Watts to show how the capstan on the foredeck near an upright boom crane is a common arrangement for hauling in fishing nets. The circular feature mistaken as the *Monitor*'s turret could easily be a circular front of a flying bridge on a fishing trawler. Our photography on Wreck #1 ended; the entire search team and ship's crew were dejected (Newton et al. 1974, 13).

Although demoralizing, this negative outcome was, as in all science, a significant positive achievement that advanced the search for the *Monitor*. Wreck #1, located at latitude 34°55.8' N, longitude 75°24.5' W, was the same wreck located by the U.S. Navy's underwater object locator (UOL) in 1950 that was reported as a possible location of the *Monitor* wreck (Midshipmen 1974, 621; Newton 1973, 1). Our photographs proved that the 1950 report was an erroneous identification.

While most of the search team was disheartened, I was not. I knew that it would have defied all odds if the first wreck we found turned out to be the *Monitor*. I did not have high expectations for success in finding the *Monitor* in only seven days of searching. I was simply pleased that in three days we had successfully found and identified a wreck. Not many marine geophysicists have ever done that. We had utilized our geophysical search equipment well and efficiently. Our photographic techniques were giving us the detail we needed. I was satisfied with our performance and glad that our surveying techniques were working.

Our geophysical search for the *Monitor* continued on 26 August. Unfortunately, upon deploying our primary search tools, the EG&G dual-channel side-scan sonar and the Varian proton-precession magnetometer, both failed to operate correctly. The cable of the magnetometer had "disintegrated beyond repair" (Newton et al. 1974, 13) and no signal was being detected from the "maggie fish," which was towed about 250 feet behind the *Eastward* to remove the sensor from the research vessel's own magnetic field. The sonar transducer for the EG&G dual-channel side-scan sonar was not functioning and needed repair. Edgerton hauled in the dual-channel transducer to make repairs, and substituted another EG&G single-channel transducer to continue the survey. The EG&G single-channel side-scan would search the starboard side of the *Eastward.* To cover the port side, we reset the *Eastward*'s hull-mounted Simrad 38 kiloHertz search sonar to look at a ninety degree angle from the axis of the ship. By using the Simrad as a side-scan sonar, we effectively had a two-channel system for typical swath mapping of the search area.

One disadvantage of using the Simrad sonar was that its recorder was in a stairwell off the wet lab on the main deck of the *Eastward,* whereas the vertical sonar PDR and the EG&G side-scan recorder were in the geophysics lab on the 01 deck. My procedure on my watch was to visit the Simrad recorder every fifteen minutes to interpret the record, while most time was spent watching the PDR and EG&G recorders in the geophysics lab. Also, we were still using the Del Norte navigator and PDR for detailed navigation grids, and the Del Norte recorder was in an alcove off the main geophysics lab.

Coming on watch at a little before noon on 27 August, I checked all the sonar recorders. We were steering a northeast course following the 39 fathom (234 feet) isobath. Ten or so minutes after noon, Kelly came in the geophysics lab and told me to come down to the Simrad recorder. "There's a contact you should look at!" Kelly had been fishing off the *Eastward* because our survey speed of five knots was ideal for trawling. In passing the Simrad recorder while going below to store his fishing rods on his way to lunch, Kelly noticed a side-scan contact on the Simrad recorder. He immediately recognized its significance (Newton et al. 1974, 14; Editorial 1976a, 17).

I accompanied Kelly down to the main deck and the Simrad recorder. There it was—the most beautiful sonar contact we had recorded yet on the cruise. It was a dark, crisp, black mark on the otherwise gray recorder

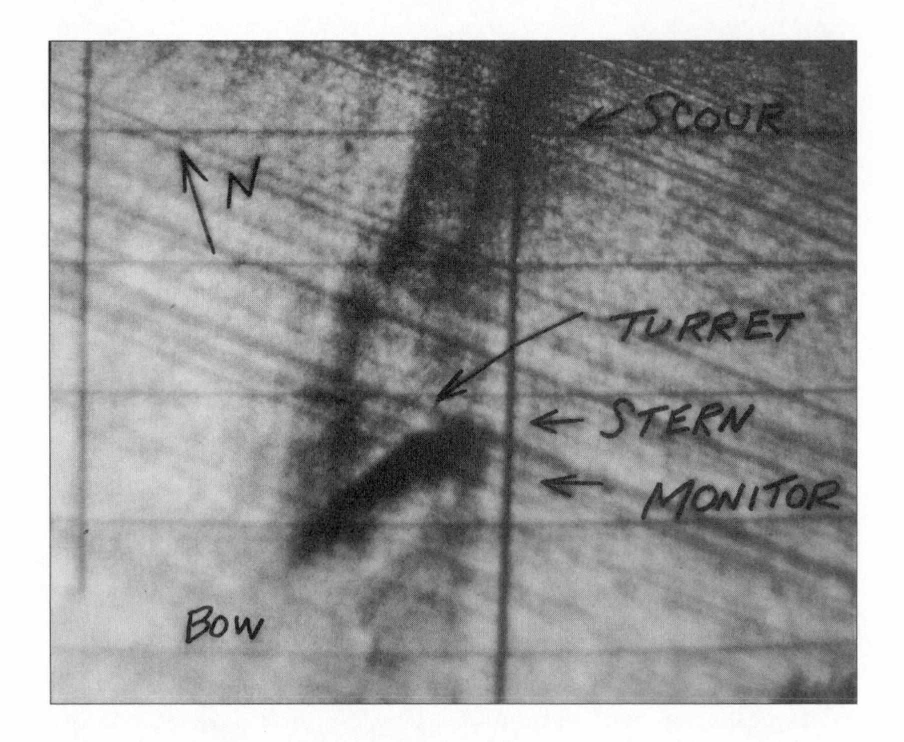

Side-scan sonar image, first seen in August 1973 during cruise E-12-73 aboard the *Eastward,* shows the complete lengthwise profile of the *Monitor* wreck. Note the approximate east-west orientation relative to the north arrow, and the scour mark northeast of the wreck made by the Gulf Stream.

Harold Edgerton

paper. Clearly, we had found another wreck. The watch stander, while enthusiastic and faithful in marking the records at fifteen minute intervals, was not a trained marine geophysicist and had not fully understood the significance of this contact. Besides, I would have seen the contact when I visited the recorder at 12:15.

I immediately estimated that the contact had occurred ten minutes earlier along our northeast track. From the wreck's reflection time difference with the sea floor reflection, giving a slant range distance, I estimated the target to be at a distance of approximately six hundred feet to our port. Quickly, I hit the wet lab's squawkbox and called the bridge. I gave Stout the time of the contact so he could estimate the distance back along our track. I gave him my estimated range, and ordered him to turn to port, proceed six hundred feet, then turn the ship on the reciprocal to our present course. Stout immediately executed the turn.

Our cruise report succinctly described the events. "Fortunately, Mr. Fred Kelly . . . passed the recorder at the appropriate moment, glanced up and recognized the potential significance of the echo. The watch chief, Dr. Sheridan, made the decision to change course to investigate the target. This chain of events and the action of reversing course proved to be of great consequence, probably being the most decisive moment of the voyage" (Newton et al. 1974, 14). Another contemporary report of the discovery stated, "The watch chief, Doctor Sheridan, made the decision to change course and investigate [the sonar contact]. 'That' says Newton, 'was probably the most decisive moment of the voyage'" (Editorial 1976a, 17). The duplicate references help to confirm my own recollections of the discovery events.

After ordering the course change I ran back up to the geophysics lab to set up the detailed navigation grid using the Del Norte and PDR coordinates. As soon as I had the grid set up, I told the PDR watch stander to maintain the depth at the thirty eight fathom isobath. I began tracking the *Eastward*'s movement back on a southwest track using the Del Norte ranges.

Suddenly the watch stander on the vertical sonar PDR recorder asked, "What is this coming up?" I looked at the record as a beautiful vertical sonar contact of a wreck appeared. I was floored! Stout had navigated the *Eastward* so well that on one pass he had returned the research vessel precisely to the target from the range of more than one nautical mile, a fantastic achievement.

The height of the vertical sonar contact appeared correct for the *Monitor*. I called Stout to hove-to, and hold and mark our position. I headed for the deck to launch the marker buoy. Prepared with proper anchor line and scope, the buoy was propped against the rail on the *Eastward*'s fantail. To get to the fantail, I had to pass through the *Eastward*'s mess. I saw Newton, Edgerton, and Watts eating lunch.

Newton called, "Did you find another wreck, Bob?"

Going out the mess door to the fantail, I yelled, "Yes, and it looks good!"

After the marker buoy was launched, Stout quickly moved upstream in the Gulf Stream current and dropped anchor. Moving the *Eastward* back on the anchor chain the ship became positioned over the wreck. Excitedly, I lowered the EG&G still camera within an hour after making

Fred Kelly lowers the *Eastward*'s EG&G still camera, which took the first photographs of the *Monitor*.

vertical sonar contact. Lowering the camera gingerly, I took perhaps six or seven shots. Then I retrieved the camera to get the photographs developed.

As the pictures were being developed and printed, the assistant in the darkroom chided me, "Can't we get a full roll of pictures next time?"

"We have to be careful not to snag the camera in the wreck, and a few good pictures in hand is better than none," I explained.

The first photographs of the wreck, recorded as Wreck #2 (Newton et al. 1974, 11, 14), were somewhat nondescript. The light source on the EG&G camera was a strobe light developed by Edgerton. Given the distance of about four feet from the light source to the target, and the distance of about seven feet from the camera to the target, the area being photographed is only about six feet by six feet. We had learned from our experience with Wreck #1 that many photographs are needed to fortuitously capture any key features. I always likened it to trying to identify an elephant by having a few photographs of the toenails, the tail, the trunk, or a tusk. Most of the elephant photographs would be of nondescript patches of skin; only a few might be diagnostic.

The first photographs of Wreck #2 showed heavily encrusted angle iron bilge bulkhead supports (Newton et al. 1974, fig. 9, fig. 11). The heavy encrustation was indicative of a nineteenth century vessel, especially when comparing the amount of encrustation with Wreck #1. This was a good sign that Wreck #2 might possibly be the *Monitor*.

After more lowerings of the EG&G still camera on later watches, what I had feared happened. The camera snagged in the wreck (Newton et al. 1974, fig. 9). This was a most unfortunate turn of events. Although we continued to photograph from the television camera's monitor, the quality and resolution of the still pictures had been far superior.

Keeping with our basic approach to collect as much data as possible with all the ship time yet remaining, we continued filming. As with the still camera, the television view and lighting limited the area seen in any one frame to about a six foot by six foot area. Dangling the television camera on a wire cable in the variable Gulf Stream current gave us little control of the camera's position. We would have to be lucky to capture a critical feature of the *Monitor*.

For three days and three nights, 28–30 August, we recorded Wreck #2 and viewed our television coverage. We continually saw well-encrusted angle iron support framing of bulkheads, flat deck plating, and some horizontal beams or shafts. As the television camera swung in the current across the wreck, we saw a semicircular feature overlain by a straight, encrusted deck-like feature (Newton et al. 1974, fig. 10).

Hung beneath the television camera frame within the camera's view was a four inch diameter magnetic compass. We routinely used a compass when doing geologic photography to provide orientation of the photographs and to provide a scale for the pictures. Next to the iron hull of Wreck #2 the directions from the magnetic compass were spurious. For scale purposes, however, the compass was useful.

Using the compass as a scale, it was clear that the semicircular feature was several inches thick, and that the straight feature above it was at least three times that thickness wide. If we were looking down at the side of an iron battleship of the Spanish-American War vintage, the straight and

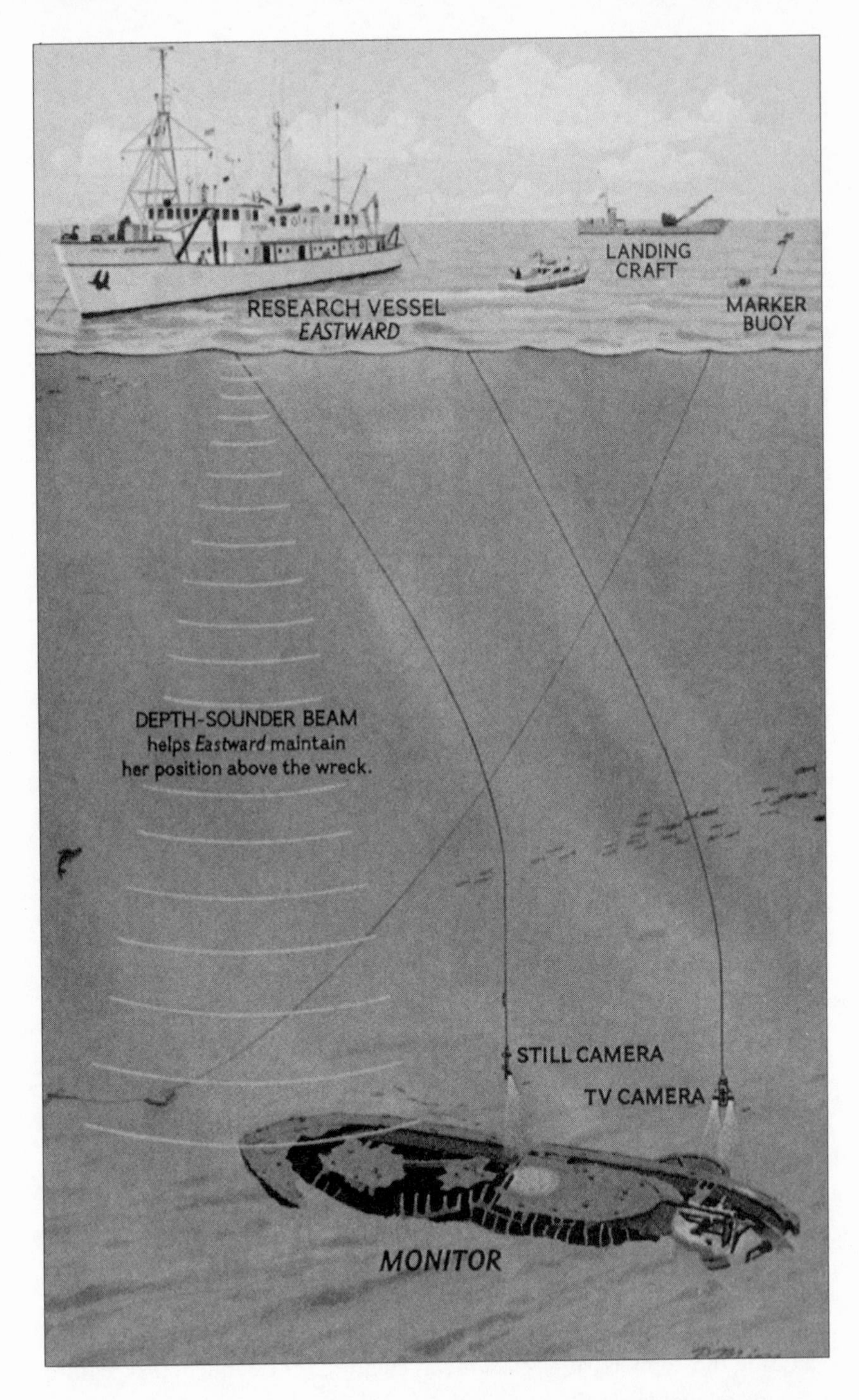

Illustration depicting the research vessel *Eastward*, anchored over the wreck of the *Monitor*, and the army reserve's LCU-1488 and J boat. Note the lowered still and television cameras.

National Geographic Magazine print. With permission.

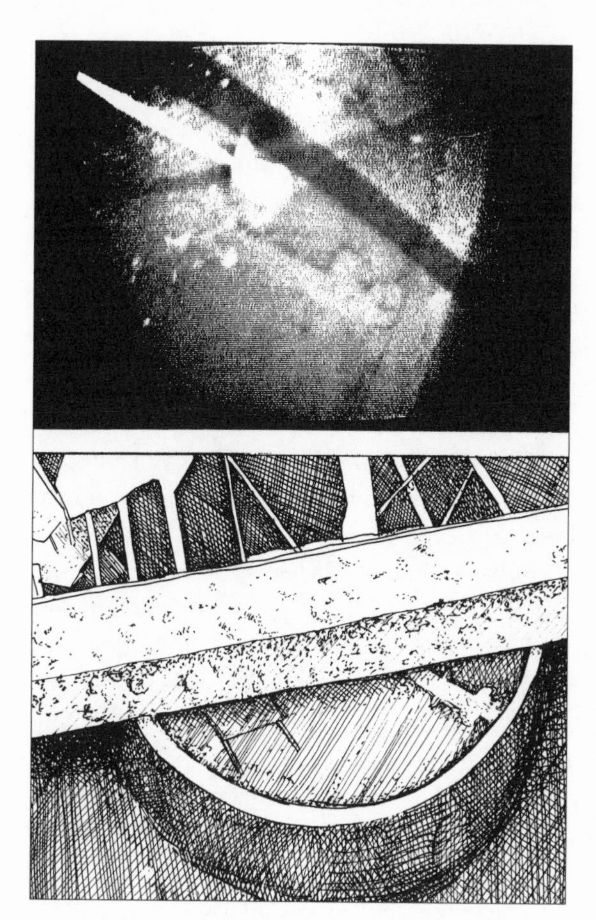

Television image of an enigmatic semicircular feature beneath a straight deck-like structure and a line-drawn interpretation of the image by Gordon Watts. Note the four-inch diameter magnetic compass, which gives a sense of scale.

Newton, J. G., H. E. Edgerton, R. E. Sheridan, and G. P. Watts. 1974. *Final Expedition Report: Cruise E-12-73*. Beaufort, N.C.: Duke University Marine Laboratory, fig. 10.

semicircular features could be a deck above a semicircular gun turret on the side hull. I have seen such gun turrets on the side hull of the battleship *Olympia* moored as a restored museum at Penn's Landing in Philadelphia. The *Olympia* was Adm. George Dewey's flagship in the Spanish-American War. Indeed, two of those obsolete *Olympia*-class battleships, the *Virginia* and the *New Jersey*, were sunk off Diamond Shoals in 1923 by Brig. Gen. William (Billy) Mitchell in his demonstration that airplanes could bomb and destroy battleships (National Geographic Society 1970, 1). Perhaps an obsolete Spanish-American War battleship was what we were seeing on the videotapes of Wreck #2.

Our speculation continued as we continued filming. We stared and stared at the video images of Wreck #2 until they were etched into our memories. Each search team member wracked his or her brain trying to relate the video images in some fashion to the photographs and construction drawings of the *Monitor* that we had available, but to no avail.

Although intensely working with the television imagery, we took a short break for a few hours to do a side-scan sonar profile. Edgerton had repaired the EG&G dual-channel side-scan sonar transducer fish, and we wanted to use it to get better sonar images of Wreck #2. I spent several hours conning the bridge to make a straight pass at a constant range from the wreck. As anchor chain was let out, the propeller and rudder were worked to move the *Eastward* very slowly past the wreck. It worked beautifully and excellent side-scan sonar images were collected. The length of Wreck #2 became evident, as was its approximate east-west orientation. The length matched the *Monitor*'s length. We even saw the scour pattern created by the Gulf Stream on the northeast, or lee, side of the wreck.

On 31 August we had to end our filming of Wreck #2 because we were scheduled to return the *Eastward* to its home port of Beaufort. We retrieved the television camera. For a few minutes we lowered a four-pronged grapnel to try to retrieve a possibly identifiable artifact. Several hard contacts were made; they bent the grapnel hooks back, but nothing was recovered. We then towed the *Eastward*'s Day dredge on the sea floor near the wreck in hopes of recovering some loose artifacts in the sea-floor sediments. Only coarse sand, some wood fragments, and coal pieces were recovered. They were not diagnostic; most nineteenth century vessels were coal burners and ships, including the *Monitor*, all used wood in their construction.

I believed that we had found an old, probably nineteenth century, vessel. My reason was based on the thicker encrustation, compared to the twentieth century trawler we had photographed at the Wreck #1 site. The sonar data indicated that Wreck #2 was about the size of the *Monitor*, and the photographs of the angle iron support brackets of the bulkheads and apparent decks indicated it was an iron ship. The coal also supported the conclusion that it was a nineteenth century vessel. All evidence led to the conclusion that Wreck #2 could possibly be the *Monitor*. However, we lacked any definitive proof. In the final analysis, we could only say that Wreck #2 at latitude 35°00.1' N, longitude 75°24.5' W might be the *Monitor*. I was happy with that conclusion.

When we docked at DUML at Beaufort, North Carolina, on 31 August

The coinvestigators on the August 1973 discovery cruise E-12-73 aboard the research vessel *Eastward*. (*Left to right:*) the leader of the cruise, John Newton of Duke University Marine Laboratory; Dr. Harold Edgerton of MIT; Dr. Robert Sheridan of the University of Delaware; and Gordon Watts of the North Carolina Division of Archives and History.

Duke University Marine Laboratory

1973, we were not besieged with newspaper and television reporters to hear our story. Given the previous publications of erroneous identifications, we were cautious. We did not want to erroneously add to the list of the *Monitor* discoveries.

Fortunately, however, the DUML's public information officer had the foresight to pose the coinvestigators on the dock in front of the *Eastward* as if we had just returned from a major discovery cruise. The resulting photograph, showing John Newton, Dr. Harold Edgerton, myself, and Gordon Watts together reading what was supposed to be a press release on the discovery of the *Monitor*, captured the moment for history.

As I drove back to Delaware from Beaufort, I continued pondering the possibility of Wreck #2 actually being the *Monitor*. No evidence ruled that out. The only unexplained item was the semicircular feature below the straight edge of what looked like a deck. An unusual feature, it was not like anything we had thus far imagined for the *Monitor*. So it was a puzzle.

As a scientist as well as a realist, I knew that it would have been very unusual for us to have actually found the *Monitor* after locating only two wrecks. There are hundreds of wrecks in the Graveyard of the Atlantic (National Geographic Society 1970, 1; Stick 1978, 75), and Wreck #2 could have been just another one. The odds were that it was just another wreck. To avoid disappointment, I kept telling myself this over and over.

6

Identification Questioned

For several months after the end of cruise E-12-73 on the *Eastward* in August 1973, the search team pondered over the photographs of Wreck #2, especially the image of the enigmatic semicircular structure beneath the straight deck-like feature. What was this? None of the other photographic evidence disqualified Wreck #2 from being the *Monitor;* the sonar and the dredged coal favored it being the *Monitor.* But nothing was apparently conclusive.

A thorough analysis of the still photographs and television tapes might be required to answer the question of the identity of Wreck #2. This task fell to Gordon Watts, the archaeologist on the team. A marine archaeologist with the North Carolina Division of Archives and History, Watts was allowed to analyze the *Eastward* data as part of his state duties even though Wreck #2 was not technically in state waters and not under the division's jurisdiction (Watts 1975, 326). Watts also used the *Eastward* data and the photographic evidence for his master's thesis under Professor William Still at East Carolina University. Luckily, Watts was able to devote a great deal of time and thought to his analysis of the photographic data that had been accumulated during the *Eastward* cruise.

Watts drew a composite diagram of Wreck #1. As stated previously, it was apparent from the television views of the gypsy-head capstan on the fore deck beneath the bridge that Wreck #1 was a twentieth century trawler. I had diagrammed the general appearance of this trawler for Watts while we were on board the *Eastward.* For his report, Watts completed a scaled, composite drawing of the photographed portions of the trawler for publication (Watts 1975, 317).

Watts then turned to the photography and videotapes of Wreck #2. According to his identification of Wreck #2,

> The majority of the data collected during the R/V [research vessel] *Eastward* cruise was in the form of random photographic and television tape records. Analysis and identification of the sites proved to be a cumulative process. First, small photo mosaics of the significant features of the wrecks were constructed. These were carefully related to drawings of the sites which were produced from the video tape and photographic data. This technique tied the individual camera passes together in the form of a composite picture (Watts 1975, 315).

His approach was time consuming yet thorough. It was several months before he started to get conclusive results.

The composite pictures were scaled using the four inch diameter of the magnetic compass that was suspended beneath the cameras so it could be captured in the photographs. Although not as precise a measurement as a diver holding a tape measure next to the objects, the compass helped determine the size of the objects fairly well (Newton et al. 1974, fig. 10). The compositing, drawing, and scaling of the pictures were time consuming. Also, "because of . . . the random and frequently erratic patterns of the camera passes, several months of analysis were required to isolate and identify the Wreck's distinguishing characteristics" (Watts 1975, 317).

The most distinguishing feature of Wreck #2 was that enigmatic semicircular feature. At one point in the analysis, Watts realized that this feature could actually be the overturned turret of the *Monitor* sticking out partially from beneath the overturned deck and armor belt (Newton et al. 1974, app. III, 1). When John Newton informed me of Watts's idea, I replied, "of course." To test his hypothesis, Watts measured his drawings of the feature. "Measurements of the structure produced an eight inch wall thickness. By extending the exposed arc 360° and using the wall thickness as a scale, a diameter of between 20 and 22 feet is obtained. Historical sources generally agree on an eight in. wall thickness and a twenty foot interior diameter for the turret" (Newton et al. 1974, app. III, 2). "If the top of the turret were constructed of railroad rails . . . the absence of the distinct [rail] pattern they would create adds

Still photograph of the *Monitor*'s overturned turret, sticking out from beneath the overturned port quarter of the armor belt. The photograph was taken by the Alcoa *Seaprobe* in April 1974.

John Newton

credibility to the conclusion that the turret is inverted" (Newton et al. 1974, app. III, 3).

The scaled size of the overhanging deck on the turret is about thirty inches, just about right for the five inches of iron backed by the thick wooden bulwark of horizontal ten inch square oak beams and vertical blocks of white pine that formed the armor belt (Peterkin 1981b, 43). The thin armor plates of the lower hull that were held on by brackets suspended from the armor belt had corroded away, leaving the interior framing exposed; the more massive armor belt remained intact, but overturned.

With these conclusions, the puzzle was solved. The *Monitor*'s hull and turret were overturned. The other features seen in the photographs now clearly made sense. The tailshaft and skeg were identified (Newton et al. 1974, fig. 8). Using compositing techniques, the turret was found near the stern of the overturned hull of the *Monitor*. The tailshaft and skeg would not be visible if the *Monitor*'s hull were upright. By examining the photographs and television tapes, Watts concluded, "because of the extreme difficulty of maneuvering the camera back over the site we were able to film only the stern of the wreck. Thus nothing is known about the condition of the hull forward of the boilers" (Newton et al. 1974, app. III, 4).

Unexplained coincidences were becoming the norm. We had defied all odds when the second wreck, the only one we could have ever documented in the last days of the *Eastward* cruise, turned out to be the *Monitor*. Then we again defied the odds when the only part of the wreck we randomly happened to photograph had the most distinguishing characteristic of the *Monitor* just peeking out from under the hull. Amazing! If we had obtained photographic coverage of the amidship area of the wreck, little in the way of distinguishing characteristics would have been seen. We were extremely lucky. The ocean never easily gives up its secrets; explorers can only do their best. Results sometimes depend on many things beyond human control. Being a religious person, and having been involved in some significant oceanographic discoveries during my career, I always say God wanted us to make these discoveries.

Reexamining the side-scan sonar data, the upraised deck of the *Monitor* faces north and the inverted deck is tilted to the south where the armor belt is being buried by sand. The sand is being carried to the northeast by the Gulf Stream and is stopped by the south side of the tilted deck and deposited. North of the raised deck of the *Monitor*, the spillover of the strong Gulf Stream current causes winnowing of the sediments and leaves a scour mark. The photographs document that the turret is holding up the northern side of the *Monitor* hull, which is some fifteen to twenty feet high above the sea floor. The side-scan sonar profiles show that the northeast side of the *Monitor* wreck is the highest part, and there is a suggestion of a reflection from the turret on the northeast. This led Watts to conclude that "the longitudinal axis of the hull is aligned southwest to northeast with the bow to the southwest" (Newton et al. 1974, app. III, 1). As discussed in succeeding chapters, the axis might actually be more east-west, but the bow is definitely on the west and the stern on the east. Cruise E-12-73's final expedition report, based solely on the *Eastward* data, included Watts's remarkably accurate drawing of the stern of the *Monitor* wreck. The hull of the *Monitor* is overturned and leaning on the overturned turret, which is partially exposed on the northeast side of the wreck. How the *Monitor* got into this particular orientation has several possible explanations. Most *Monitor* experts agree that the *Monitor* did

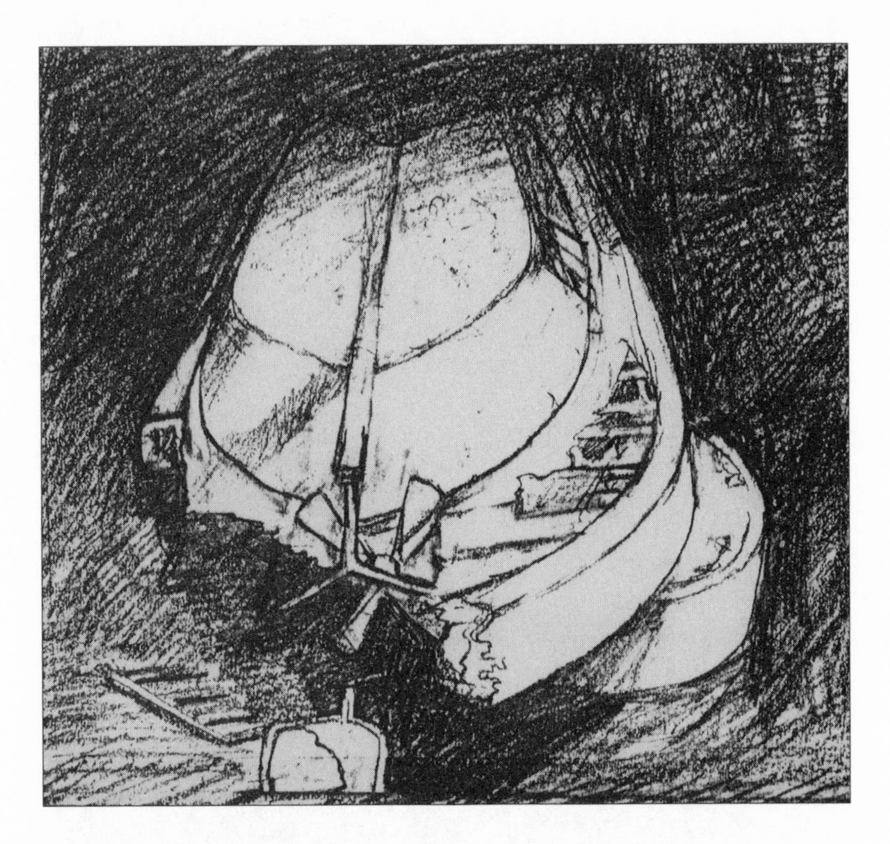

Composite drawing by Gordon Watts of the stern area of the overturned *Monitor*, as submitted in January 1974 for use in the *Eastward*'s discovery cruise report. Based solely on the *Eastward*'s data, it accurately depicts the overturned turret and armor belt.

Newton, J. G., H. E. Edgerton, R. E. Sheridan, and G. P. Watts. 1974. *Final Expedition Report: Cruise E-12-73*. Beaufort, N.C.: Duke University Marine Laboratory, fig. 8.

indeed roll over. It probably capsized early in the sinking (Newton et al. 1974, app. III, 1). It is quite understandable why this occurred. The *Monitor*, with its heavy cannons and heavily armored turret, was top heavy. Also, the hull design was not the most stable in rolling, heavy seas.

As mentioned previously, any ship without power will quickly "roll off" into the trough in a heavy sea. I have been in that situation before and can verify how quickly it occurs. Once in the trough, the rolling of the ship is violent and will eventually lead to capsizing, exactly as happened to the *Monitor*.

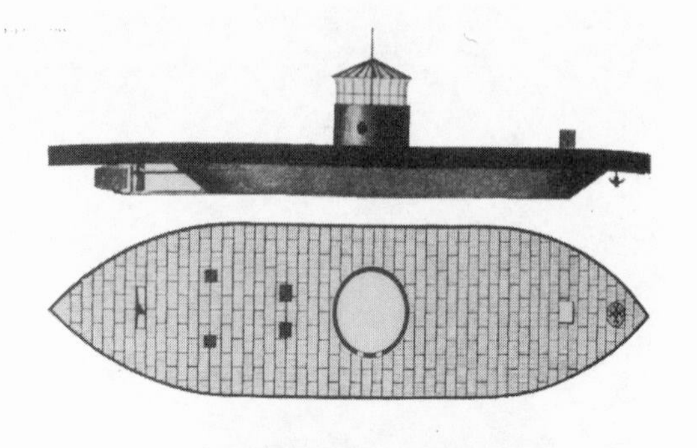

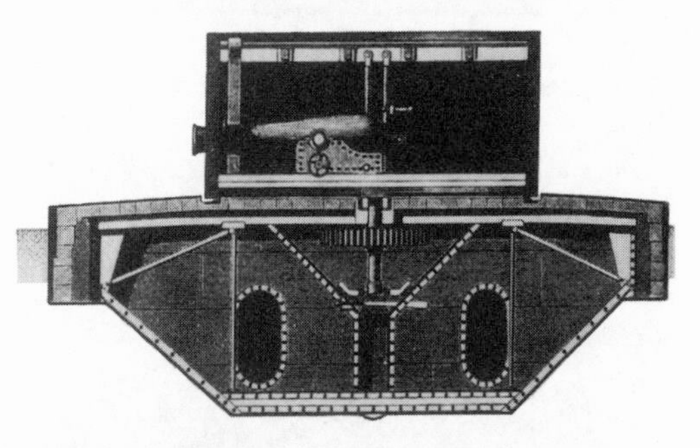

Diagrams of cross sections and plan view of the *Monitor* as depicted in a Swedish reprint of John Ericsson's article on the Monitors (Ericsson 1885, 290, 292). Note the single-chine hull of the *Monitor* as opposed to the rounded, seagoing hull of *Monitor Dictator*, a later *Monitor*-class vessel.

John Newton

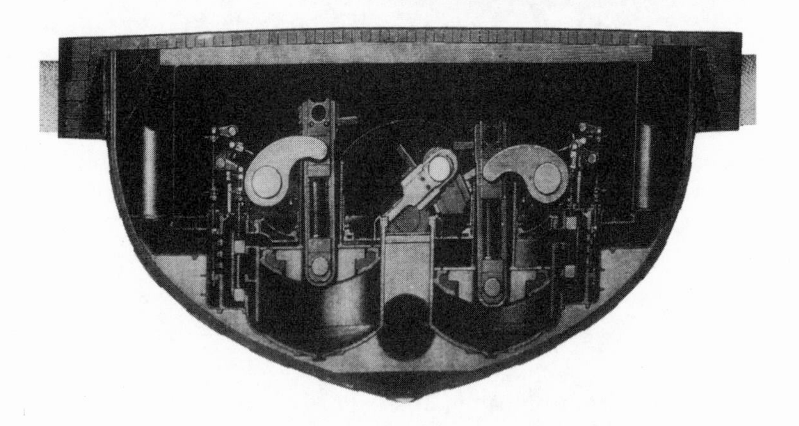

Unfortunately, the shallow-draft, single-chine hull of the *Monitor* also contributed to its instability during the violent rolling. When such a hull rolls its displacement will decrease. Given the urgency to build the *Monitor* in one hundred days, the single-chine hull design was the quickest and easiest to construct; no plates had to be curved or bent. As John Ericsson pointed out in a Swedish reprint of his article on the Monitors, this unstable hull design was not continued on the later Monitors. *Monitor*

Dictator, a later *Monitor*-class ship, had a well designed, rounded, seagoing hull (Ericsson 1885, 292). When a ship rolls with a rounded hull the displacement remains the same until a certain extreme angle is reached. The *Eastward*, for instance, was noted for its rolling; some experts say it could stand a forty-five degree roll. I had experienced some heavy rolls on the *Eastward*, from which we always came back, so I considered it a very seaworthy ship.

Most *Monitor* experts agree that the turret, being held on with some gear mechanisms and by gravity, would have dislodged quickly upon capsizing (Watts 1975, 320). To explain the location of the turret near the stern of the *Monitor* wreck requires more speculation. For example, in cruise E-12-73's final expedition report, Watts said, "because the anchor [from the *Monitor*'s bow] retarded the hull's down current progress, it would be possible for the heavy cylinder to drift slightly astern during its 200' descent" (Newton et al. 1974, app. III, 2). I disagree. The Gulf Stream current is episodically strong even down to the sea floor near the *Monitor* wreck, but the turret and guns are so heavy that they would have fallen straight down in a matter of seconds. The turret could not have been displaced down current in such a short interval of time.

In a later publication, Watts apparently retreated from the hypothesis of the sternward drift of the turret. He theorized,

> As the *Monitor*'s hull filled with sea water, the ship began to settle rapidly. Water rushing in through open engine room ventilators combined with the weight of engineering space machinery to send the ship down stern first. As bouyancy [*sic*] decreased, the weight of armor attached to the *Monitor*'s deck, armor belt, and forming the turret and the energy of wind driven seas combined to cause the ship to capsize, sending the unsecured contents of the vessel cascading aft and to starboard.
>
> Sinking by the stern at an angle of from 45 degrees to 60 degrees and rolling to starboard, the *Monitor*'s hull must have been only a short distance from, or in contact with, the bottom when the turret landed on the sand within approximately 50 feet of the stern's point of impact. As air rushed forward through the false keel and ventilation passages below the bilge ceiling to escape through the anchor well, the *Monitor* settled to the south-southwest with the inverted port quarter coming to rest on the base of the turret (Watts 1982, 4).

This scenario's details may not be entirely correct. For example, Watts's explanation suggests that the stern of the *Monitor* might have already been in contact with the bottom when the turret landed. Another scenario, which I favor, is that the hull of the *Monitor* was rolled over by the large storm waves from the southwest early in the sinking. The anchor held the bow toward the west so the *Monitor* rolled to starboard. The turret dislodged shortly after the hull rolled over and sank straight down. As the weight in the stern pulled the inverted hull down, air kept the bow area buoyed up and the anchor chain prevented the bow from moving to the east. The only motion possible was for the stern to rotate toward the west about an axis through the amidships. This brought the stern close to the original amidships position on rollover, where the turret originated. Thus, the stern landed on the bottom close to the turret, which had landed on the bottom perhaps just thirty seconds to a minute previously. The rollover to starboard favored the starboard armor belt landing on the bottom first, and the port armor belt settling to the north on top of the turret.

Cruise E-12-73's final expedition report, submitted at the end of January 1974, declared that we had found the wreck of the USS *Monitor*. John Newton called a news conference at Duke University at Durham, North Carolina, on 7 March 1974. Along with Watts, he made the announcement and distributed a news release about the discovery of the USS *Monitor* in 220 feet of water 16 miles south of Cape Hatteras.

One unfortunate thing about Doc Edgerton and I not attending the news conference at Duke University was that our roles in the discovery of the *Monitor* were not always subsequently recognized. Many news stories and referrals in history books and articles simply state that the *Monitor* was discovered by "Duke University scientists" (Davis 1975, 170; Geographica 1994, geog. 4). In reality, only one of the coinvestigators on the *Eastward* cruise that discovered the *Monitor* was from Duke University—John Newton. My being from the University of Delaware and Edgerton being from MIT were often overlooked. Because the *Eastward* was a Duke University research vessel, there was the false impression that all the scientists aboard were from Duke University. Even if such details were reported at the press conference, the pressure to ensure that the final newspaper articles were concise make these the kinds of details that are left out. But such exclusion of the University of Delaware and MIT scientists as participants in the discovery of the *Monitor* even occurred in articles by NOAA officials. Lt. Comdr. Floyd Childress of NOAA reported, "In 1973, scientists from the Duke University marine lab (led by John Newton) discovered the ship's location" (Childress 1978a, 6). NOAA lawyer John Millholland wrote, "on August 27, 1973, John Newton and his team from Duke found the ship" (Millholland 1978, 20).

Upon hearing the news of the discovery of the *Monitor*, there was some surprise and skepticism among competing groups that had also conducted searches for the *Monitor* during the 1973 summer. A private group, led by archaeologist John Broadwater, had conducted a several week long search of the Marx site north of Cape Hatteras. The U.S. Naval Academy midshipmen did aeromagnetic surveys on navy planes in the Marx area and in the area near the area covered by the *Eastward* (Miller 1978b, 29). Could anyone wonder at their skepticism, given the several previous announcements of the discovery of the *Monitor*? How could a group of academics, using technology little advanced from that used to photograph wrecks in World War II, have found the wreck of the *Monitor* in only seven days of searching? Impossible!

The Naval Academy midshipmen already had planned to conduct a photographic search for their aeromagnetic contacts in spring 1974. The Alcoa *Seaprobe*, a sophisticated centerwell vessel with a pipe-lowered, rigid camera system, offered the possibility of completely photographing a wreck (Miller 1978a, 97; Miller 1978b, 30). As part of the planning for the *Seaprobe* cruise, which was to be contracted by the Naval Intelligence Support Center, a meeting was called at the Naval Research Laboratory in Washington, D.C., on 11 March 1974 (Miller 1978a, 96–97). John Newton and Gordon Watts represented the discovery team from the *Eastward* at this meeting. They presented the results of the cruise to the assembled *Monitor* experts, showing the photographic and video evidence. They reported on the interpretation that the *Monitor* had capsized on sinking and landed on its turret. Among the naval *Monitor* experts at the meeting were Midshipman Edward Miller, one of the leaders of the Naval Academy's Project Cheesebox, and Ernest Peterkin, a retired navy captain and Naval Research Laboratory employee (Miller 1978a, 96–97).

Convinced that the *Monitor* had already been found, "the *Eastward* researchers argued that the sea time of the new venture should be used to further investigate their site. The Project Cheesebox researchers argued that the *Seaprobe*'s prime mission should be to survey and analyze all of the potential sites in their own study area" (Tise 1981, 40). It was somewhat understandable that those viewing the *Eastward* video data for the first time did not see the distinguishing features of the *Monitor* because they only had a brief look during the meeting, unlike those of us who stared at the images for days on the *Eastward* and unlike Watts who spent months analyzing the tapes. According to Miller, the Project Cheesebox representative at the meeting, "The video tapes had originally faded in and out of focus as the camera swung by the wreck from the anchored research ship, however, now they obviously had suffered greatly from the constant re-runs." He also commented, "participants [of the 11 March meeting] refrained from hasty conclusions in view of the past history of erroneous claims, desiring more irrefutable evidence" (Miller 1978a, 97). In other words, the navy experts questioned the *Eastward* team's identification of Wreck #2 as the wreck of the *Monitor*.

It was clear from the meeting that the "Duke" site, as it was then called, was to be the first site checked out by the *Seaprobe*. The plan was to use the rigid, pipe-mounted camera system to gather complete photographic coverage with high-quality, colored, still prints. The *Seaprobe*'s gripper device on the end of the pipe would be used to collect a possible uniquely identifiable artifact. Better photographs and artifacts would be the irrefutable evidence demanded by the navy's *Monitor* experts.

I am sure that the refusal of the navy experts to acknowledge the authenticity of the *Eastward*'s discovery was disappointing to Newton, who had been largely responsible for the cruise. To have the Duke site considered as just another possibility was disturbing, even if it was considered the first priority site to be visited by the *Seaprobe*. Also, the navy experts, especially Miller and Peterkin, were playing a major role in the planning and execution of the *Seaprobe* cruise. Newton now was considered just another interested participant. Without a leadership role, John was unable to get a commitment that the *Seaprobe*'s efforts would be totally devoted to collecting more data at the *Eastward* site. This was the beginning of what one reporter of the Naval Research Laboratory meeting called the "fissure among the parties" (Tise 1981, 40).

More and more, the *Seaprobe* cruise was becoming a continuation of the Project Cheesebox research of the Naval Academy. As part of that research, Miller was in frequent contact with Peterkin, whose vast knowledge of the *Monitor* aided the project's research greatly. This view that the *Seaprobe* cruise was a continuation of Project Cheesebox is borne out by the fact that the two major reports on the *Seaprobe* results were authored by Edward Miller (Miller 1978a, 1–125; Miller 1978b, 29). The discovery of the *Monitor* wreck the year before by the *Eastward* team was treated like just another ancillary piece of evidence in the larger project. As the *Seaprobe* cruise commenced, it was as if the *Monitor* had not been truly discovered yet, at least in the minds of some. Later, I felt that Miller and Peterkin considered Newton and me to have been lucky amateurs. We were clearly not as much the experts on the *Monitor* as they were, and that is true. It was as if they thought we should accept their thanks for helping them find the *Monitor* and turn the project over to them. Possibly, because we were not part of the navy, we consequently were viewed as outsiders.

Another fissure started to develop as a result of the *Seaprobe* cruise. This was the further involvement of the State of North Carolina in the project. One of the participants invited on the *Seaprobe* cruise was Dr. Kent Schneider, an archaeologist with the North Carolina Division of Archives and History. He was Watts's superior. Governmental interests were beginning to gain influence on the *Monitor* project. On the *Seaprobe* cruise, Watts would not be viewed as a member of the original discovery team, but would be working as an official of the North Carolina Division of Archives and History.

The 11 March 1974 meeting at the Naval Research Laboratory was chaired by Comdr. Colin M. Jones, the officer in charge of the navy's experimental diving unit (Miller 1978b, 30). Designated to be in charge of the *Seaprobe* cruise, Jones desired the best input. The navy mission of the cruise was to conduct an "at-sea evaluation of the [ship's] deep sea search and inspection capabilities" (Miller 1978b, 30). What better way to test the *Seaprobe*'s capabilities but to photograph and sample the *Monitor* wreck?

In addition to Jones, Miller, Peterkin, Newton, Watts, and Schneider, other *Seaprobe* participants included Chester Buchanan of the Naval Research Laboratory; Dorothy Nicholson of the National Geographic Society, which provided some funding; William Andahazy of the Naval Ship Research and Development Center; Sandra Belock of North Carolina; Dr. John Broadwater of Virginia, and Ed Jaeckel of MIT (Miller 1978a, 97; Miller 1978b, 30). Edgerton was involved in the *Seaprobe* cruise as well; he was to run a side-scan survey from aboard the LCU-1488, which had assisted in the discovery cruise the year before, to locate the *Eastward*'s site for the *Seaprobe.*

I was not involved in the *Seaprobe* cruise. Being content with the contribution I had made in finding the *Monitor* wreck, I knew that Newton, along with Watts and Edgerton, would represent the *Eastward* team well. I did not feel a pressing need to be there. I was busy preparing for another cruise on the *Eastward,* scheduled for the last two weeks of April 1974. The *Seaprobe* cruise was planned for the first week of April. I thought Newton would continue to lead future research programs on the *Monitor* wreck. The *Seaprobe* cruise to obtain complete photographic coverage of the wreck and to recover an identifiable artifact would be an important advance in that research. I was unaware until later of any fissure among the parties that was developing on the *Seaprobe* cruise.

7

Proof of Identity

Based on the 11 March 1974 meeting at the Naval Research Laboratory, it was evident that more complete photographic coverage of the *Monitor* wreck and the collection of an identifiable artifact were desirable to prove the identity of the wreck to the navy experts. The photographs and the artifact were the objectives of the Alcoa *Seaprobe* cruise. A pre-cruise meeting was held on 15 March between Jones, Peterkin, and Buchanan (Miller 1978a, 97). Their role was to prioritize the potential *Monitor* wreck sites to be photographed. "Eleven contacts were selected on the basis of the magnetic data and the *Eastward* survey. Each was assigned a corresponding number of priority; the first site to be looked at would be the Duke position" (Miller 1978a, 97).

Departing from Morehead City, North Carolina, on the evening of 31 March, the *Seaprobe* arrived near the Duke position on the morning of 1 April. Edgerton, aboard the LCU-1488, made contact with the wreck with his side-scan sonar. The *Seaprobe* moved into position and recorded a vertical sonar contact with a relief of eighteen feet at 0842 (Miller 1978a, 97).

Immediately the *Seaprobe* got into position for lowering the photography pod on the drill-string pipe from the derrick. The *Seaprobe* was

> an ultrasophisticated research vessel designed to recover 200-ton payloads from 6,000-foot depths.... In conducting pinpoint search and recovery operations, the vessel acts as a dynamically positioned

> working platform able to "hover" over a site on the ocean floor without the use of any ground tackle. The ship is capable of this because of its unique propulsion system—twin cycloidal propellers fore and aft which can direct their thrust 360 degrees, making it as simple to move sideways as foreward and backward (Miller 1978b, 30).

With its hovering capability, the *Seaprobe* held station over the *Monitor* wreck while the drill-string pipe was coupled together from the ship's derrick. The photographic pod was attached to the pipe and lowered through the centerwell (Miller 1978a, 97), a process that took several hours. After the photography pod was lowered, the *Seaprobe* maneuvered very slowly to a position over the wreck. There were two 35 mm still cameras and a television camera with accompanying lights on the pod. Using the television monitor in the ship's lab, the final positioning over the *Monitor* wreck was established in the late afternoon at 1605 (Miller 1978a, 97).

As the researchers on the *Seaprobe* stared intently at the television views from the hovering pod, the still cameras were automatically shooting frames every eight seconds (Miller 1978a, 97). The television views were similar to what we had looked at for days on the *Eastward* the year before. According to Miller the first appearance of the wreck to the *Seaprobe* researchers made them

> aware of the extremely fragile condition of the wreck. Long submersion in salt water had severely eroded the iron plates and portions of the hull had completely collapsed. What was left was the skeletal remains of a ship, it's [*sic*] identity shrouded beneath the encrustation and marine growth of over a century. The question was "Is this the *Monitor* or is it the old Staten Island ferry rumored to have sunk in the area?" (Miller 1978a, 97).

As we had experienced on the *Eastward* the year before, the identity of the wreck was not readily apparent to the *Seaprobe* participants based on their first television views.

The *Seaprobe* team was organized into watches to work around-the-clock in processing the developed photographs from the still cameras. Recording and cataloguing each picture was required for the later construction of a photo mosaic. The television tapes also had to be logged and catalogued. For three days, from 1–4 April, the photography continued. A huge number of pictures was collected. "In total, more than 1,500 high quality vertical-view photographs were taken, of these, approximately 1,200 were black and white with the remainder in color. Additionally, several hours of video tape were made of the wreck" (Miller 1978b, 32).

The *Seaprobe* photographs from the stern area of the wreck were identical to the videotape images recovered by the *Eastward* team a year before. They showed the turret peeking out from beneath the overturned port quarter of the armor belt and deck. The corrosion of the missing bulkhead plating of the bottom hull was evident in the photographs as well as the skeg and propeller. All the features in the *Seaprobe* photos were identical to the interpreted drawing in the *Eastward*'s 1973 cruise report.

New photographic coverage of the amidship and bow areas of the *Monitor* wreck was recovered by the *Seaprobe.* From the new photos, onboard interpretations included, "The stern section [of the lower hull] is still intact up to the main athwartships bulkhead. Forward of this, in the vicinity of the crews' berthing, the hull has completely collapsed" (Miller 1978a, 102). Farther forward of the crew's berthing area, the lower hull was still intact over the area of the officers' staterooms and above the overturned pilothouse. In the photographs, the bow area of the main deck appeared to be intact, as was the distinct circular anchor well (Newton 1975, 52; Watts 1975, 327).

Viewing the photographs and videotapes on the *Seaprobe,* Newton and Watts, convinced they had discovered the *Monitor* the previous year while on the *Eastward,* felt vindicated. The naval experts on the *Monitor* were starting to appreciate that the *Seaprobe* data was verifying the previous identification. But they still were tentative. According to Miller, "The final proof, however, had to wait until nearly two months later, when Naval Intelligence photographic experts completed the photomosaic, showing the entire wreck for the first time" (Miller 1978b, 32).

Despite the tentative nature of the naval experts' conclusions, members of the press were taken to the *Seaprobe* by boat to conduct interviews at the *Monitor* site on 4 April. A relatively cautious announcement stated "that all the evidence to date indicated that the *Monitor* had been located" (Miller 1978a, 103). Although not present on the *Seaprobe* cruise,

I was involved in subsequent press interviews and press coverage of research cruises to the *Monitor.* The *Seaprobe* press visit was the beginning of these media events.

Possibly the original discovery team members should have held a press conference when we returned from the first discovery cruise. Having the *Eastward* as a backdrop would have helped with the press. I learned that the media and the public are often impressed with marine technology. Also, I feel that the press responds better to governmental agencies, as opposed to academics. The U.S. Navy and State of North Carolina officials on the *Seaprobe* cruise certainly gave it an air of official authenticity and elevated the *Seaprobe* cruise in the media's eyes. Newton told me that he was worried because the media were so impressed with the *Seaprobe*'s sophisticated technology that the accomplishments of the less sophisticated *Eastward* would be ignored. Media coverage, and the emphasis and lack of emphasis that comes with that coverage, began to feed the fissure that started to evolve on the *Seaprobe* cruise.

After the press visit, the *Seaprobe* prepared to leave the *Monitor* site. The *Seaprobe* left to attempt to identify a nearby unknown wreck that had been marked by a magnetic anomaly recorded by the navy aeromagnetic survey done for Project Cheesebox (Miller 1978a, 103).

Newton was disappointed that the *Seaprobe* was not going to remain at the *Monitor* site longer and continue its work. The original plan was to use the *Seaprobe*'s controllable gripper on the end of its pipe to collect an artifact from the *Monitor* wreck. An artifact uniquely identifiable as from the *Monitor* would confirm the identification. In addition, an iron artifact would provide evidence of the extent of corrosion of the *Monitor*'s metallic parts. Unfortunately the *Seaprobe* was diverted to another wreck before the attempt to recover an artifact was made. Disappointed by this, Newton left the *Seaprobe* to join Edgerton on the LCU-1488. They attempted to dredge artifacts from the *Monitor* wreck (Miller 1978a, 103), but after dragging the dredge near the wreck several times nothing was recovered except sand and coal fragments.

On the afternoon of 5 April the *Seaprobe* returned to the *Monitor* site. The weather had worsened and the seas were rough. The "weather prevented the recovery of any artifacts" and any further work by the *Seaprobe* on the *Monitor* wreck (Miller 1978a, 103). The *Seaprobe* left the *Monitor* site and returned to port at Morehead City, North Carolina, on 6 April. In his discussions of the *Seaprobe* cruise, Miller never mentions what was found when the *Seaprobe* diverted from the *Monitor* operations on 4 and 5 April (Miller 1978a, 103; Miller 1978b, 32). Searching with the *Seaprobe* for a wreck identified by the navy aeromagnetic survey was likely not that easy, even with the *Seaprobe*'s sophisticated equipment. It is possible that no wreck was found.

Having no firsthand knowledge about the fissure that started on the *Seaprobe* cruise, I can comment only from the few remarks made by Newton. Clearly, he became upset during the *Seaprobe* cruise. I surmised that he felt his authority was usurped. In subsequent years, I became aware that Watts, Miller, and Peterkin were truly experts on the *Monitor*. Watts was a professional historian, and Miller and Peterkin had extensive historical knowledge. Based on my observations of Watts, Miller, and Peterkin at many *Monitor* meetings, I thought they probably knew more about the *Monitor* than anyone else. Certainly more than John Newton or I did. Based on the forward and preface of Miller's book on the *Monitor* published in 1978, Watts had developed a friendship with Miller and Peterkin. Watts spoke highly of Miller in Miller's book, crediting Miller for his extensive research on the *Monitor* (Miller 1978a, xiii). Possibly Miller and Peterkin may have felt Newton, Edgerton, and I merely assisted Watts. From Newton's perspective, I imagine this possible attitude would have bothered him. Newton was the leader of the *Eastward* cruise, the cruise that discovered the *Monitor*! I believe the *Monitor* would never have been discovered without his leadership. I did view myself as a "helper" in the discovery of the *Monitor*, so being considered an assistant did not upset me. Later, I did get upset, however, with what I perceived as Watts's, Miller's, and Peterkin's attitudes toward Newton.

In April 1974, however, I was not aware of any fissure developing among Watts, Miller, Peterkin, and Newton. I innocently thought that Newton was continuing his research on the *Monitor* with the blessings of his employer, Duke University Marine Laboratory. I considered the discovery of the *Monitor* a major oceanographic achievement, and, as a consequence, thought the *Monitor* was the logical object of future oceanographic research. I believed Newton would continue as the leader in that research.

Newton radioed me aboard the *Eastward* on 3 May 1974 to request that I make a dredging station at the *Monitor* site. Chief scientist on the *Eastward* at the time, cruise E-6B-74 had just spent two weeks doing a geophysical survey on the Delaware continental shelf and we were returning to the *Eastward*'s home port of Beaufort, North Carolina. On the homebound leg the *Eastward*'s track would pass directly over the *Monitor* site (Sheridan 1977, 12).

On the radio, Newton told me that the *Seaprobe*'s gripper had not been used to collect an artifact from the *Monitor*. No details were discussed so I did not know why an artifact had not been recovered. Did they try to recover an artifact and fail in the effort? What had happened? I did not know and Newton did not tell me. John did say that he had tried to dredge for an artifact from the LCU, but was not successful in recovering anything. He asked me to try dredging from the *Eastward*. I agreed, and I advised him that I could only spend four hours on the attempt. We had an estimated time of arrival (ETA) already scheduled for our return to Beaufort, and we were determined to make it. Allowing four hours for dredging would not jeopardize our arrival time. Also, under the protocols of the *Eastward* Cooperative Oceanographic Program, it was proper and acceptable to take a station for an ancillary project if the request was made by that project's principal investigator and the ancillary work was a minor effort.

In the oceanographic community, taking advantage of a ship of opportunity is a common practice. Often a scientist, on another research vessel passing your area of interest, will retrieve what might later be determined to be a critical piece of data: a sediment core, a seismic profile, a water sample, a bottom photograph, or, as in this case, a dredge sample. This is an efficient and productive use of our country's academic oceanographic research fleet. Most oceanographic scientists are cooperative and oblige such requests.

The recovery of even a minimal artifact from the *Monitor* wreck, if possible, could be critical to prove our case about the discovery and identification of the *Monitor*. It was hoped that a piece uniquely identifiable as being a part of the *Monitor* might be recovered. Metallurgical analysis could identify the vintage of any iron collected and determine the corrosion effects after more than one hundred years on the ocean floor.

On the 1973 *Eastward* cruise, a Day dredge was used. Normally used to drag through sand to collect benthic fauna and flora, it is relatively lightweight. With its wire mesh body and sheet-metal frame for a mouth, shell fish are frequently recovered. We had towed the Day dredge slowly off to starboard and aft with about five hundred feet of cable out to provide scope and to keep the dredge on the bottom. Towing speeds were usually about two knots through the water; in the currents around the *Monitor* site our ship was just making headway over the seabed at about a speed of one knot. In 1973, the *Eastward* had been maneuvered slowly around the marker buoy near the wreck and, as mentioned previously, only coarse black sand, coal pieces, wood fragments, and shells were recovered.

With only four hours allotted for the dredging attempt on 4 May 1974, it was critical that we locate the *Monitor* wreck with the *Eastward*'s sonar as soon as possible. We did not have the benefit of the marker buoy as had been the case during the 1973 dredging. Our best effort had to be expended on our first try.

To improve our dredging results, I decided to use a rock dredge rather than the Day dredge. Heavier, the rock dredge has a chain-mail bag behind steel plow-like cutting-edge blades on the upper and lower part of the dredge's mouth. I thought the heavier frame would sink deeper into the sand than the Day dredge. Perhaps heavier pieces of loose iron plate from the wreck might be slightly buried by a few feet of sand. Being lighter, the Day dredge may have possibly bounced along the bottom rather than digging in. Or maybe the Day dredge was so light that it might have been deflected by a heavier piece of metal plate. I thought the stronger plow-blade edges of the rock dredge might force the plate into the dredge's chain retrieval bag. Moreover, should the rock dredge hit the hull of the *Monitor*, the sharper blades would more successfully break off a small piece more cleanly than would the mouth of the Day dredge. I followed the old axiom: "It is safer to use a sharp knife than a dull one."

To locate the wreck we used our standard Loran A navigation equipment. One channel gave us a good northwest-southeast set of lines, so we knew when we were about twenty-five hundred feet northeast or southwest of the wreck. The gentle southeastward slope of the sea floor at the *Monitor* wreck site was consistent so the water depths of one fathom (six feet) deeper than the wreck or shallower than the wreck's depth would be about eight hundred feet southeast or northwest of the wreck, respectively. Within these limits it was possible to use the *Eastward*'s side-looking search sonar and vertical sonar to find the wreck.

While I manned the side-scan sonar, Capt. Harold Yeomans ably steered the *Eastward* along a south-southwest course toward his anticipated Loran position of the *Monitor* wreck. At about 1200 hours on 4 May, after reading a Loran line we knew to be south of the wreck, I told the captain that the vertical sonar, which we had on a 0.25 second sweep rate for maximum depth resolution, indicated the wreck was off to our starboard. At the 0.25 second sweep, the one fathom resolution desired would be 0.01 of the sweep scale, which was feasible to record and see on the record. Yeomans agreed that the wreck was off to starboard, so we reversed course to starboard. Cruising north-northeast for a few minutes, we managed to pass directly over the wreck as indicated on the vertical sonar. This was a remarkable achievement, attesting to Yeomans's navigational skills. We had located the wreck using ordinary navigation within an hour after first entering the search pattern.

Our cruising speed of six knots was too fast to close range on the wreck, so we returned to the same Loran rates recorded when we were directly over the *Monitor.* The *Eastward* slowed to two knots, and we launched the dredge. As usual we circled slowly until we had a side-scan contact off the starboard beam. A jury-rigged Styrofoam marker buoy was jettisoned immediately over the spot where we thought the wreck was. Then the *Eastward* changed course to circle back near the wreck. The side-searching sonar was then locked onto the target for relative navigation in closing range.

As the *Eastward* came directly over the *Monitor* wreck, we knew from past experience with the cable-slung cameras that the dredge was somewhere aft and not at the wreck itself. We then maneuvered relative to the marker buoy to drag the dredge slowly near the wreck. This went on for nearly ten minutes while the sonar contact was intermittent. Then high tensions were recorded, up to ten thousand pounds, indicating that the dredge was snagged on something, perhaps the main deck, or perhaps the turret, or maybe a large object some distance from the main hulk. James Davis, the Duke University liaison officer, skillfully worked the dredge cable controls, carefully ensuring that the tension never exceeded ten thousand pounds. As is standard procedure, the ship moved back on the cable. The gentle rolling motion of the ship then worked the dredge against the taut wire until a small piece of plate was sharply broken off or the dredge slipped free.

Soon the tension on the dredge cable dropped, but not with the abrupt snap as if a piece had broken off, but more like the wire angle had changed and pulled the dredge back off its hangup. For a few more minutes the dredge was moved through the sand near the wreck as we opened range. After approximately twenty-five minutes on the bottom the dredge was brought up.

It was evident that most of the dredge sample was coarse, black-speckled, tan sand and shell hash from the sea floor around the wreck. Some sponge and coral fragments provided evidence of the abundant life around the wreck. All the artifacts in the dredge haul were carefully removed after a photograph was taken of the general sample.

As in the previous dredging attempts, coal pieces and wood fragments were present. In this haul we happily found small fragments of iron and one larger piece of heavy iron plate. Seventy-two items were recovered, including many postcard sized, thin spall flakes of brittle rusted iron, a slotted piece of iron, a threaded nut, and, best of all, what appeared to me to be a circular porthole cover about one foot in diameter.

The circular item was thoroughly encrusted with about two inches of calcium carbonate crust, incorporating sediment and shell fragments that were cemented into the crust. When I picked up the circular piece and removed it from the dredge I was impressed with the weight. Clearly this was not the limestone rock it resembled. The complete encrustation layer indicated that the piece was not broken off from the hull; the encrusting layer was not chipped through to a broken, bare iron surface. Instead, it appeared that the piece had fallen to the sea floor as the wreck was sinking, subsequently becoming encrusted in the sediments as a loose piece. I was delighted. I felt we had just recovered the first significant iron artifact from the *Monitor* wreck site.

The artifacts were placed in buckets of fresh water to prevent any further oxidation by exposure to air and the change in environment, following the same instructions that James Davis had been given when he was preparing to receive artifacts at Duke University Marine Laboratory from the *Seaprobe* cruise. Having completed our mission in recovering a piece of iron plate from the wreck of the *Monitor*, a minimum type sample for proof of identification and documentation of corrosion, we departed the wreck site at 1500 hours. Within several hours the artifacts were at the Duke University Marine Laboratory. They were labeled, photographed, and packaged. Newton was ecstatic to finally have the first artifacts from the *Monitor*. He arranged to have the porthole cover sample treated for preservation at Jack Zbar's laboratory in South Carolina. Zbar is well known for his work in preservation of marine artifacts for the Smithsonian Institution. Newton personally drove the artifacts to South Carolina to

First significant artifact retrieved from the *Monitor* wreck site. Shown after cleaning, it was recovered by the *Eastward* crew on 4 May 1974 during a dredging operation. The decklight cover consists of two circular pieces of plate, each one inch thick, held together by four bolts. This uniquely identifiable artifact provided "ironclad" proof of identification (Newton 1975, 60; Sheridan 1977, 10; Sheridan 1979, 256).

John Newton

deliver them directly to Zbar; he felt he could not chance any loss or damage in shipping (Editorial 1976a, 18).

Chemical dissolution of the calcareous crust exposed the rather well preserved iron. The heavy ten inch diameter object is constructed of two iron discs, each one inch thick, bolted together with four bolts. The upper disc plate is larger than the lower disc to provide a lip that would rest on the depressed sill around the porthole that the plate covered, allowing the cover to fit flush with the deck when in place.

Newton and I interpreted this disc-shaped artifact to be a deck cover for one of the light portholes that were constructed through the main deck into the ceilings of the officer's and crew's staterooms (Newton 1975, 60; Sheridan 1977, 10; Sheridan 1979, 256). Two inches thick, the decklight covers prevented damage by the glancing shots from enemy ships during battle; the flush fit prevented any tripping hazard on the deck. Thick heavy glass was beneath each decklight cover. The decklight covers were removed during the day to allow light into the state-

Photograph of the *Monitor* taken in July 1862 by James Gibson (Peterkin 1981c, 49). The opened decklight covers are seen on the deck between the turret and the pilothouse, next to the portholes of the officer's and crew's staterooms (Sheridan 1977, 10). Note the pilothouse's slanted metal shield added to prevent hits such as that which wounded Lt. John L. Worden. Dents are visible in the turret from the hits inflicted by the *Merrimac*'s cannon balls during the Battle of Hampton Roads.

John Newton

rooms, and the glass portholes were opened for ventilation. At night, the decklight covers were placed on the portholes to keep light from escaping when targeting by shore snipers was a concern.

Largely intact, the decklight cover was uniquely identifiable as part of the *Monitor*. The decklight covers were visible in photographs of the *Monitor* taken by James Gibson in July 1862 (Peterkin 1981c, 49; Sheridan 1977, 10). Gibson also made at least one set of eight stereo-pair glass-plate pictures of the *Monitor* while the ship was on blockade duty in the James River. In one of Gibson's photographs the decklight covers are seen opened and sitting on the deck next to the portholes between the turret and the pilothouse. Plans and drawings of the *Monitor* depicted the circular decklight covers (Watts 1975, 302). Nine portholes are indicated to have decklight covers. Newton and I concluded that when the *Monitor* capsized upon sinking, these decklight covers fell to the sea floor and were scattered around the wreck site; probably the decklight covers were intermittently buried a few inches or a foot in the loose sand.

To provide a visual to accompany the *National Geographic Magazine* article by John Newton on the discovery of the *Monitor,* the cleaned decklight cover was photographed. The photograph's caption refers to the artifact as "ironclad proof of discovery" (Newton 1975, 60).

Newton and I were pleased to have recovered the first identifiable artifact from the *Monitor* wreck site, using the relatively primitive and simple technology of dredging. Along with the original photography of the *Monitor* wreck in 1973, the decklight cover was all that was needed to claim our discovery of the *Monitor* and prove its identification. Equally important for us, the discovery and proof data were collected by crews that had used the same ship, the *Eastward.*

Naturally, Newton and I were feeling that the media was becoming too enthralled with the sophistication of the *Seaprobe*'s technological capabilities. We felt the impression was being made that only with sophisticated and complex photography systems could the identity of the *Monitor* wreck be verified. Newton and I were worried that the role of the *Eastward* in the discovery and identification of the *Monitor* wreck would become marginalized. The successful collection of the first identifiable artifact from the *Monitor* restored the importance of the *Eastward* in the project. Also, within days of the recovery of the decklight cover, its significance as proof of identification became evident. There was no need to wait months for the *Seaprobe*'s photomosaic to be constructed to verify the discovery of the *Monitor* wreck.

8

Meetings, Meetings, Meetings

After identification of the *Monitor* wreck was proved in May 1974, there was a burst of bureaucratic activity by governmental agencies. North Carolina's historic preservation officer nominated the *Monitor* wreck to be placed on the National Register of Historic Places on 12 June (Tise 1981, 41). The presumption was that the placement on the National Register would provide the *Monitor* with some form of protection through the National Historic Preservation Act of 1966. Section 106 of the act requires that all federal actions, funding, or licensing affecting any "building, structure, or object" on the National Register shall be reviewed by the National Advisory Council on Historic Preservation (Pepi 1978, 8). Of course, this vehicle for protection only applies to federal actions, funding, or licensing. If private interests wanted to do something with the *Monitor* wreck without federal funding, section 106 did not apply. Thus, if the *Monitor* came under private ownership, protection would be circumvented.

Ownership of the *Monitor* wreck is currently complicated, just as it was in 1974 when North Carolina state bureaucrats began their attempts at regulation of the wreck. In the 1950s there had been hope that the *Monitor* would be found within the decade. As discussed previously, there were the reports that the U.S. Navy's underwater object locator had found the wreck in 1950 as well as the discovery publicized by Robert Marx in 1955. Marx indicated that the *Monitor* wreck was near the shore and in shallow water. The possibility of a nearshore, shallow water location of the wreck was attractive to some who dreamed of a future recovery of the *Monitor*. A "group of citizens who wanted to salvage the ship and establish it as a national monument" petitioned the U.S. Navy to declare the *Monitor* obsolete and to decommission the ship; the group could then take over ownership (Millholland 1978, 19). Decommissioning is what occurs before private individuals purchase an obsolete submarine or battleship for a dollar in order to begin a museum restoration. On 30 September 1953 the U.S. Navy formally abandoned the *Monitor* as a lost, obsolete ship in order "to remove the legal barriers" for the interested group (Millholland 1978, 19). From that point forward, the U.S. Navy no longer had any jurisdiction over the *Monitor*. The *Monitor*'s title resides, instead, with the General Services Administration (GSA). Anyone now could place a bid with the GSA for the title of the *Monitor*.

Many states enacted laws that give the respective state ownership over historic wrecks in their state waters. State officials, such as state archaeologists or state historic preservation officers, can take possession of all antiquities recovered from historic wrecks if they are in state waters. The federal Antiquities Act requires that U.S. citizens secure a permit from the Department of Interior before they "gather, recover, damage or destroy antiquities from lands owned or controlled by the United States." Millholland stated that this law is based on the theory that the U.S. government has the right to control the actions of its citizens even outside the United States (Millholland 1978, 19–20).

The U.S. District Court, however, in the case of the bullion-laden *Atocha* discovered on the Florida continental shelf outside of state waters and outside of the U.S. territorial sea (twelve nautical miles from shore), ruled in 1975 that the United States only controlled natural resources there, not wrecks. This distinction was explicitly addressed in the Geneva Conventions on continental shelves that separated the regulation of natural resources from the regulation of wrecks and their cargos (Millholland 1978, 20). The salvage of wrecks in international waters is regulated by longstanding maritime salvage laws. Typically, the salvagers, risking their investment in the salvage attempt, would negotiate with the current title holder of a wreck for a portion, usually half, of the value of the ship and cargo. The U.S. government paid $275,000 for the *Monitor* in 1862. But what is its value today? The *Monitor* lies sixteen miles south of Cape Hatteras in international waters. It is outside the U.S. territorial sea; it is outside the United States. Can the traditional maritime salvage laws apply to the *Monitor*?

On 4 September 1974 the governor of North Carolina nominated the *Monitor* to be the nation's first marine sanctuary (Tise 1981, 41). Marine sanctuaries are a concept that was established in the Marine Protection, Research, and Sanctuaries Act of 1972. According to NOAA lawyer John Millholland, "[T]his act authorizes the Secretary of Commerce to designate areas of ocean water—essentially from high tide to the edge of the continental shelf—as marine sanctuaries, so as to preserve such areas for their conservation, recreational, ecological or aesthetic values" (Millholland 1978, 20). As a response to the nearly quadrupling of the price of foreign crude oil by the Organization of Petroleum Exporting Countries (OPEC) in the early 1970s, petroleum exploration had increased on the U.S. continental shelves. The Marine Sanctuaries Act was meant to protect particular marine environments from damage by drilling. Environments, such as coral reefs and fish spawning areas, might be negatively affected by drilling and production structures on the sea floor. The Marine Sanctuaries Act allows the restriction of access, under the supervision of NOAA, into designated areas called national marine sanctuaries.

The Marine Sanctuaries Act was not written as a means to protect wrecks, or to restrict access to wrecks, although there was some intent to preserve resources on the continental shelf. These resources were originally visualized as natural resources, not historical or archaeological resources. But the *Monitor* wreck is, indeed, a very important historical resource on the continental shelf, so the Marine Sanctuaries Act can logically be seen as an appropriate means to restrict access. Moreover, the creation of a marine sanctuary for the *Monitor*, with the restriction of access to that volume of ocean, would give some protection to the wreck without dealing with the complicated issues of jurisdiction and ownership. The sanctuary is actually the ocean volume around the wreck, but not the wreck itself.

The restriction of access applies to U.S. citizens, who presumably would be most interested in the *Monitor*. However, salvagers from other countries, sailing from foreign ports, would not be restricted by the U.S. government's Marine Sanctuaries Act. Only specific treaties with specific foreign countries would cover those situations (Millholland 1978, 31).

I was unaware of any of the bureaucratic maneuvers to gain control over the *Monitor* wreck in 1974. Perhaps naively, I just presumed that studies of the wreck and the *Monitor* site would continue as a major oceanographic research project. I was so happy that we had actually found the *Monitor,* and I had so many ideas about what kinds of research should be done next, that I never thought access to the wreck might be restricted. I thought the government would be encouraging access to the *Monitor* and continued research. When I learned about the laws and acts discussed above, I felt they were rather negative; the various laws specified what could not be done, rather than what should be done.

Thinking back on it now, I was surprised that North Carolina government officials were so eagerly interested in playing an active role in restricting access to the *Monitor.* The *Monitor* wreck is not in North Carolina; it is not even in the United States. So why was North Carolina so immediately involved in the *Monitor* wreck? Besides, the *Monitor* was a Union warship, not a Confederate ship. Wouldn't a Confederate ship be more in line with North Carolina's historical interest? I definitely consider the *Monitor* the most historically important wreck off Cape Hatteras, and North Carolina obviously saw some importance also. Indeed, the presence of the *Monitor* off Cape Hatteras is usually included as a tourist attraction in any publicity about Cape Hatteras and the Graveyard of the Atlantic.

On a less altruistic level, some North Carolina governmental agencies possibly viewed the *Monitor* discovery as an opportunity to enhance their own importance. For example, over the years since the discovery of the *Monitor,* the North Carolina Division of Archives and History has been consistently involved in the regulatory process over the wreck. The *Monitor* discussions have certainly increased the division's prestige. Some of the division's officials have gained rewarding personal exposure that they might not have had otherwise. Also, the old axiom "follow the money" applies. The North Carolina Division of Archives and History has received various contracts from NOAA specifically related to the *Monitor.* The division's involvement with the *Monitor* has been financially rewarding. History will judge whether North Carolina's involvement has made a positive or a negative impact on the *Monitor*'s fate.

On 30 January 1975, the 103rd anniversary date of the launching of the *Monitor,* the *Monitor* was designated the first national marine sanctuary by the secretary of commerce (Millholland 1978, 31). NOAA thus became the leading federal agency in control of the *Monitor* wreck. The Marine Sanctuaries Act is sufficiently powerful; it permits NOAA to "control any activities permitted within the designated sanctuary" (Millholland 1978, 31). According to Millholland, "[T]he law carries enough authority to prevent any disturbance of the site by U.S. citizens. More importantly, it establishes a management system to ensure that desirable research activities will be conducted in such a way as to ensure that the site and any artifacts recovered from it will be preserved to provide the maximum degree of educational and scientific value over the long term" (Millholland 1978, 31). I note that the emphasis is on the control on how the research at the site is conducted, not on ensuring that "desirable research" will be conducted. Also, there is an emphasis on the control of the use and final disposition of any artifacts from the *Monitor.* I was concerned that NOAA, in its regulatory role, might be more concerned about control of the *Monitor* wreck than encouraging proper research and development of the site.

To their credit, most NOAA officials realized that they could not unilaterally make decisions on what was "desirable research" and what was a proper use of the *Monitor* artifacts. NOAA has over the years, however, exerted broad discretion in making many decisions. In preparation for the designation of the *Monitor* as the first marine sanctuary, NOAA needed advice from agencies and individuals with firsthand knowledge of the *Monitor,* experience with the wreck, and interests in the future development of the site. A meeting was convened for discussion of the future role of NOAA and the *Monitor* with the Smithsonian Institution as the host. The meeting was held on 29 October 1974 (Tise 1978a, 15).

The meeting was well attended. I drove from Delaware to Washington, D.C., and found my designated parking area underneath one of the Smithsonian Museum buildings. The meeting room was in one of the rooms of the lower level of the National Museum of History and Technology building. Working my way to the meeting room I passed a display of the preserved and restored wooden hull of a small lake warship used by the Americans in the Revolutionary War. Other displays in this area showed the divers and underwater salvage techniques used to recover the Revolutionary War vessel. It struck me that we were in the right place for a meeting about the *Monitor.*

The chair and host of the meeting was Dr. Philip Lundeberg of the Smithsonian Institution; he was the curator of the Division of Naval History of the Museum of History and Technology. Lundeberg was certainly of sufficient rank and prestige and had the credentials in naval history to chair this first national meeting on the *Monitor.* Other attendees included John Newton, Doc Edgerton, Gordon Watts, Dr. Kent Schneider, and

Ernest Peterkin. Representing the Navy Historical Center was Vice Adm. Edwin Hooper. NOAA was represented by Robert Kifer, assistant administrator of the Office of Ocean Management. Charles McKinney, from the Department of Interior, also attended.

Each of the representatives of the state and federal organizations made presentations describing their interests in the *Monitor* and their organizations' qualifications to play a role in the *Monitor*'s future. Lundeberg reminded us of the Smithsonian's role as the caretaker of the nation's artifacts, as the nation's "attic." Indeed, in the very Museum of History and Technology building where we were meeting, there were numerous displays of the U.S. Navy's history, including large models of the *Monitor* and the *Merrimac*. As one of the nation's most important artifacts, the *Monitor* wreck's future was rightfully of concern to the Smithsonian Institution. Lundeberg explained that the attic was full, however. There was no more room on the "mall" to have a national monument to the *Monitor*, with the wreck on display, in Washington, D.C. Current policy was to construct such new monuments away from Washington where they would form their own public attraction.

McKinney reminded us that the National Park Service was in charge of our national monuments, including many Civil War battlefield sites. The Park Service rangers have the well recognized "Smokey Bear" hats that are seen at the Civil War monuments. If the *Monitor* was retrieved and displayed in a national monument, the National Park Service would have an understandable role and responsibility.

Hooper expressed the U.S. Navy's interest in the *Monitor* as perhaps its second-most-famous ship as the USS *Constitution*. Indeed, the navy had already expended funds on the Alcoa *Seaprobe* cruise to verify the location of the *Monitor* wreck site. There were two small naval museums, one at Anacostia Naval Yard in Washington, D.C., and one at the Naval Academy in Annapolis, Maryland. Hooper visualized one of these museums as housing and displaying the *Monitor* artifacts in the future. In fact, he presented a letter of agreement to NOAA, the organization in charge of the *Monitor* wreck as the nation's first marine sanctuary, that the U.S. Navy would be given jurisdiction over all artifacts to be recovered from the *Monitor* in the future. According to John Millholland, the NOAA lawyer, the U.S. Navy had reached an understanding with NOAA and had "agreed to provide curatorial support for the sanctuary; this involves cataloging any artifacts recovered and, where both agencies agree that it is appropriate, preserving or displaying them" (Millholland 1978, 21).

Speaking for the North Carolina Division of Archives and History, Dr. Kent Schneider expressed the need for protection of a major historical resource. The wreck's position is off Cape Hatteras; the wreck is part of the lore of the Graveyard of the Atlantic, and the state would naturally like to continue that status. The research on the *Monitor* wreck would undoubtedly involve North Carolina universities, North Carolina ports, and North Carolina vessels and crews. Eventually, as has come to pass, tourist diving trips to the *Monitor* wreck would be run out of the Outer Banks, so the *Monitor* wreck has contributed to the Outer Banks' tourism. There were hopes on the part of some North Carolinians that a *Monitor* museum might someday be established in the Outer Banks–Cape Hatteras area.

As part of section 106 of the National Historic Preservation Act, any action at the *Monitor* site requires review by the National Advisory Council of Historic Preservation. This would bring yet another group into the consideration of the future of the *Monitor*. The review process by this council was discussed at the meeting.

At the Smithsonian Institution meeting, a management procedure was worked out to support NOAA in its role as the administrator of the newly formed Monitor Marine Sanctuary, once it was designated by the secretary of commerce on 30 January 1975. An advisory committee, composed of one member each from five different federal and state agencies, would report to NOAA on future activities at the *Monitor* wreck. The members of the committee would represent the Smithsonian Institution, the Department of Interior, the U.S. Navy, the Advisory Council on Historic Preservation, and the North Carolina Division of Archives and History (Sheridan 1977, 12). While each one of these federal and state agencies, including NOAA, had some reason to be involved in the future of the *Monitor*, the net effect was the imposition of a cumbersome layer of bureaucracy. Each committee member would have his or her own motives, motives that would inherently be in conflict. In addition, each agency's representative on the committee would expectedly take a very cautious approach to the future of the *Monitor* to avoid approving actions that might jeopardize their agency's position.

NOAA was in charge of the *Monitor* only because the wreck site was in the ocean. What would happen if the wreck was recovered? Then there would no longer be a sanctuary for NOAA to administer. If the *Monitor* were recovered, would it go to the Smithsonian, the U.S. Navy, or the Department of Interior? If the *Monitor* were recovered and not placed in a museum in North Carolina, the state would lose a potentially profitable tourist attraction. Also, the North Carolina Division of Archives and History would then no longer be involved. For all these rather obvious reasons, I had some misgivings about how the advisory committee would work. How could the members be impartial on the question of recovery of the *Monitor*?

As researchers who intended to continue research on the *Monitor* for scholarly and academic purposes, John Newton from Duke University, Doc Edgerton from MIT, and I, from the University of Delaware, felt there was no apparent need at that time for us to be involved in the governmental regulation of the *Monitor* wreck. As long as we could continue our research, we were content to work with the advisory committee and NOAA. Also, we had ideas about what positive steps should be taken to develop the *Monitor* wreck site. We felt we should be allowed to formulate and initiate research plans. I felt the governmental agencies had mostly negative charges—to "prevent" this or that action from occurring in the Monitor Marine Sanctuary. Newton, Edgerton, and I felt that we were the "players" in the game and that NOAA and the advisory committee were the umpires or referees.

The next meeting was convened by NOAA on 14 May 1975 (Tise 1978a, 15). On sabbatical leave, I was working for the Office of Marine Geology of the U.S. Geological Survey in Woods Hole, Massachusetts. I drove to Washington, D.C., with a stopover at Delaware to get some paperwork on the *Monitor*. Meeting in a downtown office building of the Department of Commerce, the other academic experts—Newton and Edgerton—attended. Other attendees were Watts and Schneider of the North Carolina Division of Archives and History, Peterkin of the U.S. Naval Research Laboratory, Lundeberg of the Smithsonian Institution, the NOAA lawyer, Millholland, and Edward Miller, now an ensign in the U.S. Navy, representing the Navy Historical Center. This was my first encounter with Miller and Millholland.

Ostensibly, the meeting's purpose was to develop a research plan for the Monitor Marine Sanctuary. Schneider chaired the meeting. Being advisory to NOAA, it was proper protocol that the advisory committee members run the meeting. Given that the Smithsonian Institution, Interior Department, and the Navy Department were federal agencies with conflicting interests with NOAA, having Schneider, representing a state agency, chair the meeting might have been a good approach. But I felt uneasy. Why should one state have so much influence on the future of the *Monitor*? The *Monitor* is truly a national historic treasure. Didn't NOAA realize the power it would hold over the committee and its decision-making process? Any state would probably feel compelled to agree with NOAA's proposals to ensure that it received grants and contracts. Also, having a state involved would garner the support of those senators and congressmen whose constituents might receive NOAA's largess.

The advisory committee would be the review committee for future proposed research in the sanctuary. Millholland went over the legalities and procedures of a proposal review process. To prevent financial exploitation of the wreck, only nonprofit educational research groups would be issued permits. Permits would be issued only for "desirable research" (Millholland 1978, 31), in which all the data would eventually be made public, either in reports or in publications in the scientific literature. All "artifacts obtained in the research shall be made available to the public" (Millholland 1978, 21). Proposals would first be reviewed by a technical review group to ensure the technical feasibility of the research, the quality and responsibility of the researchers, the relevance of the research to the development of the site, and the proposed use and disposition of the recovered data and artifacts. The technical review group would have objective experts with knowledge of the site in the areas of archaeology, naval history, oceanography, marine geology, ocean engineering, salvage, and museum preservation. After review by the technical review group, the proposals would go forward to the advisory committee for their evaluation and approval (Millholland 1978, 31).

But how could the advisory committee decide what proposed research would be desirable research? This judgment would have to be made by considering how the proposed research fit into a master plan for the future of the *Monitor*. The meeting participants expressed many ideas as to what a master plan should include. Newton, Edgerton, and I just logically presumed that the ultimate goal of any master plan would be the possible recovery of the *Monitor* wreck. All the photography of the wreck, and the recovered decklight cover, indicated substantial corrosion and disintegration. Newton, Edgerton, and I had much experience with submerging equipment in the ocean, and with dealing with the power of storm waves and currents. Corrosion by salt water is a rapid, relentless process. The ocean is a very unforgiving environment. This is especially true off Cape Hatteras where complex currents and storms, including frequent hurricanes, occur. The corrosion and battering of the *Monitor* necessitated the recovery of as much of the wreck as possible, as soon as possible. Seemingly self-evident, Newton, Edgerton, and I expected no debate on this issue at this meeting.

When the *Monitor* recovery topic arose at the meeting, grave concerns were expressed, especially from Watts and Miller. "The *Monitor* wreck is too disintegrated and fragile to be salvaged by ordinary means." "The salvage technology does not exist to lift the *Monitor*." "The preservation technology is not available to deal with such a large iron vessel." I was surprised and somewhat skeptical. While I am not an expert on the salvage of wrecks, I thought our nation's ocean engineering technology was among the best in the world. I knew in 1975 from my own experience in marine geophysics, and with my acquaintance with the offshore petroleum exploration and drilling industry, that our commercial marine technology was awesome. With enough financial incentive, I felt technology could be invented to solve almost any problem. We had just landed the first men on the moon in 1969, only six years ago. If technology could be mustered to achieve that, then raising the *Monitor* should be entirely feasible.

In this discussion, Edgerton was his usual exuberant and enthusiastic self. He said, "Well if we can't recover the entire *Monitor* wreck, let's at least recover the turret which is the best preserved and most historic part of the vessel. Let's make that our first priority." Miller replied, "If the turret is recovered, there goes the *Monitor*." Yes, I knew that because the turret was then supporting the main deck and lower hull, the removal of the turret might cause the deck to fall and break apart. Obviously, however, even then I knew that the main deck and lower hull would have to be jacked up to support the weight while the turret was moved and recovered. Similar to a wheel that is supporting a car's weight, the car is jacked up before replacing a flat tire. Watts stated his opinion that the archaeological integrity of the *Monitor* wreck had to be maintained until a thorough archaeological study of the site could be completed. Nothing should be removed from the site until its precise location and condition on the sea floor was measured, documented, and recorded. Such archaeological studies would require enormous amounts of diving time in difficult conditions. He felt the turret should not be moved before the required dives could be completed.

Nothing concrete was resolved at this meeting with regards to specific plans for the future of the *Monitor.* It was concluded, however, that a master plan was needed. Newton informed the group that he was pursuing, with Duke University, the establishment of a "Monitor Research Center" that would be housed at the DUML. From such a center, which he would direct, a master plan would be developed. Lundeberg said he would approach the Smithsonian Institution to set up a "Monitor Research Institute" to encourage researchers to conduct studies of the *Monitor* (Tise 1978a, 15).

After this meeting, I felt that I should get more involved in the planning process for the future of the *Monitor.* It seemed to me that I knew as much about the *Monitor* wreck and the site as many others. Also, I was more knowledgeable about the Pleistocene and Holocene geology of the North Carolina continental shelf than all but a few other marine geologists. Sediments from these ages were most likely lying directly under the *Monitor,* and these most recent geological environments had controlled the creation of the sea floor at the wreck site. I wrote a letter to Kifer and Schneider volunteering my expertise to sit on the technical review group as the group's expert in marine geology. In September 1975, I received a letter from Schneider: "Bob Kifer concurs that you should be a member of the technical review group for the Monitor Marine Sanctuary. Please consider this letter, then, as confirmation of your membership in this group.... [M]embers of the review group who author a proposal or who would participate in research proposed in a permit proposal can not comment on that proposal" (Schneider 1975, 1). I hoped that participating in the technical review group would keep me informed about future actions with the *Monitor.* Also, I hoped to exert as much influence as I could to get something positive done with the wreck.

A major turning point occurred in fall 1975. Newton failed to convince the Duke University administration to set up a *Monitor* research center at DUML. As a consequence, Newton decided to resign his position as marine superintendent of DUML and set up his own organization to work on the future of the *Monitor* (Tise 1978a, 15). Called the Monitor Research and Recovery Foundation (MRRF), "The MRRF is a charitable, educational, scientific, and cultural organization dedicated to the furtherance of research concerning USS Monitor and the future preservation of this historic ship" (Newton et al. 1976b, 32). This move by Newton was a major investment on his part. To risk his financial future on such an enterprise, and to dedicate himself to what we knew even then would be years of effort, was a great sacrifice on his part.

Newton called me and asked if I would serve on the board of trustees of the newly formed MRRF. Jumping at the chance, I said yes. This would offer me an opportunity to contribute to future positive actions at the *Monitor* site. More important, I quickly accepted the board position to lend my support to Newton in his personal effort. I owed him my gratitude for inviting me to participate in the initial discovery cruise in 1973. I recognized and respected Newton's abilities to lead and organize a project to recover the *Monitor*. Joining me on the MRRF board of trustees were Dr. Harold E. Edgerton of MIT, one of the codiscoverers of the *Monitor* wreck; Dr. William N. Still Jr., of East Carolina University, who was a naval historian with expertise on Civil War ironclads; Carl J. Clausen, of the American Institute of Nautical Archaeology, who was a professional diving marine archaeologist; and Warren J. Davis, of the Wheatly, Mason, Wheatly, and Davis law firm, who had some experience in marine admiralty law. Newton organized the MRRF with himself as the salaried executive director and with A. David Cloud Jr. as treasurer (Newton et al. 1976b, 32). With the officers identified and in place, "The [MRRF] was incorporated under the laws of the State of North Carolina on October 20, 1975. Tax exempt status was accorded to the Foundation on November 24, 1975" (Newton et al. 1976b, 32). We held our first board of trustees meeting on 20–21 December 1975 in Beaufort, North Carolina, at a motel near Newton's home. The headquarters office of the MRRF was at his residence, but the organization's official address was a Beaufort post office box number (Newton et al. 1976b, 1).

One of the first actions we took at the MRRF meeting was the election of the board officers. I was elected president of the board, and Newton served as executive vice president. I gladly accepted my position, feeling that such a professionally related service role was appropriate at this point in my career. As a tenured, associate professor at the University of Delaware, my professorship position allowed me to diversify my research and professional activities. The future research at the *Monitor* site would require marine geological and geophysical research that I was planning to do. I planned to eventually publish the results of the geological and geophysical research on the *Monitor* site in the peer-reviewed, refereed *Journal of Field Archaeology*, so my research on the *Monitor* was entirely proper for my professorship position.

Additionally, at that time I had just completed a two month leg, as co-chief scientist, on the drilling vessel *Glomar Challenger* in the summer of 1975. The *Challenger* was a state-of-the-art deep-sea drilling vessel with dynamic positioning capabilities similar to those of the Alcoa *Seaprobe*. Rather than using cycloidal propellers as the *Seaprobe* did, the *Challenger* utilized fore-and-aft thrusters that jetted water sideways through the hull to move the ship sideways while the main propellers moved the *Challenger* forward and backward. Thus, the *Challenger* could move in any direction horizontally and maintain its position over one spot for the entire two month cruise without anchors.

The *Challenger* was a sister ship of the *Glomar Explorer*, designed and operated by Global Marine, Inc., one of the most important deep-sea drilling companies at that time. As discussed in later chapters, the *Glomar Explorer* was the most sophisticated salvage ship ever constructed. The *Challenger* and *Explorer* had several features in common: dynamic positioning, centerwell deployment of drill strings from large derricks, and heave compensation. Normal drilling ships, such as the *Challenger*, had to hoist about twenty thousand feet of drill string with about a two million pound capacity. The *Explorer* had to hoist recovered vessels as well as the drill string, so its hoist capacity was as much as fourteen million pounds (Crooke 1976, 4; Editorial 1976b, 68). I felt that my experience with modern marine technology, which was relevant to future development of the *Monitor* site, had grown significantly by 1975. I was confident that I could contribute something to the MRRF as its board of trustees' president.

At the December 1975 MRRF meeting, we approved a master plan for the future of the *Monitor*. The plan evolved from board member discussions that included "representations of the following fields of knowledge: Civil War History, Marine Archeology, Oceanography, Engineering, Admiralty Law" (Newton et al. 1976b, 11). The plan was brief and somewhat generalized to provide flexibility. To be locked into a rigid, detailed master plan in the early stages of development of the *Monitor* site was not considered wise by the MRRF board. New data, once recovered, would obviously lead to new questions and new requirements for future work. The MRRF master plan was a framework of logical phases that would meet "the requirements of government, private interests, and especially the interests of researchers who will actually carry the burden of the many tasks that need to be accomplished" (Newton et al. 1976b, 11).

The 1975 MRRF master plan detailed six phases. It read:

> Research plans have evolved by taking into careful consideration the constraints applied by man and nature in these 220 feet depths. The plans involve a six phased effort that will draw upon the most recent technological developments thoroughly tested and de-bugged, to give a high probability of success to the endeavor.
>
> Completion of Phase I, the discovery and identification, leads naturally to Phase II, charting of the site and environmental studies. It is now believed the Monitor slipped under the sea by the stern, capsizing underwater. It is known from historical sources that several fittings on deck were loosened by the storm. These objects probably rained down on the sea floor, spreading debris over a wide area of the site. Other artifacts within the turret and immediately below decks may have been cast loose in the Sanctuary. The charting of the distribution of the remains of the Monitor can be accomplished by an undersea sled or submarine equipped with precision cameras, magnetometer, sonars, and seismic profiler. This will be supplemented by diver observation, photography and materials testing. Strings of current meters will measure the flow of water; samples of the water and sea floor, in the vicinity of the wreck, will be taken to analyze the nature of Monitor's grave.

Evaluation of environmental factors would be considered for impact on the subsequent diving operations. The plan continued:

> Divers, especially trained for the mission and led by archeologists, will descend to the site of the ship in Phase III, site testing. A series of experiments designed to acquire the necessary data for an archeological evaluation and an appraisal of the structural integrity will be carefully performed. Accessible compartments of the ship will be entered, photographed and video-taped. The sterile overburden, if

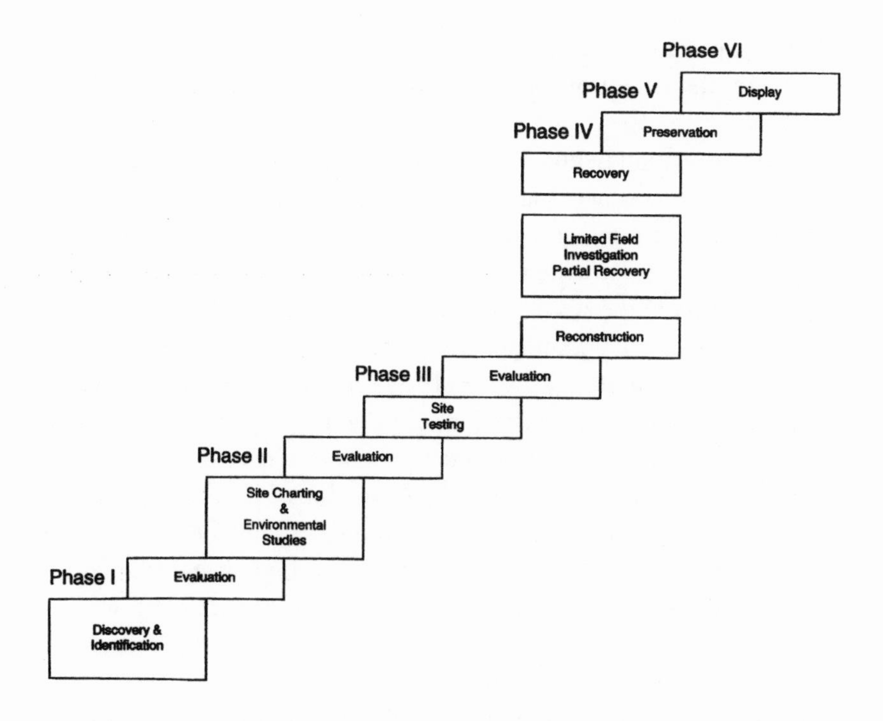

Block diagram of the Monitor Research and Recovery Foundation's "Master Plan for Monitor." Developed at MRRF's first board meeting in December 1975, the plan was used for research proposals in 1976 and 1977.

Newton, J. G., R. E. Sheridan, H. E. Edgerton, W. N. Still, and C. J. Clausen. 1976a. *Request for a Research Permit for a Baseline Magnetic Profiling of the Monitor Marine Sanctuary.* Beaufort, N.C.: Monitor Research and Recovery Foundation, 5; Newton, J. G., R. E. Sheridan, H. E. Edgerton, W. N. Still, and C. J. Clausen. 1976b. *A Proposal for Environmental Engineering Studies and Site Charting at the Monitor Marine Sanctuary.* Beaufort, N.C.: Monitor Research and Recovery Foundation, 13.

present, will be whisked gently into suspension and blown away to reveal artifactual remains and structural evidence below. The area exposed will be thoroughly recorded both on videotape and photogrametrically on motion picture film. This will freeze the exact provenance of the artifacts to the structure and to each other. It is planned, once the record has been made, to remove very small samples. Possibly as few as ten artifacts representing dissimilar metals and other materials will be removed for preservational analyses. Engineers, or trained divers, will take small samples of the armor

> belt, supporting wood and other structural members to determine strength, the extent of corrosion and applicable preservation techniques.
>
> The evaluation period following their diving activity will offer a time to decide which stage, or combination of stages shown in Phase IV, [complete recovery, limited field investigation partial recovery, or reconstruction,] will be most appropriate considering the condition of the wreck. At this point, the results of archeological, oceanographic and engineering research will be meshed with recovery plans offered by the world's most capable lifting engineers. Iron objects that are submerged in sea water for more than a century often disintegrate when exposed to air unless they are properly treated. Preservation of the more than 300 tons of iron in the ship will pose an immense task. In Phase V, [preservation], the ship must be dismantled piece by piece while it remains underwater [though not necessarily at its present depth]. Each iron part must be subjected to a multi-stage electro-chemical process needed to remove salts from within the metal. In the final step, a thin iron oxide coating will be superimposed on the metal to ensure that the iron will be stabilized in air. The preservation of other materials (plant products, animal products and other metals, etc.) will also require careful attention, depending on the degree of deterioration. The variety of objects to be preserved is quite diverse because the ship is a small microcosm—a time capsule—of the life and period of the Civil War. The men aboard had all the utensils required for living, the weapons for fighting and the tools for working (Newton et al. 1976a, 5).

Whatever was recovered would be dealt with in Phase VI, display. Where and how the preserved parts of the Monitor were to be displayed were questions that were hard to answer then. Whatever the display mode and location, the MRRF felt it should be commensurate with the *Monitor*'s importance to the Civil War, to naval architecture, and to U.S. naval history (Newton et al. 1976b, 13).

With the MRRF's master plan in hand, we were all enthusiastic about proceeding with the project. We felt ready to approach NOAA and the advisory committee to explain and defend, if necessary, "our proposals for research within this framework" (Sheridan 1977, 12). We requested a meeting with NOAA and the advisory committee to present our long-range plan for the *Monitor* and to propose future research and recovery activities. There was a sense of urgency that something should be done with the *Monitor* wreck as soon as possible. The MRRF board was well aware of the hostile environment for wrecks near the edge of the continental shelf off Cape Hatteras. Also, we were well aware that it was necessary to continue activities to develop the *Monitor* site without a long hiatus. The recent publication on the *Monitor*'s discovery and identification in 1975 in the *National Geographic Magazine* needed to be exploited (Newton 1975, 48–61). Positive publicity is vital. Moreover, 1976 was the Bicentennial Year for the United States. What better way to celebrate our history than to begin the steps to recover the USS *Monitor*?

The next national meeting on the *Monitor* convened on 15–16 January 1976 (Tise 1978a, 15). The group met in a small conference room in one of the Smithsonian Institution's buildings on the mall in Washington, D.C. The MRRF board members would make their case on the future of the *Monitor*. The NOAA and advisory committee representatives were present as well. Although I did not see any senators or congressmen present, a few of their staff members identified themselves and their legislators' interests in the *Monitor*. They would take significant notes back to their bosses about the gist of the meeting.

Once again, a representative of the North Carolina Division of Archives and History chaired the meeting. Dr. Larry Tise, the director of the division and the state's historic preservation officer, was an eloquent speaker and writer, qualities that reflected his background as a historian. The head of a major North Carolina bureaucracy, he impressed me with his air of authority. He was well versed in the state and federal regulations and laws regarding historic resources, and he easily bandied about the numerous acronyms (alphabet soup) of the historical *cognoscenti*. Tise set the stage for the meeting with his serious introduction. I felt a little intimidated by him.

The MRRF officers made their presentations. Newton gave an introduction and general overview of the master plan. Clausen, the professional diving archaeologist, discussed the MRRF's ideas on site-testing procedures and marine archaeological practices to be done at the *Monitor* wreck. I followed with the discussion of the plans for site charting and environmental studies of the site, including the need for a magnetometer survey, a sub-bottom high-resolution seismic reflection survey, sediment coring, water sampling, and near-bottom current measurements. The MRRF's intent was to submit a request for a long-term, three-year permit over the period of 1976 through 1979 for the purposes of carrying out Phases II and III as listed in the master plan (Newton et al. 1976a, 5; Newton et al. 1976b, 13). This longer-term authorization of the MRRF research by NOAA would give the foundation authenticity and credentials, which were necessary before approaching various private funding sources. Approval from the NOAA advisory committee would have aided the MRRF immensely.

As discussed by Tise,

> following two days of intense deliberations about the general future of the *Monitor* and the specific plans drawn up by the *Monitor* Research and Recovery Foundation, the conference in plenary session chose not to endorse the plans of the foundation. It instead recommended to the National Oceanic and Atmospheric Administration in a formally adopted resolution that a *Monitor* Marine Sanctuary Advisory Council be established to coordinate and initiate planning for future research on the *Monitor* for its eventual recovery and display (Tise 1978a, 15).

This negative response was disheartening. It was clear that the governmental agencies on the advisory committee wanted to create a master plan by themselves, rather than accept what had been proposed from the private sector through our foundation.

The new "advisory council," responsible for initiating planning on the future of the *Monitor*, added a new layer of governmental bureaucracy, and with it the commensurate delay in beginning the much needed research on the wreck site. The new council would become another "player" by initiating plans, rather than being a "referee" review group that would evaluate plans submitted from the private sector. This change in policy opened the door for the archaeologists, engineers, and historians of state and federal agencies to initiate and carry out research in direct competition with the scientists and researchers from academia, such as those in the MRRF. The schism among the researchers had widened further.

NOAA did not close the door completely on the MRRF as a result of the January 1976 meeting, however. The NOAA policy became more *ad hoc;* research proposals were evaluated on an individual cruise-by-cruise basis. The MRRF was able to execute two important cruises utilizing ships-of-opportunity in 1976 and 1977. They accomplished part of the MRRF's Phase II master plan, site charting and environmental studies. Without NOAA's endorsement of these cruises, the MRRF would have lost momentum and the opportunity for vital publicity that is needed to attract private funding.

9

The Wreck's Environment

As of 1975, some inferences about the environment of the *Monitor* wreck and the condition of the wreck could be made from the side-scan sonar imagery, the dredged decklight cover, and especially the photographic coverage from the Alcoa *Seaprobe* cruise. Side-scan sonar profiles showed the scour mark of the northeast-flowing Gulf Stream current on the leeward, down-current northeast side of the wreck. The scour indicates that the bottom currents are, at least episodically, strong enough to transport and winnow medium sand, similar in grain size to some sand recovered in previous dredges. This means that bottom currents must exceed the transport threshold of sand particles at speeds of about one third of a knot and higher. The photography and side-scan sonar revealed the buried starboard armor belt, which is on the upstream side of the wreck; it acted as a dam to the sand transport.

Photography of the wreck showed that corrosion had been extensive. The ocean's salt water had acted on the cast and wrought iron of the *Monitor* for more than 110 years. Thick pieces of plate, such as the two inch thick decklight cover, thoroughly encrusted with a calcium carbonate ($CaCO_3$) cemented, limestone layer, were still fairly well preserved (Newton 1975, 60; Sheridan 1977, 10; Sheridan 1979, 256). Knowing that the original construction of the decklight cover was two pieces of one inch thick plates of ten inches in diameter held together by four bolts, the measured dimensions of the recovered and cleaned plate give an indication of the amount of corrosion. About one fifth of an inch of corrosion on the outer surface of the plates corresponds to about a 26 percent volumetric corrosion (Sheridan 1977, 12; Sheridan 1979, 256). This was not that bad and it gave some hope that other thicker pieces of iron were not that badly corroded. Based on the photography, however, many of the thinner plates, of the hull especially, were completely corroded by 1974.

The corrosion of the *Monitor* by the saltwater environment was clear, as discussed by Gordon Watts and Edward Miller in their reports on the Alcoa *Seaprobe* photography. As most researchers believe, the extensive damage to the stern and the breakage of the armor belt there was probably caused by the impact on sinking rather than subsequent corrosion. This indicates that the sea-floor sediments are pretty firm at the wreck site. In 1975 Watts wrote that "aft of the only substantial athwartships bulkhead, located almost amidships, the lower hull exists in an excellent state of preservation. Plating on the bottom of the hull remains virtually intact as does the vertical plating of the stern. Along the port side of the lower hull a considerable portion of the athwartships plating is either missing or badly damaged" (Watts 1975, 319). Miller concurred in 1978 when he wrote that "the stern section [of the lower hull] is still intact up to the main athwartships bulkhead" (Miller 1978a, 102).

Forward of the athwartship bulkhead, the lower hull "seems to have collapsed almost entirely. This includes not only the plating but stanchions, braces, framing, and the transverse floor 'timbers' which are of considerable size and strength" (Watts 1975, 322). "The bow section of the lower hull in the vicinity of the captain's state room, anchor windless room and the chain locker is also still standing" (Miller 1978a, 102). Both Watts and Miller noted that the engine and machinery structures in the stern area probably contributed to the support of the lower hull. Similar vertical structures in the bow section aided in holding up the hull. But amidships, where the larger open area of the crews berthing was located, there was less vertical supporting structure. This was the weakest part of the hull, and thus under normal corrosion the collapse of the hull there, before the areas to the bow or stern, was understandable.

Watts, however, wrote that "it would be questionable to assume that the structural differences between the . . . sections of the lower hull were responsible for the excessive damage found [amidships]" (Watts 1975, 322). Rather, he speculated that the amidships hull collapse was "the result of depth charges during World War II" (Watts 1975, 322). Watts was not specific as on what evidence he based this speculation; he only stated that "the damage more closely resembles that which results from an explosion of considerable force" (Watts 1975, 322). Miller later referred to Watts's speculation, but Miller was more cautious and skeptical. He stated, "[A] theory of possible depth charging of the wreck during World War II has been offered as an explanation for the collapse of the center section, but further careful on-site study will be needed to verify this" (Miller 1978a, 102).

Another reference to this possible depth charging appeared in a 1978 publication by Ernest Peterkin. He stated "forward of the midship traverse [*sic*] bulkhead, the hull is almost completely collapsed. Examination of photography indicates that the 15-inch floor timbers in this area are scattered in all directions, several lying fore and aft. This distribution indicates to me that some force greater than the sinking impact or gravity has acted on this area. A World War II depth charge attack may offer an explanation" (Peterkin 1978, 26). Peterkin referred to some specific evidence for an explosion, but firm evidence for an explosion has not yet been unearthed.

I personally am doubtful about the speculative depth charge attack. The only fifteen inch wide beam-like feature I see in the amidships area of the Alcoa *Seaprobe* photomosaic does lie more or less fore and aft. It looks more like part of the flooring support of the hull at the chine break. The fifteen inch wide beam is tilted to the southeast slightly and attached to the chine part of the collapsed hull. This orientation is easily explained by the sliding downhill of the collapsed hull portion toward the starboard armor belt. This sliding downhill dragged the attached east end of the fifteen inch beam downward to give it a southeast orientation. I believe that corrosion and gravity explain this feature and the general collapse of the amidships hull.

Subsequent to the speculations by Watts and Peterkin on the depth charging, divers have collected what I consider evidence against a depth charge attack. The dive results will be discussed in later chapters, but suffice it to say that several delicate glass objects, such as a lantern, glass jars, engine room oil-lamp chimneys, and an intact mercury-tube engine room thermometer, have been collected from within and near the wreck of the *Monitor.* Such delicate glass artifacts would have been shattered by the concussion of a depth charge explosion.

I personally have had some experience with exploding depth charges, so I can appreciate their energy and concussion capabilities. While I was a Columbia University graduate student in 1963, I was on a cruise on the research vessel *Robert Conrad,* the second year of the ship's operation by Lamont-Doherty Geological Observatory. On our way from New York to the Caribbean, we stopped at the naval ammunition depot in Earle, New Jersey, to load explosives. In my career, I have been on three different ships that loaded explosives at the familiar port of Earle. On that 1963 *Conrad* cruise, we loaded about ten tons of half-pound blocks of TNT for seismic reflection profiling, and about ten to fifteen 300-pound Mark 7 depth charges for SOFAR (sound fixing and ranging) channel studies. Dr. Maurice Ewing, Lamont's director and one of my former geophysics professors, was studying the SOFAR channel. Columbia University had a SOFAR station on Bermuda that was part of a global network that listened to shots in the SOFAR channel. Periodically, Ewing would radio the *Conrad* and direct us to drop a depth charge in the channel.

As a geophysics graduate student I had to learn to use these explosives as sound sources. When we were to drop our first depth charge, the *Conrad*'s chief scientist, Chuck Frey, and I rolled a Mark 7 to the fantail rail platform. We armed the depth charge with half-pound blocks of TNT and, for redundancy, two detonator caps with two waterproof fuses. The fuses were about one hundred inches long to give enough burn time for the *Conrad* to proceed a safe distance at a speed of ten knots, and for the depth charge to sink into the SOFAR channel. We pulled the fuse lighters and pushed the Mark 7 over.

Standing on the fantail and counting the seconds, we waited for the report of the depth charge. When the charge exploded, the concussion was enormous; it felt like the *Conrad*'s fantail lifted out of the water and vibrated and shook. Immediately, the *Conrad*'s engineer came running on deck from the engine room. He yelled "What the hell is going on! Our pipes in the engine room have sprung leaks! My ears are ringing!" This was the first time such large shots had been used from the *Conrad.* Also, Chuck Frey had neglected to inform the engine room about what was happening. Needless to say, we put longer fuses on the subsequent depth charge shots.

A nearby depth charge explosion is powerful and damaging. There does not have to be a direct hit to damage a submerged submarine or a sunken ship. If such a depth charge had hit the *Monitor* wreck, the delicate glass objects would have been shattered. Besides, what are the odds that a depth charge would have hit the *Monitor*'s hull exactly at its weakest point amidships?

One of the reasons I discuss the depth charge theory is because it had reinforced a false impression about the damage to the *Monitor*, namely, that the greatest damage was man-made and not due to the natural harshness of the *Monitor*'s *in situ* environment. A myth had developed that the *Monitor* was safe in its grave under the ocean. And consequently, there was no urgency to recover the *Monitor* wreck so long as further man-made damage could be prevented. For example, in the final chapter of Civil War historian William C. Davis's book on the *Monitor* and the *Merrimac* in 1975, he stated that the *Monitor* "will be safe enough in the watery home that has held her for over a century" (Davis 1975, 170).

The MRRF took it for granted that everyone knew the corrosive, high wave energy, strong current environment of the *Monitor* wreck site was not good for the wreck. To the MRRF members, this seemed obvious. We were interested in documenting any and all possible environmental threats to the *Monitor* wreck, and the rates and temporal changes of these environmental stresses. But we were also interested in documenting those aspects of the environment that would impact on the development activities of the site, such as future diving projects and any excavation related to possible recovery. Are there times when the currents are mild and of constant direction to allow divers and submersibles to work? Where are the possible larger artifacts of the *Monitor*, such as the two Dahlgren cannons? Did they fall out of the overturned turret on sinking? Are these larger iron artifacts buried in the sediments around the wreck? Could excavation devices penetrate the sediments under the *Monitor* wreck? What is the density of the sediments? This information had to be known in order to estimate the weight of material to be excavated. What is the nature and thickness of the calcareous encrustation on the wreck and iron artifacts? Has the encrustation sealed the iron to prevent further corrosion? The MRRF wanted to address these questions by completing Phases II and III of the organization's master plan.

I was awarded research ship time on the *Eastward* in June 1976 as part of the Cooperative Oceanographic Research Program funded by the

National Science Foundation (NSF). The project involved seismic reflection profiling of the Delaware–New Jersey continental shelf. The track of the *Eastward* to and from the Delaware–New Jersey area took the research vessel right over the *Monitor*, thus offering us the chance to use the *Eastward* as a ship of opportunity to carry out site charting and environmental studies.

John Newton took the lead in producing a MRRF permit proposal for the *Eastward* cruise to the *Monitor* wreck site in 1976. Twenty copies of the proposal were submitted to Dr. Robert M. White, the administrator of the National Oceanic and Atmospheric Administration (NOAA) on 30 March 1976 (Newton et al. 1976a, 1–23). The primary goal of the *Eastward* visit to the *Monitor* was to conduct a baseline magnetic anomaly map of the *Monitor* wreck site. No previous near sea-level magnetic anomaly profiles had been taken at the site. The main reason for the magnetic survey was stated in the proposal: "[I]t is evident from ... previous studies that the wreck has been buried on the south side by [six to seven feet] of sand. It is known that certain parts of the Monitor, such as the deck-light cover that was recovered from the sand, fell away from the wreck to be buried [Sheridan 1976, 41; Newton, 1975, 60]. These buried parts will not be detected photographically but would be [detectable] magnetically" (Newton et al. 1976a, 2).

The magnetic survey was viewed by the MRRF as an essential part of Phase II, site charting and environmental studies, of the foundation's master plan; the plan was described and included as a block diagram in the permit proposal. The proposal read:

> The objectives of the proposed research are threefold:
>
> 1. To measure the total intensity of the earth's magnetic field 20 to 30 feet below the sea's surface and
>
> 2. To identify regional geological anomalies and gradients in the area and
>
> 3. To identify the near sea-level anomalies caused by the Monitor wreck and debris fragments
>
> This will be accomplished by spending approximately 12–24 hours in the Marine Sanctuary. The magnetic profiling will involve

5 or more crossings of the wreck site in a northeast-southwest direction (parallel to the regional magnetic field and depth contours) and 5 or more crossings of the wreck in directions perpendicular to these courses. A Varian proton precession magnetometer sensor will be towed at approximately 6 knots with about 250 feet of cable trailing astern. The sensor of the instrument would tow at a depth between 20 and 30 feet in this configuration below the surface. Spacing of the crossings will be approximately 200 feet apart centered on the wreck and accuracies of ±1 gamma are expected.

Navigational control for this survey will be based on the use of Loran C, SATNAV [satellite navigation], side search and vertical sonar contact with the wreck of the Monitor. The sonars to be employed are UQN-1 with precision fathometer recorder for vertical profiling and Simrad BASDIC [bottom and azimuthal sound detection indicator] for horizontal ranging. Accuracies of absolute position will be within 150 feet by Loran C, and of relative sonar position with respect to the Monitor wreck will be within 30–50 feet.

As an ancillary part of this magnetic survey, it is planned to run the 3.5kHz [kiloHertz] sub-bottom profiler at the same time. These data will give acoustic profiles of the sedimentary layers directly beneath the wreck of the Monitor, and provide evidence of possible near-surface faults, buried channels, or hard [older] sub-strate that might exist in the site.

The cruise plan, as presently scheduled, is described below:

Depart Beaufort, N.C., 0800 June 9, 1976

Arrive Monitor Marine Sanctuary 1600 June 9, 1976

Begin northeast-southwest transect across the Sanctuary

Secure magnetometer cable and proceed to site off Delaware 0200 June 10, 1976

Arrive Monitor Marine Sanctuary, stream cable for southeast-northwest transects across the Sanctuary... 2300 June 16, 1976

Secure magnetometer cable and proceed to Beaufort 0900 June 17, 1976 (Newton et al. 1976a, 6–7).

One of the requirements of any permit proposal to NOAA for work at the *Monitor* wreck site was an evaluation of the risks to damage of the wreck. The MRRF proposal stated the risk of the magnetometer survey: "The risk of contact between magnetometer sensor and the wreck is nil. In thousands of miles of magnetic profiling with this equipment, the towing cable and sensor have never been lost, nor has it ever come in contact with the sea-floor" (Newton et al. 1976a, 9). In my experience with towing "maggies" on several research ships in the Atlantic, the Caribbean, and in the Antarctic oceans, the only contact we ever made with the sensors was with an occasional shark that confused the maggie with a fish. Teeth marks on the sensors and cables have been found, but no sensor or cable has been cut off. The magnetometer survey, coupled with the sub-bottom profiling, were considered a nonthreatening remote-sensing activity and easily permitted in the marine sanctuary.

Regarding the availability of the data, the MRRF proposal stated:

> A report, summarizing preliminary results of the cruise, will be provided to the Administration of NOAA within a month after completion of the work at sea. It is anticipated that the basic data will be available to the scientific community at the end of the cruise. (That is, for planning purposes only and at the costs of making duplicate copies available.) However, the investigators reserve the right to protect their proprietary interests in the event any part of these data prove to be publishable. In that event, publication will be accorded to these data within three years of the end of the work at sea (Newton et al. 1976a, 10).

The details of the permit proposal document the rigorous proposal and permitting process for research at the *Monitor* wreck site. Also, the statements made in the MRRF proposal were all complied with, both in the execution of the magnetometer survey and in the reporting and publication (Sheridan 1978, 35–36; Sheridan 1979, 254–57). It is important to state that in the cruises that I led under MRRF permits, we successfully completed our proposed research and we followed our cruise plans as precisely as possible. The foundation was proving that it was a credible, reliable research institution that deserved to be the leading organization in future work on the *Monitor* wreck site.

On 27 May 1976 the MRRF received a permit for the magnetic profiling from Robert Knecht, assistant administrator for coastal zone management at NOAA. "The research permit application for a baseline magnetic profiling of the Monitor Marine Sanctuary has been favorably reviewed. . . . The permit is valid for the magnetic profiling survey only, and for the period June 1, 1976–June 30, 1976. A NOAA observer is not required for this permitted activity" (Knecht 1976, 1).

The following discussion of the operations of the *Eastward* on the magnetic and high-resolution seismic reflection (3.5 kiloHertz) survey of the *Monitor* site is based on my cruise report, which was completed within thirty days of the cruise and submitted to NOAA. The research was carried out on the *Eastward* cruise E-4-76. We entered the Monitor Marine Sanctuary on two occasions to carry out the permitted studies. The first time was on 9–10 June 1976 from 1800 hours in the evening to 0500 hours the next morning; approximately eleven hours were spent surveying the wreck. On the return leg of the cruise, surveying was again conducted in the sanctuary from 1630 hours to 2045 hours on 16 June.

The longer period of time used in the first survey on 9–10 June was caused by the futile search for the wreck in an erroneously plotted position. As stated in the permit request, the primary navigation system to be used in this survey was the Loran C, supplemented with vertical and side-looking sonar and satellite navigation. The *Monitor* was approached based on its Loran C coordinates on the area's NOAA Loran C navigation chart. After searching in this area with a grid survey, however, it was clear that the wreck was not present at the expected coordinates. The bathymetry measured on the precision depth recorder indicated depths of about 213 feet at the expected coordinates, which were shallower than the known 220 feet depths at the *Monitor* wreck. This indicated that we were northwest of the true *Monitor* wreck position.

After spending five hours on the futile search, I consulted Capt. Harold Yeomans, a veteran of two past cruises to the *Monitor* site and an excellent navigator. We reestablished the search to the southeast along a new set of Loran C lines where the water depth was slightly deeper and near the 220 feet target. Within two hours at the new search area, the side-looking sonar picked up the wreck and the range was closed systematically until the wreck was crossed with both the vertical sonar and the magnetometer.

Given the inaccuracies of the Loran C navigation charts, we decided to use the raw Loran C rates centered at the *Monitor* wreck site to establish a relative navigation grid for the survey. The wreck was centered on the Loran C coordinates SS7-W-1616.05/SS7-Y-54506.0. This position was refined by the crossings of the wreck on the northeast-southwest lines, and confirmed by the reoccupation of the position on the return leg to carry out the northwest-southeast crossings. The numbers on the Loran C lines are rates in microseconds and could be resolved to tenths of microseconds. The Loran C lines formed a good orthogonal grid with the SS7-Y lines oriented northwest-southeast and the SS7-W lines oriented northeast-southwest. The Loran C system appeared to give good results during both surveys within the Monitor Marine Sanctuary as evidenced by the repeatability of the positions and the lack of jumping of the rates even to a tenth of a microsecond. Sky waves did present a problem.

Our exercise was instructive about the absolute accuracy of Loran C in the *Monitor* site area. When converting the raw Loran C microsecond rates at the *Monitor* wreck to absolute latitude and longitude computed from those rates using software in the Loran C receiver, the absolute position was off by four tenths of a nautical mile, or about twenty-four hundred feet. This was far from the accuracy advertised of plus-or-minus 150 feet for the Loran C equipment. As it turns out, the conversion software for the measured Loran C rates assumes perfect hyperbolic shapes for the radio field lines from the master-and-slave shore stations. However, near land, as we were sixteen miles off Cape Hatteras, there are distortions in the Loran C radio waves so the perfect hyperbolic shapes of the Loran C lines do not occur.

For example, if you were to take the commercially available Loran C charts of the *Monitor* area published by NOAA, which assumed perfect hyperbolic shapes, and used the Loran C lines printed on the chart to go to the *Monitor* wreck, you would wind up being about twenty-four hundred feet away from the wreck. This was good news for us, because in 1976 many fishing and diving boats had the now affordable Loran C navigation; they could have more easily found the wreck and exploited it.

Satellite navigation in 1976 was based only on a few satellites so that a satellite, or "bird," might be available every ninety minutes or so. My experience was that a single underway fix, if it was at a poor angle with the bird, could be off by as much as three miles! After remaining on-station for several days, or even months as we did on the *Glomar Challenger* in the Deep Sea Drilling Project in 1980, however, the absolute accuracy from satellite navigation was down to plus-or-minus two hundred feet because of the statistical averaging of many repeated satellite passes. Most satellite navigation equipment was expensive and not routinely available on fishing or diving boats. Even with satellite navigation technology, it did not aid us in finding the location of the *Monitor* wreck, and it did not aid us on the *Eastward* magnetometer survey.

Today, navigation is another story. The current global positioning system (GPS) has as many as twenty-four satellites in orbit, so continuous, multiple satellite fixes can be made. Absolute navigation is accurate to plus-or-minus thirty-five feet with standard, affordable antennas and receivers. Until recently, the satellite fixes were degraded by the Department of Defense so that commercial GPS was restricted to plus-or-minus thirty-five feet accuracy, unless a base station was used to get "differential GPS." I have been involved in seismic surveys using differential GPS navigation that was accurate to plus-or-minus seven feet. Now with the removal of the military degradation, standard GPS is accurate to plus-or-minus seven feet. Any fisherman or diver can easily locate the *Monitor* wreck today. This is relevant because, as discussed in later chapters, violations of the Monitor Marine Sanctuary by unauthorized vessels and personnel have occurred.

Other than the navigational difficulties on cruise E-4-76, the geophysical survey went smoothly. I was grateful to my University of Delaware students who conscientiously recorded data and monitored the sonar; their diligence and efforts made the survey successful. The students were Daniel Belknap, Robert Minck, Michael Schilly, James St. Lifer, George Magruder, Arthur Johnson, David Pate, Everly Keenan, Holly Lanan, Charles Diggins, and James Buckland. Jim St. Lifer used the magnetics data for a master's thesis at the University of Delaware (Sheridan 1979, 254).

Measurements of the total magnetic field intensity were measured by the Varian proton-precession magnetometer with accuracies of plus-or-minus one gamma. Noise levels evident by the flutter in the recorded values were along the order of plus-or-minus one gamma. Smoothly varying values over known geologic anomalies, such as the nearby east coast magnetic anomaly (ECMA) with values about twenty to thirty gammas higher in the southeast part of the survey, confirmed the correct operation of the magnetometer.

To make a measurement with the proton-precession magnetometer, the hydrogen protons in the kerosene in the sensor must first be polarized. On the Varian, the duration of the polarization/measurement cycle is selectable. I selected the lowest possible duration of polarization of two seconds. With two seconds for a measurement after each polarization, that gave a measurement every four seconds, or fifteen measurements every minute. The *Eastward* was making an overground speed of five knots, the minimum speed needed to maintain a straight course in the Gulf Stream current. This corresponded to a speed of about five hundred feet a minute, thus yielding one magnetic field intensity measurement about every thirty-three feet along the track. At that ship speed we crossed the *Monitor* magnetic anomaly in about a minute, so we could resolve the shape and amplitude of the anomaly with about fifteen measurements. This was sufficient to obtain all the detail needed to successfully map the magnetic anomaly from the *Monitor* wreck.

The results of the magnetometer survey were good. The analog data from the Varian recorder were digitized and coordinated by the recorded ship time as to geographic location. The position of the magnetometer sensor, some 250 feet behind the ship and offset by the current slightly, was taken into account to give the correct geographic location of the actual magnetic field measurement. Magnetogram data from Fredericksburg, Virginia, indicated quiet magnetic conditions and a difference in baseline of only six gammas between the 9 June measurements and the 16 June measurements. The measurements were adjusted to account for this change between the different crossings, and the values were forced to agree at line crossings. Also, spurious magnetic readings during changes in course caused by the *Eastward*'s own magnetic field were ignored. We were successfully able to construct a contour map of the total magnetic field intensity at the *Monitor* wreck.

> Generally, the total magnetic field [intensity] varies from 53,850 gammas on the north and west to 53,870 gammas on the south and east, with a regional gradient at the [*Monitor*] wreck site of 1.2 gammas per [330 feet]. This gradient is part of the local geological effect

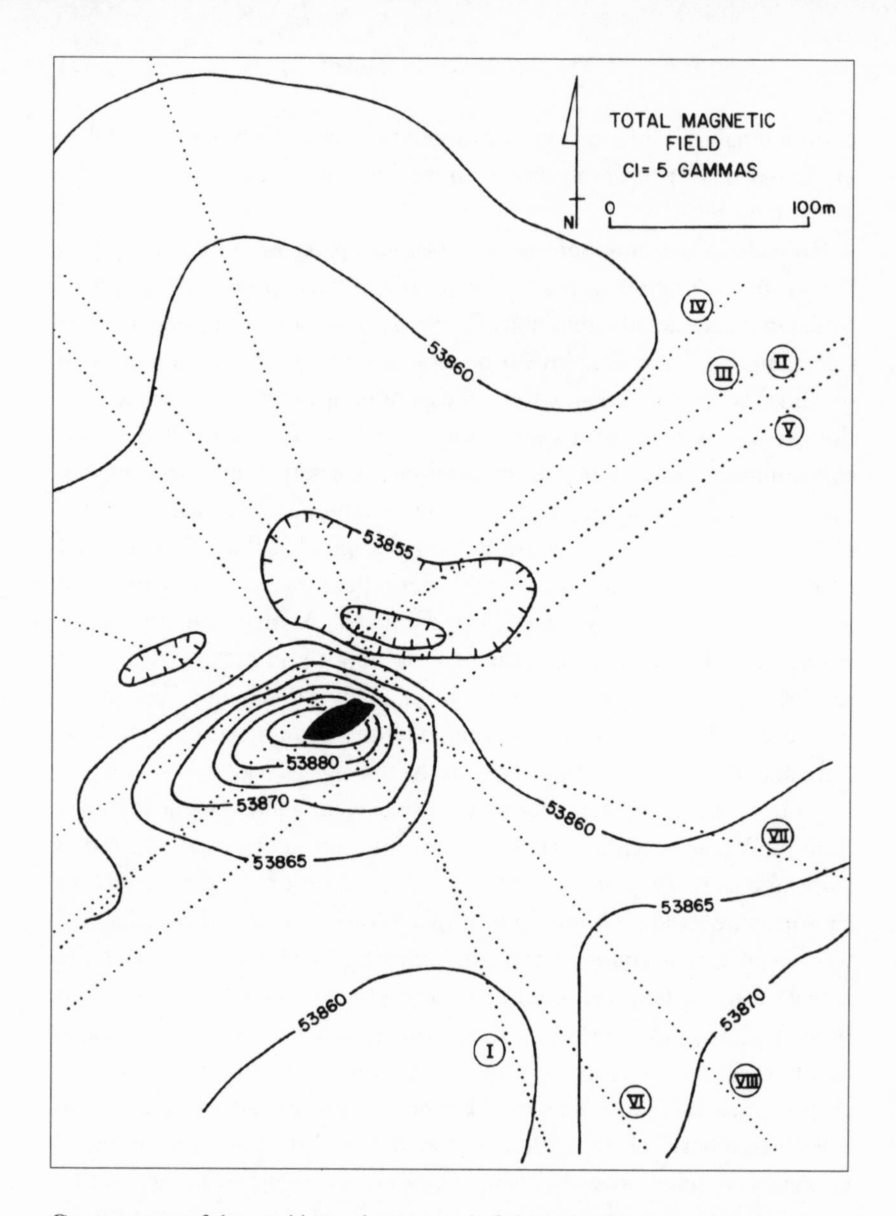

Contour map of the total intensity magnetic field at the *Monitor* wreck site, constructed by Dr. Robert Sheridan from data collected on the June 1976 *Eastward* cruise E-4-76. Note the negative trough north of the wreck and the positive peak over the wreck. The southwest orientation of the wreck's bow on the diagram is based on an erroneous previous publication by Watts (Watts 1975, 327). The diagram's bow actually should point nearly due west.

Sheridan, R. E. 1979. Site Charting and Environmental Studies of the *Monitor* Wreck, *Journal of Field Archaeology* 6:254.

> called the East Coast magnetic anomaly. A positive peak value of 53,889 gammas was measured over the south side of the wreck with a negative trough [value of 53,851 gammas] just north of the wreck. This characteristic positive-and-negative doublet forms an asymmetric peak-to-[trough] anomaly of 38 gammas [for the *Monitor* wreck] (Sheridan 1979, 255).

The positive-and-negative couplet was just what was expected. All magnetic bodies have two fictitious magnetic poles, one north-seeking and one south-seeking. These fictitious poles enhance the earth's magnetic field making it higher (positive anomaly), and detract from the earth's field making it lower (negative anomaly). At the latitude of the *Monitor* wreck the earth's field has a steep northward inclination; therefore, the negative anomaly is generally north of a magnetic body and the positive anomaly is over and to the south of a magnetic body, just as the map shows.

On the magnetic field map of the *Monitor* wreck site (Sheridan 1979, 254), submitted in 1978 for publication, I indicated the location of the wreck as a black symbol with its bow pointing southwest on a bearing of approximately 250° T. My data was based on Watts's recent orientation (Watts 1975, 327, 324). Watts had included a north arrow with the photomosaic of the Alcoa *Seaprobe* photography, and had also made an explicit statement in the text "that the wreck is aligned south-west to northeast" with a southwest direction for the bow. Even when I put in the black symbol for the *Monitor* wreck on the magnetic field map 1979, I felt uneasy. In the preliminary reports on this magnetic field map, I had put the *Monitor* wreck symbol with the bow pointing due west, or 270° T. This was what I thought we had found by the side-scan data from the *Eastward* during the discovery cruise in August 1973 (Newton 1975, 57). The 270° T orientation for the bow would better fit the positive anomaly contours on the magnetic field map. Later publications now seem to indicate that the approximate 270° T direction for the bow is correct. For example, the diagram in the NOAA operations manual for the 1979 diving project shows a drawing of the wreck with a north arrow that indicated the bow pointed approximately 270° T (National Oceanic and Atmospheric Administration 1979, app. 5, fig. 1). This was quite different from the north arrow in the 1975 publication (Watts 1975, 327). Also,

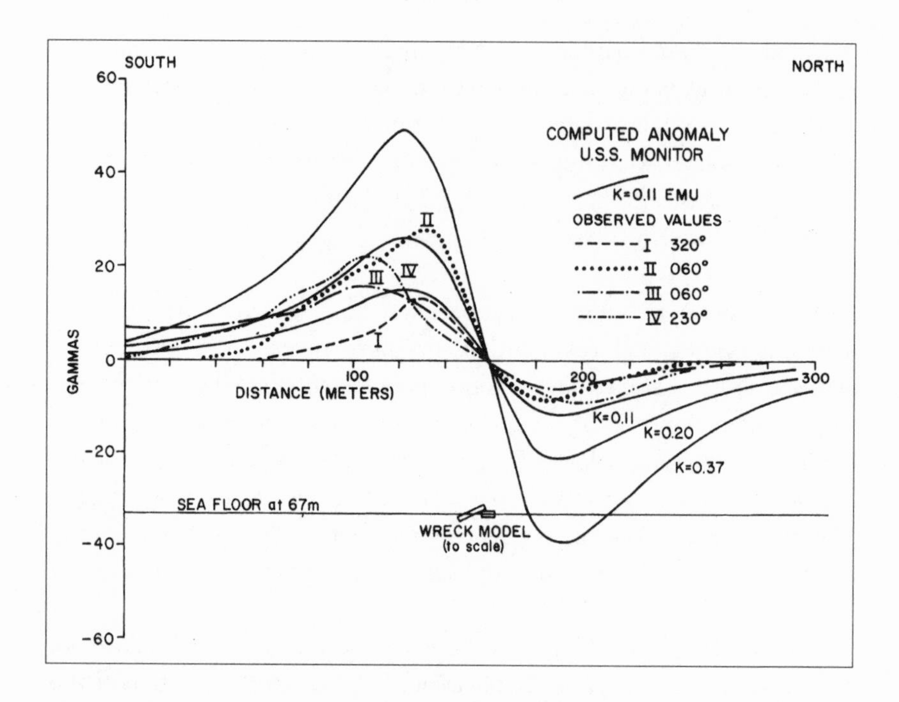

Comparison of the observed magnetic anomaly profiles over the *Monitor* wreck with computed values for a model of the wreck with iron of different values of effective magnetic susceptibility, K. The observed peak anomaly is lower than predicted because of the 60 percent corrosion of the *Monitor*'s iron.

Sheridan, R. E. 1979. Site Charting and Environmental Studies of the *Monitor* Wreck, *Journal of Field Archaeology* 6:256.

the 1987 expedition's report stated, "The longitudinal axis lies approximately west at 275° T" (Arnold et al. 1991, 305). I have never heard an explanation for why the alignment of the axis of the *Monitor* wreck was stated incorrectly in Watts's 1975 article or read any explanation for this discrepancy in later publications. Perhaps magnetic compasses were used on the Alcoa *Sea-probe* photography pod and the *Monitor* wreck site area's magnetic anomaly caused the false directional readings?

Another interesting thing about the magnetic field map of the *Monitor* wreck site is that it revealed the contrasting possibilities that exist for a single magnetic profile crossing. Depending on the orientation and position of the magnetic profile line within about one hundred feet of the wreck, the single-line anomaly could be totally negative if just north of the wreck and totally positive if just south of the wreck for lines oriented northwest-southeast. This is very instructive, especially to antisubmarine warfare (ASW) specialists who might use the shipborne magnetic anomaly detection (MAD) technique to identify submarines. Hopefully, the publication of the magnetic anomaly map of the *Monitor* wreck will alert future ASW experts to what the *Monitor* anomaly looks like, and it will not be mistaken for an enemy submarine lying on the bottom!

In the 1979 publication on the magnetic and seismic profile results, a technique was described that used the magnetic anomaly to estimate remotely the corrosion state of the *Monitor*:

> The general characteristics of the baseline magnetic field of the *Monitor* wreck are consistent with computer calculations for simplified models of the wreck. Slabs of the proper width and thickness for the *Monitor* occupied by a shell of outside armor were assumed as a model of the wreck. Calculations were made for a N-S crossing for iron with three different effective magnetic susceptibilities (K = 0.11, 0.20, and 0.37 emu [electromagnetic units]). The possible remnant magnetization of individual parts of the *Monitor* wreck is neglected because of the cancelling effects of components interacting with each other. Comparing the observed values with the calculated ones shows good agreement in general shape, which is dependent on the depth, tilt, volume, and iron content of the *Monitor*; all [of which are] well known values. The amplitude of the magnetic anomaly indicates that the volume of iron in the wreck, presumed to be present based on historical records, has an effective magnetic susceptibility of 0.32 emu.
>
> The effective bulk susceptibility determined for the model is apparently much lower than expected for wrought iron, implying that the volume of iron which originally sank has been extensively oxidized and that only a portion remains. Using equations
>
> $$H = \frac{2KHoV}{R^3} = \frac{2K'HoV'}{R^3}$$
>
> [for the peak magnetic anomaly, H] where K is the model susceptibility and V is the model volume, presumed to be the total original iron content of the *Monitor*; and K' is the true susceptibility of the

iron and V' is the volume of iron remaining in the high magnetic metallic or magnetite phases, it is possible to estimate the volume of iron remaining [in the pristine state] after corrosion.

$$\frac{V'}{V} = \frac{K}{K'}$$

Compared to a value of K' = 0.85, which is to be expected for closely packed magnetite and wrought iron, the K = 0.32 value implies that ca. 60% of the iron of the *Monitor* is corroded and oxidized to the low and nonmagnetic iron phases of hematite and goethite.

This amount of corrosion is reasonable in light of the corrosion observed on iron artifacts recovered from the *Monitor.* The iron decklight cover recovered in 1974 consists of two thick plates (each [1 inch] thick) held together by four bolts. Ca. [one fifth of an inch] of corrosion on the outer surface of this [plate] corresponds to a 26% volumetric corrosion. It is not unreasonable that the remaining iron is oxidized by 50% to the non-magnetic phases, leaving 37% of the original iron in the metallic and magnetite phases (Sheridan 1979, 256).

This was another good use of the magnetic measurements of the *Monitor* wreck.

One of the objectives of the magnetic survey was to locate buried parts of the wreck of the *Monitor.*

No anomalies larger than 3 gammas . . . were observed beyond [330 feet] from the *Monitor* wreck. Using the approximate equation for the positive peak anomaly from a body in high magnetic latitude of

$$H = \frac{2KHoV}{R^3}$$

where H = the positive peak magnetic anomaly of 3 gammas, K = the magnetic susceptibility 0.85, Ho = the earth's magnetic field at the *Monitor* of 53,800 gammas, R is the slant distance to the body, the minimum detectable size, [volume V,] iron fragment of the

> wreck can be calculated. For this survey of a maximum line spacing of [595 feet] and vertical distance between the sea-floor and sensor of [190 feet] the maximum R is calculated as [345 feet]. With R of this value, V is calculated as Ca. [1,368 cubic feet]. This value indicates that no iron fragments larger than [about 10 feet] on a side exist outside a distance of [330 feet] from the main hulk. The twin 11-inch Dahlgren guns and their carriages are about this volume and might be detected by a 3 gamma anomaly (Sheridan 1979, 257).

This meant that the Dahlgren cannons, if they did fall out of the turret on sinking, are close to the wreck. Personally, I believed they did not fall out of the turret. The fall of the turret was so quick that there was not a lot of time for the cannons to separate; water pressure, buoyancy, and whatever clamps held the gun carriages to the turret's floor-rails should have kept the guns in the turret.

The information gathered from the 3.5 kiloHertz sub-bottom seismic reflection profiles on cruise E-4-76 was very interesting. The acoustic system, hull-mounted on the *Eastward*, penetrated sediments up to fifty feet deep beneath the *Monitor* wreck. Layers as thin as three feet could be resolved. Four prominent reflectors were observed beneath the sea floor that appeared highly reflective, or "acoustically opaque" in seismic reflection profiling jargon. This high reflectivity of the sea floor implied that the sediments were consolidated slightly more than normal, recently deposited sediments. All four reflectors were inclined to the southeast and truncated at the sea floor (Sheridan 1979, 258).

These acoustic characteristics are similar to what we have observed on other parts of the continental shelf, for example, off Delaware and New Jersey. Sediments of the Pleistocene age are buried under a thin cover of Holocene age sediments deposited within the last ten thousand years. The truncation of the reflectors at the *Monitor* site is "definitive evidence for erosion of this part of the shelf edge, where the sediments are just beginning to dip [southeast] towards the continental slope" (Sheridan 1979, 258). This erosion occurred during the transgressive processes associated with the most recent Holocene sea level rise; processes of wave and current erosion truncated the older Pleistocene sediments deposited when the sea level was lower. The Gulf Stream current has persisted in this area throughout the Holocene Epoch and

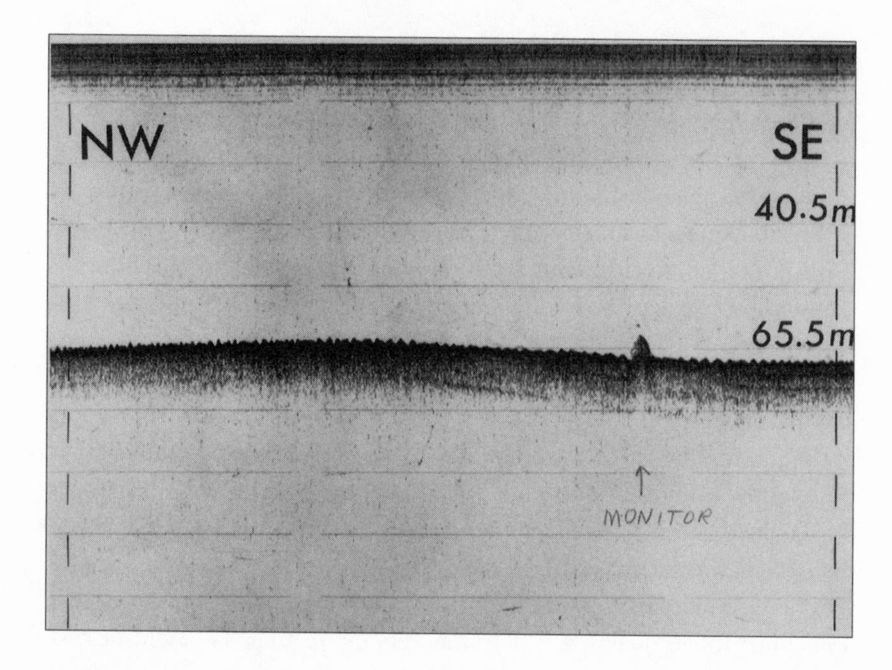

High-resolution 3.5 kiloHertz sub-bottom seismic reflection profile across the *Monitor* wreck. Note the truncation of the southeast sloping reflectors that occur beneath the wreck. This indicates that the sediments of the reflectors are of an older Pleistocene age and are undergoing erosion at the site.

Sheridan, R. E. 1979. Site Charting and Environmental Studies of the *Monitor* Wreck, *Journal of Field Archaeology* 6:258.

has maintained the erosion there. The interpretations were possible solely from the *Eastward*'s 3.5 kiloHertz sub-bottom seismic reflection profiles, and were stated in the cruise report to NOAA in 1976 and in a later publication on the site charting and environmental studies of the *Monitor* wreck (Sheridan 1979, 258).

The erosion by the Gulf Stream involves sediment traction and suspension with grain-by-grain processes. "These grain-by-grain processes at the wreck site would not be threatening to the *Monitor* because the wreck could settle as sand was gradually washed away beneath it, and it would continually be exposed on the sea floor" (Sheridan 1979, 258). While there is no threat of burial at the site, episodic strong flows of the

Gulf Stream with high bottom current velocities might transport sand to create a sandblasting effect on the wreck.

Further examination of the 3.5 kiloHertz profiles north of the *Monitor* site showed that the acoustically opaque sub-bottom Pleistocene sediments extend beneath the accreting Holocene sediments that are building south toward the *Monitor* from the Diamond Shoals (Sheridan 1979, 259). Alongshore sand transport on the Outer Banks' barrier islands converges at Cape Hatteras to create the Diamond Shoals sand-shoal complex, which builds outward like a large sand delta. If it were not for the persistent Gulf Stream erosion that keeps the *Monitor* site clean, the Diamond Shoal sands would have buried the *Monitor* wreck after slightly more than one hundred years. We are so fortunate that the *Monitor* sank where it did. If it had sunk a little farther north it would have been within the toe of the Diamond Shoals sand complex and buried by now. The wreck could be seen acoustically, however, even if buried about ten to twenty feet; there would have been the same good magnetic anomaly, but to whom would researchers have turned to get the hundreds of thousands of dollars needed to excavate the sand to prove the identification by photography?

There was no evidence of faulting of the sub-bottom reflectors at the *Monitor* wreck site. However, some of the largest growth faults on the U.S. Atlantic continental margin exist off the Carolinas and Georgia under the outer continental shelf. These faults have been growing since the Cretaceous period, for more than one hundred million years, by the slow slippage of a salt layer under the weight of thousands of feet of sediments and sedimentary rock. The salt is creeping out, just as toothpaste is squeezed from a tube, to form salt domes under the continental slope off the Carolinas. Subsequent to 1976, there have been seismic reflection profiles recorded by the U.S. Geological Survey that show these Carolina growth faults intersecting the sea floor in some places. This implies that the process of movement on these faults is continuing. Justifiably, I made a statement in my cruise report to NOAA and in my publication on the *Monitor*'s environment that "release of seismic energy by faults such as those [discussed above] might still affect the *Monitor* wreck site" (Sheridan 1979, 259). Of course, it is understandably difficult to predict when the next earthquake will occur!

Another phenomenon with relevance to the potential instability of the

Atlantic margin continental slope and shelf edge was discovered after my results on the *Monitor* site acoustic profiles were published in 1979. Methane gas hydrates have been found under the continental slope and rise. Gas hydrates are mixtures of water and methane in ice structures that occur beneath the sea floor when the conditions of the sediments (impermeable and rich in organic carbon), the hydrostatic pressure, and the sea-floor temperature are correct for the hydrate stability. Seismically these gas hydrates have been mapped from Florida to New Jersey under the Atlantic continental rise.

I was fortunate to be a co-chief scientist on leg 76 of the Deep Sea Drilling Project when we first successfully tested and sampled these Atlantic margin gas hydrates using a special pressure core barrel from the drilling ship *Glomar Challenger* in fall 1980. The little crystals of methane hydrate ice occur in the pore spaces between the sediment grains. In the case of the U.S. Atlantic margin, the sediments are organic rich, impermeable muds. Such muds are usually weak and are prone to slumping. However, the gas hydrate ice crystals effectively cement the sediment grains together and increase the rigidity of the bulk sediments. Now there is a theory that, because of several processes, the gas hydrates can rapidly disassociate over large areas of the sea floor, and the rapid loss of strength in the sediments causes the sediments to collapse under their own weight with resulting down-slope slumping. Such slumping on the slope and rise has been theorized to also affect the continental shelf edge where large blocks of the sea-floor sediments can be dislodged. If this theory proves true, the *Monitor* wreck lies in a potentially unstable environment.

After the 1976 *Eastward* cruise, the MRRF wanted to continue research on the *Monitor* as part of Phase II, the site charting and environmental studies, and to begin Phase III, the site testing. Another permit proposal was submitted on 29 June 1976 (Newton et al. 1976b, 1–86). The MRRF requested a longer-term permit for the interval from 1 August 1976 to 1 February 1979. With such a long-term permit, adequate time would be available to plan cruises, select the best weather windows, make cruise preparations, and, most important, to secure long-term funding for the research.

The MRRF planned to continue Phase II in 1977 with studies of the bottom currents, the age, lithology, and engineering properties of the sediments, and with the first horizontal photography of the wreck, which would give information on the thickness of the limestone encrustation. At the beginning of Phase III, the MRRF planned to make the first direct observations of the wreck from submersibles and by divers. For the diving and submersible work, John Newton contacted Edwin (Ed) Link, who was then the vice president of the Harbor Branch Foundation of Fort Pierce, Florida. Link was the inventor of the "Link trainer" used extensively in World War II to train pilots in the movable, mock cockpit. As a fellow inventor, Link was a personal friend of Doc Edgerton, who facilitated the relationship between the MRRF and the Harbor Branch Foundation in 1976 and 1977 (Edgerton 1977, 1).

Link sent a commitment letter to Newton on 18 March 1976:

> Harbor Branch Foundation's offer of one of [their] research submarines with support ship, including certain equipment and crews, to participate in the research efforts in the Monitor Marine Sanctuary... The [Harbor Branch] Foundation's interest in the Monitor is solely motivated by a desire to be helpful in this research and the recognition it could bring to [Harbor Branch Foundation's] achievements in providing equipment and technology needed to assure success of an operation of this kind which involves the national interest (Newton et al. 1976b, 33).

Harbor Branch Foundation was an accomplished submersible and diving group. In the MRRF proposal for August 1976 through January 1979, the details of the Harbor Branch Foundation's support ship, the research vessel *Johnson,* were given. This specialized ship was named after Seward Johnson, of the New Jersey Johnson and Johnson family. The Johnsons had donated extensive funding to the Harbor Branch Foundation to develop its programs. In addition to the support ship, the submersible *Johnson-Sea-Link* was described in detail in the proposal, as was the lockout diving capability to depths of five hundred feet (Newton et al. 1976b, 58).

In February 1977 NOAA, after the review process, issued a permit to the MRRF: "The Monitor Research and Recovery Foundation, Inc.... is hereby granted permission to conduct scientific research within the Monitor Marine Sanctuary described in the Foundation's Application for

'Environmental Engineering Studies and Site Charting at the Monitor Sanctuary' dated 29 June 1976, . . . for a period of 14 months beginning 20 August 1976" (Office of Coastal Zone Management 1977, 1).

Under the auspices of this permit to MRRF, I was fortunate to make a cruise to the *Monitor* site in April 1977 during cruise 77-3 aboard the research vessel *Cape Henlopen*. We continued the environmental studies of the wreck as part of Phase II of the MRRF's master plan. The *Cape Henlopen* was newly constructed as a diverse research vessel for the University of Delaware and had been christened in 1976. I was on the faculty committee that helped design the *Cape Henlopen*, so the vessel was capable of seismic reflection profiling at slow speeds and heavy coring devices could be recovered while on station. The *Cape Henlopen*'s high speeds of up to fifteen knots allowed physical and chemical oceanographers to gather needed samples over widespread areas in short time intervals.

During 1977, ship time on the *Cape Henlopen* was not fully booked by outside users, so some ship time was reserved for University of Delaware faculty for educational training of students. These educational cruises were funded by a gift from the Exxon Educational Foundation. I applied for a training cruise to return to the *Monitor* wreck site to accomplish five objectives:

1. measure long-term near-bottom current variations at the wreck site;
2. recover a piston core of the upper [20 feet] of sediments beneath the *Monitor;*
3. measure the physical and engineering properties of the sediments;
4. determine the stratigraphy of the sediments as a record of sedimentation or erosion rates; and
5. obtain horizontal photographs and television views of the deck encrustation and underside of the *Monitor* (Sheridan 1979, 254).

My application was accepted and I was awarded the ship time from 4 through 8 April 1977.

Within thirty days after the trip I submitted my cruise report to NOAA. On the *Cape Henlopen* cruise, I was joined by Doc Edgerton and

The research vessel *Cape Henlopen* of the University of Delaware was on station at the *Monitor* site in April 1977 to do current measurements, take a piston core, and capture the first horizontal photography of the wreck (Sheridan 1979, 254).

University of Delaware

John Newton as coinvestigators. Built for high speed, the *Cape Henlopen* was narrow abeam; this restricted space and there was only enough bunk space for twelve scientists. The bunk space was needed for students, technicians, and the NOAA observer, so John Newton stayed ashore and worked on the vital logistics of the cruise. He joined us on site after the *Cape Henlopen* was anchored over the *Monitor* wreck site.

University of Delaware students James St. Lifer, James Demarest, Daniel Belknap, Sandra Shaeffer, Kim Curlin, Doug Lynch, and Jack Cox ably performed their research duties. MIT technicians Robert Magee and James Scholten assisted Edgerton with his television and photographic work. The onboard NOAA observer was Lt. Comdr. Floyd Childress. Along with Newton, Dr. William (Bill) Still Jr. of East Carolina University and James Stegall, vice president of the Del Norte Company, came aboard the *Cape Henlopen* at the *Monitor* site. Del Norte Company

Views from the *Cape Henlopen* decks during a typical Cape Hatteras storm (up to sea state 6) on the way out to the *Monitor* wreck site. The piston core is shown in the upper view, and the tractor tire filled with concrete anchor weight for the current meter is shown in the lower view.

had donated the use of the highly accurate microwave navigator. Capt. Russell Preble ably commanded the *Cape Henlopen* in all aspects of cruising, holding station, anchoring, and navigating in this complex and demanding cruise. The *Cape Henlopen* boatswain, Jack Stuart, was extremely helpful in rigging the heavy piston core and the near-bottom current meter; he also was in charge of operating the many deck winches and the "cherry picker." Stuart also built a substantial one thousand pound anchor, a tractor tire filled with concrete, for the current meter.

Cruise 77-3 of the *Cape Henlopen* was remarkable. All objectives were accomplished in the limited time, even as our time constraints were made worse by a typical Hatteras storm. After leaving port from Lewes, Delaware, at 0900 hours on 4 April, we benefited from the high fifteen knot cruising speed and the ship was off the Chesapeake Bay mouth by 1630 hours. Then the journey slowed, first for fog, then for stormy seas from the south that were reminiscent of the storm that sank the *Monitor*. We battled the storm all night and into the next day, winding up twenty miles north of Diamond Shoals at 1200 hours on 5 April. We had ten foot swells with five foot waves on top and gale force winds with gusts up to fifty knots. We were in sea state 6, just as the *Monitor* had been when it sank!

We knew about the storm from weather forecasts, but we decided to go into it from Delaware, hoping we would be close to the *Monitor* site to begin our work as soon as it cleared. For comfort we rode with the storm and wound up sixty miles north of Cape Hatteras. After the storm abated, we passed Diamond Shoals at 0700 hours on 6 April and arrived at the *Monitor* site at 0730 hours.

Using the raw Loran C rates from the June 1976 *Eastward* cruise, we focused in on the wreck rapidly, making contact with the 7 kiloHertz Raytheon vertical sub-bottom profiler on the second pass. The vertical sonar contact was shown to Childress, the NOAA observer, to document our relative navigation and ensure the location of the current meter and the piston core relative to the wreck. At 1030 hours *Cape Henlopen* moved to the current meter location about a nautical mile southeast of the wreck, and we launched the meter.

We then returned to the wreck and made passes with Edgerton's EG&G side-scan sonar. *Cape Henlopen* left the wreck site to make a rendezvous off Hatteras Inlet to pick up the Del Norte navigation receiver and a trigger-arm come-along for the piston core. The U.S. Coast Guard was very helpful on this cruise, using their thirty-four foot rescue vessel to transport and transfer items. Also, the U.S. Coast Guard gave permission and assistance in installing the microwave transponders for the Del Norte navigator on Hatteras Lighthouse and Diamond Shoals Light. Later, the U.S. Coast Guard rescue helicopter carried an NBC news cameraman over the *Cape Henlopen*.

We returned to the piston core site about three fourths of a nautical mile southeast of the *Monitor* wreck, and took a core at 2230 hours on 6 April. It was a good core with twenty feet of penetration and twenty feet of recovery. *Cape Henlopen* then began its approach to the *Monitor* wreck site for the photography phase of the cruise.

To photograph the wreck we needed to three-point moor the *Cape Henlopen*, with one anchor off the bow, and one anchor off each of the stern's K frames, one to starboard and one to port. For this close work and to be sure of the camera's position, we needed very controlled motion of the ship to plus-or-minus ten feet. The Del Norte navigator provided that accuracy.

After much work in setting the anchors, Edgerton's new horizontal-looking television and still camera pod was lowered at 1305 hours on 7 April. Our positioning was so good that on the first lowering the camera landed on the overturned flat-bottomed hull plating in the area of the engine room!

To move the camera pod, we had to move the ship very gradually and by plus-and-minus ten foot distances. This was done using the Del Norte navigator, which had been set up in the electronics laboratory. Preble took his station there with a relative grid; via headphones he ordered Stuart on the K frame winches to haul in the starboard anchor while letting out the port anchor to move the *Cape Henlopen* sideways. Preble tracked the movement of the ship on the Del Norte grid. Also, with the television monitor in the *Cape Henlopen*'s wet laboratory, Edgerton could see where the television pod was looking and request changes in location.

While at anchor over the *Monitor* wreck, John Newton, Bill Still, and Jim Stegall transferred by raft from the cabin cruiser *Sara Kay* at about 1500 hours. Still, a prominent naval historian and ironclad expert, examined the television footage and the real-time video to advise us on what

John Newton climbed the ladder up the fantail of the *Cape Henlopen* after rowing a raft to the research vessel. He and others visited the research vessel while it was anchored over the *Monitor* during television and still photography activities.

University of Delaware

we were seeing. Newton also viewed the television data and I showed him the piston core, which was split and being studied in one of the *Cape Henlopen*'s laboratories. Stegall checked on the Del Norte receiver's installation, which he had guided us through over the radio. He verified that the Del Norte was in correct working order. Our three visitors left before dark that evening.

We continued to photograph the wreck for a few more hours and achieved good results. We hauled in the camera and anchors by 1945 hours and the current meter at 2130 hours on 7 April. We next made a 7 kiloHertz sub-bottom profile from the *Monitor* wreck to the piston core site; this showed a continuation of the same acoustic character between the two locations. At 2215 hours we departed the *Monitor* site and arrived at Lewes, Delaware, at 1430 hours on 8 April 1977.

The piston core results were excellent. "Upon opening the plastic core liner, the bedding contacts appeared sharp and near horizontal indicating

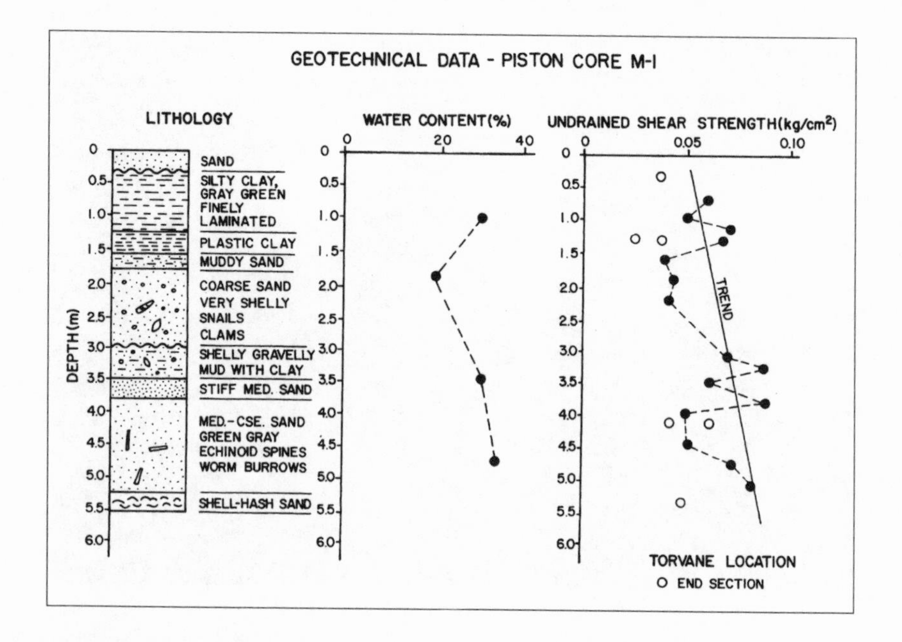

Piston core results show the stratigraphy, the water content, and the shear strength of the sediments to a depth of twenty feet beneath the sea floor at the *Monitor* site. The lithology of the sediments indicates they were deposited when the sea level was lower, during the Pleistocene Epoch. Shells collected were dated as being approximately 115,000 years old.

Sheridan, R. E. 1979. Site Charting and Environmental Studies of the *Monitor* Wreck, *Journal of Field Archaeology* 6:260.

the correct [vertical] position of the core and little disturbance of the sediments . . . [the core was] described geologically and tested for water content and undrained shear strength before the cores had a chance to dessicate" (Sheridan 1979, 259). Two upward-fining (decreasing grain size) lithologic units bounded at the top by unconformities were recovered. These are typical of regressive facies deposited during sea-level lowerings of the Pleistocene Epoch. The sandier units with pelecypod and gastropod shells represent inner shelf and estuarine deposits that grade upward into shallower water mud and clay deposits. Certainly the finely laminated clay, just beneath the foot or so of sand forming the sea floor, was deposited in an enclosed environment like a quiet water bay or

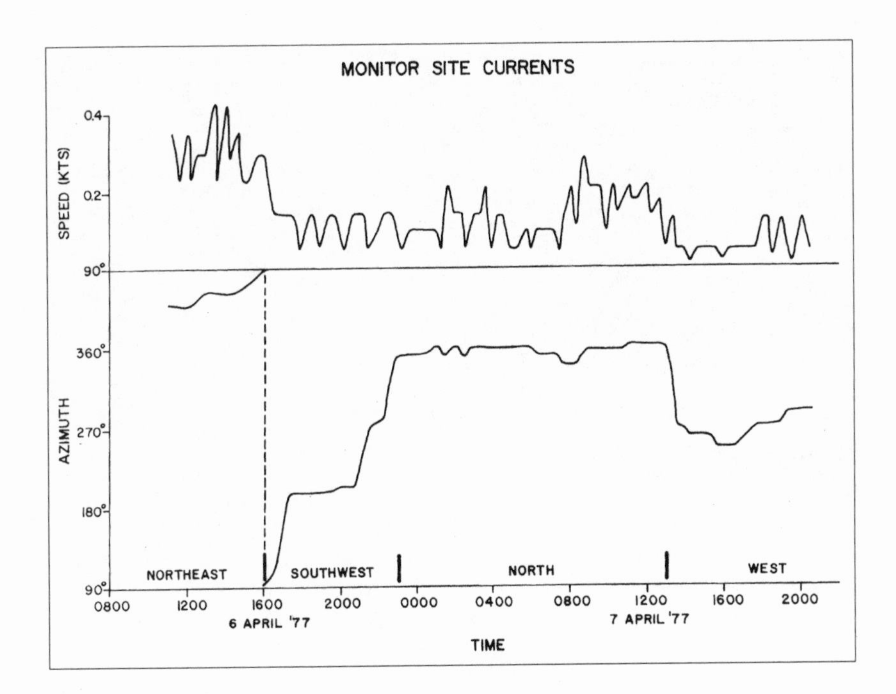

Current measurements showing the speed and direction over a thirty-six hour period at the *Monitor* site. The northeasterly directed current is the stronger Gulf Stream current; the southwesterly directed current is the weaker Labrador current. The boundary between these currents moves back and forth over the *Monitor* wreck every few hours.

Sheridan, R. E. 1979. Site Charting and Environmental Studies of the *Monitor* Wreck, *Journal of Field Archaeology* 6:262.

lagoon. This would be only a few feet deep, analogous to the present-day Pamlico Sound (Sheridan 1979, 260). The only time the sea level was so low at the *Monitor* site was during the Pleistocene Epoch, which proves the conclusions made previously from the 3.5 kiloHertz profiles (Sheridan 1979, 258). "Shells in the sand have been dated by the amino acid racemization technique and given an approximate age of 115,000 years B.P." (Sheridan 1979, 259), which positively proves their Pleistocene age. The older sediments are being eroded and nearly exposed at the *Monitor* wreck site.

The water content measurements, varying between 15 to 40 percent, are typical of slightly compacted older sediments, as are the slightly higher

The first horizontal still photograph of the bottom hull plating in the area of the engine room. This was the first indication of the thickness of the limestone encrustation by coral growth, barnacles, and pelecypod shells. The gentle currents at the time allow the sea bass and smaller fish to school easily (Sheridan 1979, 262).

Harold Edgerton

undrained shear strength values. The lithologic units with more clay content have the higher shear strength, or cohesion (Sheridan 1979, 260). This is good news and bad news. The clayey units will hold the sediments together and prevent crumbling, as sands will do, in any possible future excavation. This is good. But the cohesion of the clays, their stickiness, will cause higher entry and pullout forces for any excavation device. That is bad. The water content percent controls the density of the sediment, and thus the weight of any volume of sediment involved in possible future excavations. The *Cape Henlopen* piston core gave this basic environmental information vital for recovery plans (Sheridan 1979, 261).

The current meter was mounted about eight feet above the sea floor to measure near-bottom currents at a depth where divers and submersibles would operate as part of the MRRF's Phase III operations. After the storm had abated, the current measurements showed that over a thirty-six hour interval "the current velocities were not very fast with values generally measured between 0.2 and 0.4 knots. These relatively mild currents would not create unreasonable hazards to future diving and submersible operations near the sea floor around the *Monitor* wreck. Another observation is that the current direction maintains itself steadily for several hours and then changes direction relatively abruptly, sometimes between the 20-minute sampling intervals, to take up a new direction" (Sheridan 1979, 262). The northeasterly flowing Gulf Stream was alternating with the southwesterly flowing Labrador current.

"It should be noted that the north-NE (Gulf Stream) currents are faster (more than 0.2 knots) than the [Labrador] currents to the west and southwest (less than 0.2 knots). Interestingly, the stronger Gulf Stream current has a great enough velocity part of the time (more than 0.3 knots) to transport medium-to-fine sand. The westerly and southerly [Labrador] currents, however, are below the threshold velocity to move sand" (Sheridan 1979, 261). This asymmetry in the transport means that the net transport of sand is in the direction of the Gulf Stream, as indicated by the by now widely known scour mark northeast of the *Monitor*.

The abrupt shifting of the boundary between the Gulf Stream and Labrador currents across the *Monitor* wreck explains these current observations. There are times when the currents are mild and of constant directions for several hours. This gives enough of a time window for submersible and lockout dives. The dives could last for up to an hour, but generally will be about thirty minutes at the *Monitor* wreck's depth.

From the *Cape Henlopen*, Harold Edgerton's specially designed camera took the first horizontal photographs of the wreck and the first horizontal television views of the overturned main deck of the *Monitor*. A view under the bow area of the wreck was recorded on television tape. Most notable was the fact that there was little evidence of debris hanging from the main deck, as if that deck were largely intact beneath the thick encrustation.... The initial horizontal view of the *Monitor* give the first appreciation of the thick coral and sponge encrustation of the wreck. In profile, the encrusted [hull] looks much like a coral reef. The abundant fish photographed during the *Cape Henlopen* cruise were schooled in a very relaxed manner, not struggling against stiff currents to maintain their position over the wreck. This observation also indicates relatively mild currents, a finding that agrees with the current measurements recorded when the photo was taken" (Sheridan 1979, 262).

The thickness of the encrustation first revealed on the *Cape Henlopen* cruise is another good news–bad news factor. The encrustation seals the underlying iron and prevents or slows down the corrosion process. This is good. But the weight of the limestone accumulating as a reef could eventually stress the lower hull and cause a collapse of the hull and possibly the main deck as well. This is bad.

After the *Eastward* and the *Cape Henlopen* cruises, the MRRF felt that it had determined many of the environmental factors relevant to the rate of degradation of the wreck and to the possible threats to its future from natural processes. The MRRF felt it had some facts relevant to future operations and excavations for the development of the *Monitor* wreck site, including future recovery efforts.

10

Site Testing

The Monitor Research and Recovery Foundation (MRRF) enjoyed a great deal of positive publicity from the success of the *Cape Henlopen* cruise in April 1977. In many interviews with the printed and television press, I described the results and was further prodded to explain their significance. The detection of mild and constantly directed currents, at least for several hours, had direct bearing on future diving and submersible operations on the *Monitor* wreck. For development of the site this information was vital. Of course, the word "recovery" in the foundation's name made it clear that its members were interested in the development of the *Monitor* site to the point of retrieval of the wreck intact or at least retrieval of its major parts.

The taking of the piston core sample and measurement of the sediment's physical geotechnical properties were pertinent to any excavation beneath the wreck. For the press I described possible recovery concepts that would involve excavating the sediments. Naturally, this was the part of the project that the press realized would intrigue the public the most. Indeed, to the American public in 1977, recovery seemed logical. An NOAA publication noted, "[T]he question most often asked is can the Monitor be raised?" (Childress 1977, 3). Newspaper articles about the *Cape Henlopen* cruise included significant coverage of several recovery proposals.

One recovery proposal, involving excavation of the sediments, had been put forward in 1976 by Global Marine Development, Inc. (Global Marine Development Inc. 1976, 5). R. Curtis Crooke, president of Global

Marine, provided MRRF a copy of a proposal to recover the *Monitor* intact using the *Glomar Explorer.* The plan was to construct a submerged vehicle to be lowered by the *Glomar Explorer;* the vehicle would be designed to scoop up the *Monitor* wreck and approximately fifteen feet of the sea-floor sediments beneath the wreck. The *Cape Henlopen* piston core data were favorable to such a concept (Sheridan 1979, 264). The weight of the sediments involved in such a lift and the breakout and pull-out forces caused by the shear strength (cohesion) of the sediments were within the fourteen million pound lift capacity of the *Glomar Explorer.* In 1976, Crooke was riding the wave of the bicentennial enthusiasm for historic preservation projects (Global Marine Development Inc. 1976, 1). The recovery of the *Monitor* would have been an ideal project to rally national support. Private proponents and supporters, however, needed the encouragement and approval from the various government agencies involved.

Outside of the discussion of the *Glomar Explorer* in the press in 1977, as part of the publicity of the *Cape Henlopen* cruise, the only other mention of this proposal in 1977 was in an article published in the fall issue of *Sea History, the Journal of the National Maritime Historical Society* (Sheridan 1977, 12). The article served as an announcement of the *Glomar Explorer* plan to the professional maritime historical community. With all the press exposure given to the possibility of recovering the *Monitor* in 1977, there was great excitement; the MRRF was probably in its best position to affect events during this time.

To maintain momentum, it was essential to begin Phase III, site testing, that summer. MRRF members were enthusiastic about the planned dives using the Harbor Branch Foundation's submersibles and lockout divers. Doc Edgerton, in his usual exuberance, wrote a letter to his friend Ed Link on 22 April 1977, almost immediately after he returned from the *Cape Henlopen* cruise. He enthusiastically outlined plans for that summer's use of the Harbor Branch Foundation's submersibles:

> Enclosed is a copy of my report "Monitor Search Trip Report" Covering April 4–8, 1977. I can send a copy of the video tape to you, if you think it would be useful in planning our next expedition in your submersibles.
>
> The currents were not serious when we were on the Monitor station. We must remember that this site is on the edge of the *wander-*

> *ing* Gulf Stream. Prof. Bob Sheridan had a current meter in the area and will advise you of his results.
>
> Horizontal photography will be of great value to the continued study of the Monitor. You may recall that one edge of the ship lies across the turret, holding the ship above the bottom by some 5 feet at the stern end.
>
> Also I suggest that a lock-out dive might be considered—for example, to pick up the Duke University underwater camera/strobe equipment which is on the wreck with exposed film. The divers could use a cable cutter to clear the camera from the 200 feet of cable that was used to suspend the camera from the ship. The cable may be snarled in the wreck.
>
> The Monitor Research & Recovery Foundation . . . has a permit in hand to do exploratory work at the Monitor site with cameras and other systems. Prof. Sheridan is president of this foundation. I have written to him asking that he send you a copy of the permit and an invitation to participate in an August 1977 effort. Please telephone him, if you have any comments about the permit. We will have time to request permit modifications, if we act promptly.
>
> We all appreciate the great capability of your diving systems and your willingness to use it for this important archaeological and historical project. Please give my personal regards to Mr. Johnson when you discuss this project with him (Edgerton 1977, 1).

I was pleased to receive a copy of the letter; the MRRF members were all eager to get on with the first submersible and diver visits to the *Monitor* wreck. Although Edgerton referred to me as president of the MRRF, I was only the president of the board of trustees, not the organization's chief executive officer. The role of the trustees, in practice, was to decide on policy, and give guidance to the salaried executive director, John Newton. Edgerton obviously expected the head of the MRRF to invite Link to participate in the August 1977 effort. Newton would be the individual to negotiate with Link about the arrangements for the diving cruise. In fact, Newton had negotiated with Link in 1976. Newton had already received Link's commitment letter, which allowed the use of the support ship *Johnson* and the submersible *Johnson-Sea-Link* for a *Monitor* wreck site cruise (Newton et al. 1976b, 33). Use of the Harbor Branch Foundation's facilities and equipment had been a major part of the MRRF's proposal to NOAA, under which we had received our permit. I thought Link had already been "invited" to assist the MRRF in the diving project on the *Monitor* in August 1977.

A phone call from Edgerton clarified the "president" situation. He said that Link preferred not communicating or working directly with Newton. All the MRRF members recognized John Newton as the organization's leader and knew that he would be the chief scientist on the planned August diving cruise. The MRRF researchers expected the Harbor Branch Foundation's submersibles and divers on the *Monitor* site to assist in the research, thus advancing the MRRF's master plan. Unfortunately, conflicts between Link and Newton had surfaced. Later, I reviewed possible reasons. Was it possible that Link felt he should have been in charge of the cruise? Did Link feel that Harbor Branch Foundation would be considered nothing more than glorified bus drivers delivering the MRRF researchers to the *Monitor*? Did Link think Harbor Branch Foundation should have a more primary role and thus be better able to demonstrate their capabilities? Edgerton, however, explicitly told me that Ed Link refused to work with John Newton.

Then Edgerton surprised me further. He suggested that I represent the MRRF on the diving cruise as chief scientist. In this way, the existing NOAA permit to the MRRF could be used. I was dumbfounded—what should I do? As a question of scientific ethics, I felt I could not replace John Newton. It was "his" project and he had scientific proprietary rights. I was involved in the *Monitor* research only through his invitation and I recognized his leadership in the project. To replace him would be a betrayal. I told Edgerton that I would not do it.

In the marine sciences and the exploration of the oceans, there are scientists, like Ed Link, that are instrumentalists. They develop and perfect tools to achieve certain results or collect certain kinds of data. With these tools they naturally try to employ their techniques on as many projects as possible. Instrumentalists are not intimately involved in the research results that they help collect, nor are they dedicated to solving a particular research question. They mainly are interested in employing their tools. I liken them to the "have gun, will travel" professionals of other disciplines. Often, instrumentalists move in on continuing research projects, and sometimes they succeed in taking over some projects because of their superior tools. Was this possibly what was happening with the *Monitor* project?

After my rejection of Edgerton's offer to be chief scientist on the August 1977 diving cruise with Harbor Branch Foundation, the organization's offer to assist the MRRF never materialized. Link began negotiating directly with NOAA to conduct the diving work at the *Monitor* site. Several complications ensued. Harbor Branch Foundation was a nonprofit, educationally based foundation, so it was qualified to get a permit from NOAA for research on the *Monitor*. However, the permitted research must fit into a master plan of the permittee. The permittee must be interested in the *Monitor* as an archaeological and historical research project, not just to exploit a famous wreck as a way to show off its capabilities. With this principle as one of the criteria to receive a permit, it would take months for Harbor Branch Foundation to bring on board expert archaeologists and *Monitor* historians to write a proper permit proposal. The proposal would have to be reviewed by NOAA's technical review group and then by the governmental advisory committee. This would require a month or more.

While the time was available for Harbor Branch Foundation to submit a proposal through channels and get a permit, they did not do it. No proposal was submitted or reviewed. Instead, Link and Edgerton went directly to NOAA with an enticing offer. Harbor Branch Foundation offered NOAA free use of its ships, equipment, and personnel to dive at the *Monitor* site. NOAA itself, therefore, had to become the research investigator. Because NOAA had neither archaeologists nor historians with expertise on the *Monitor*, it designated the North Carolina Division of Archives and History as a coinvestigator. Gordon Watts was named the archaeologist in charge of the scientific and historical research of the diving project. And so the worst possible ethical situation had happened. The government agencies in charge of the review and permitting process for the Monitor Marine Sanctuary became active researchers on the *Monitor*. NOAA was now in direct competition with the MRRF. This made me feel uneasy about potential conflicts of interest arising in the future.

This debacle was a devastating blow to the MRRF. Failure to execute the cooperative diving program with Harbor Branch Foundation was irrefutable evidence that the MRRF would not be leading the research on the *Monitor*. Ethically, NOAA should have refused Harbor Branch Foundation's offer, and told them to cooperate with the MRRF, which was the sole permit holder for research on the *Monitor*. Instead, NOAA dealt a deadly blow to the MRRF.

The NOAA–Harbor Branch Foundation diving cruise took place from 16 July to 2 August 1977 (Childress 1977, 2; Childress et al. 1977, 1; Childress 1978b, 42). The diving operation was actually a feasibility test of the diving techniques that could be used around the *Monitor* wreck, with an emphasis on safety. To provide redundancy in divers and submersibles, two support vessels and two submersibles were used. The support vessel *Johnson* was teamed with the submersible *Johnson-Sea-Link II;* the support vessel *Sea Diver* was teamed with the submersible *Johnson-Sea-Link I.* One team would be used as a backup in case of equipment problems. In addition, photography was done extensively, not only from the submersibles but also from a cable observation and rescue device (CORD). Lockout dives from the submersibles used highly trained divers, who used mixed gases (helium and oxygen) that diminished the threat of bends. Dive times could be longer, and a dive master in the submersible controlled the gases to ensure safety.

Participants in the cruise included Gordon Watts; Doc Edgerton; navy representative Donald Rosencrantz; Comdr. Philip Johnson, Lt. Comdr. Floyd Childress, Chester Slama, and Sue Froeschie from NOAA; and Roger Cook, the operations director of Harbor Branch Foundation (Childress 1977, 2). The first week of the cruise was spent using side-scan sonar and the Loran C and Del Norte navigation to locate and survey the wreck and its immediate surroundings. The CORD remote vehicle provided television views of the *Monitor* on 22 July (Childress 1977, 3). More than forty-five minutes of video were recorded during the cruise (Childress et al. 1977, 13; Childress 1978b, 44). The first submersible dives were made on 25 July after the support vessel *Johnson* and *Johnson-Sea-Link II* arrived on the site to join the *Sea Diver* and *Johnson-Sea-Link I* (Childress et al. 1977, 3; Childress 1978b, 42). "Bottom conditions, currents, and low visibility, and surface conditions, wind and sea state, hampered the operation two days and cut the mission short on a third" (Childress 1977, 3).

Despite the typical Cape Hatteras weather, many important dives were made. Watts had his first opportunity to examine the *Monitor* wreck directly from a submersible. "During the initial examination of the wreck site on July 25, 1977, a considerable amount of material associated with the site was noted on the sea floor north of the *Monitor.* The first, and perhaps most striking, object to be located was the remains of a brass navigational lantern found forty feet north of the turret" (Childress et al. 1977,

3). The lockout divers examined the turret and found it filled with sand. The pendulum gunport covers were closed, with shafts protruding from holes in the pendulum covers. These shafts might have served as seals to the holes during the *Monitor*'s last stormy voyage. The divers also observed the pilothouse and the engine room. It appeared that much of the engine room machinery was still intact (Childress et al. 1977, 4). While sweeping away the sand and shell hash around the lantern, the lockout diver confirmed the existence of the gray clay immediately below the sand (Childress et al. 1977, 4). This is exactly what the MRRF had found from the piston core sample taken during its April 1977 cruise (Sheridan 1979, 260). The sand and shell hash forming the sea floor around the wreck is an ephemeral, thin veneer over the clay.

Three of the submersible dive missions were made specifically to photograph the wreck (Childress 1978b, 43). Slama, a photogrammetric specialist, set up stereo-pair cameras and strobe lights on the submersibles. The submersibles covered a grid to produce a three dimensional image of the wreck. "Approximately 4000 black and white and color 35mm stereo photographs were taken vertically and obliquely under controlled conditions" (Childress et al. 1977, 13; Childress 1978b, 44).

On 1 August the plan was to use the lockout divers and submersibles to recover some objects from the wreck (Childress 1977, 3). Based on the precruise plan, two objects were to be recovered: the EG&G still camera that was snagged in the wreck during the *Eastward*'s discovery cruise, and a piece of bottom hull plate that was lying on top of the camera (Childress 1977, 3; Childress 1978b, 44). The camera, made of aluminum and stainless steel, was a hazard to the wreck. It could cause corrosion to the *Monitor*'s wrought iron because of the galvanic reaction between the dissimilar metals. Edgerton also thought he could still develop the camera's film. The iron hull plate was obviously displaced by the snagging of the camera and its location was not vital to the archaeological integrity of the *Monitor*. More important, the recovered hull plate would offer an opportunity to conduct tests with destructive analyses on a not so crucially unique artifact.

During one dive, a unique lantern was discovered near the wreck. After consultation with NOAA's advisory committee, recovery of the lantern was authorized (Childress 1977, 3; Childress et al. 1977, 4). Diver observations of the lantern showed it was of well-preserved brass and red glass, two materials vastly different from the hull plate wrought iron. The lantern's recovery would be valuable, providing a sample to assess the preservation of the materials (Childress 1978b, 42).

Unfortunately, the Cape Hatteras weather prevented any recovery attempts on 1 August. Postponed to the next day, conditions were much better with good bottom visibility. In the *Johnson-Sea-Link II* submersible, Childress and Watts

> watched, 10 feet from the lantern, as [Richard] Roesch, [a Harbor Branch Foundation diver] swam over from the other sub with a plastic bucket. He gingerly scooped up the lantern, placed it in the bucket and swam back toward the dark hulk of the wreck. [Watts's and Childress's] submarine moved back over the wreck as Roesch transferred the bucket into the pressurized diving chamber in [the *Johnson-Sea-Link I*]. Then taking two lifting bags, he swam up over the edge of the Monitor's armor belt and down into the wreck to recover, first, the bottom plate, and then the camera system. The two inflated lifting bags, looking like two huge yellow balloons, floated slowly to the surface with their cargo (Childress 1977, 3).

Edgerton was on board the support vessel *Johnson* during the dives that recovered the camera, plate, and lantern. On the *Johnson*, he was able to examine the camera and artifacts, and he took some colored slides of them. In a short note, he sent me copies of the slides. The camera was thoroughly corroded after only four years in the ocean. This illustrated the harshness of the corrosive sea water on the *Monitor* wreck. Despite Edgerton's hope that the film could be developed, all the pressure seals had deteriorated and the chambers had leaked.

The red-glass and brass lantern was beautifully preserved, with little corrosion or damage. Its location on the sea floor forty feet north of the turret indicates it might possibly be the signal lantern that was raised on the *Monitor*'s turret to signal the abandon ship command. An enormously valuable artifact, it is a man-made, physical representation of a historic event. Artifacts, much more so than a collection of words in a history book, make historical events real. The red-glass lantern testifies to the fateful sinking of the *Monitor* on a stormy night in December 1862.

The Smithsonian Institution volunteered to cover the cost of and supervise the preservation of the lantern (Childress et al. 1977, 5). The lantern was kept in the proper solutions, except for occasional viewing

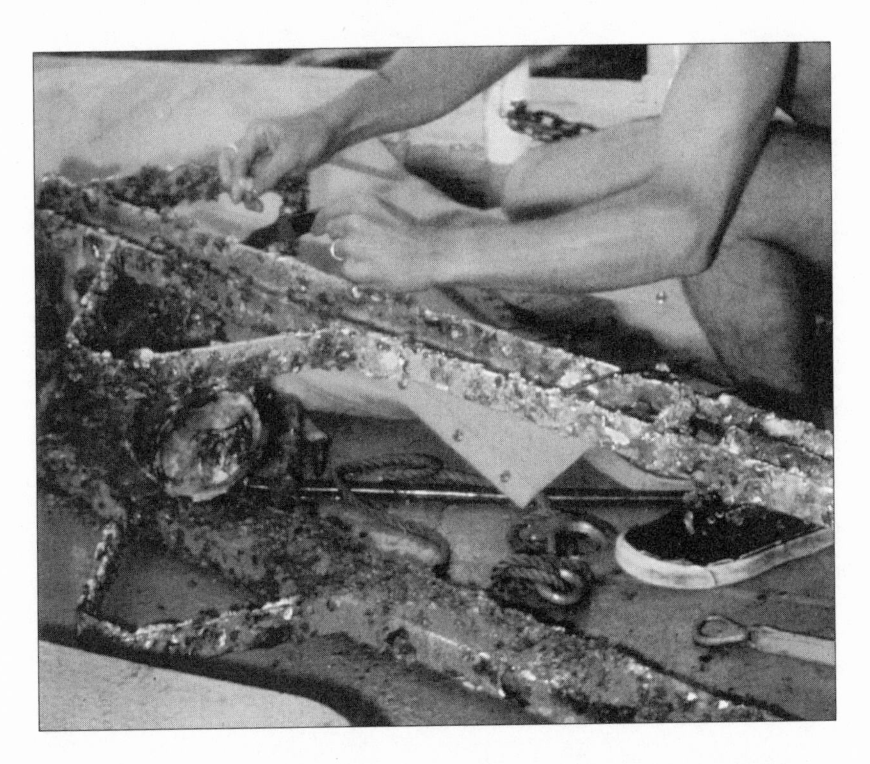

Photograph of the recovered EG&G camera recovered at the *Monitor* site in August 1977. The camera had been snagged in the *Monitor* wreck during the 1973 discovery cruise. Note the extent of corrosion after only four years in seawater.

Harold Edgerton

and photography (Childress 1977, 3), for transportation to shore on the *Johnson*. It eventually arrived at the Smithsonian Institution's Museum of History and Technology for preservation (Childress 1978b, 44). It required thousands of dollars and several years of preservation processing before the lantern was displayed for the first time in the museum at the U.S. Naval Academy. A spectacular piece, I first saw the lantern there in the early 1980s.

Of greater importance scientifically, the bottom hull plate showed extensive evidence of corrosion. Originally about one half inch thick, the recovered plate was paper thin. As much as 50 percent of the area of the original plate was missing, presumably from corrosion to the point where all the iron had been dissolved and carried off in solution. An accretionary

Photograph of the recovered navigation red-glass lantern found forty feet north of the *Monitor* turret. This is probably the lantern that was signaling the tow ship that the *Monitor* was sinking.

Harold Edgerton

layer of organic growth and rust covered what had been the upper surface of the plate (Peterkin 1977, 7).

Analysis of the plate, using destructive techniques, was the first step in the planned MRRF's site testing phase of the research on the *Monitor*. The North Carolina Division of Archives and History was awarded a contract from NOAA to coordinate and supervise the analyses of the plate (Childress 1978b, 44). Watts was in charge of the project. The plate was transported to the Naval Research Laboratory in Washington, D.C., for preliminary analysis (Peterkin 1977, 1). The plate was weighed, photographed, x-rayed, and studied through microscopes. Ernest Peterkin interpreted the photographed plate, based on the rivet hole spacings and alignments. The barnacle-encrusted surface was interpreted to be the outside-facing side of the plate; it was facing upward on the overturned hull. The barnacles needed to be on the outside of the hull to grow. The longer side of the recovered plate was aligned fore-and-aft, but which edge of the plate was fore or aft could not be determined (Peterkin 1977, 5).

Photograph of the recovered wrought iron plate from the bottom of the *Monitor*'s hull. The black pad beneath the hull plate is three feet wide. Note the extensive corrosion and rust encrustation. Much of the plate is completely gone.

Harold Edgerton

C. D. Beacham conducted the x-ray radiography and microscopic study of the plate. Beacham concluded that the plate was thoroughly encrusted with rust, and corroded to the point of perforation in many places. The plate was too thin to measure its thickness in many places. Using the estimated plate area of 9.5 square feet, and the measured weight of 60 pounds, the density of iron could be used to compute an average thickness of about 0.15 inch (Peterkin 1977, 13). Beacham's microscopic analysis of small loose fragments of rusted iron from the plate in polished and thin sections showed "fibers" of silicate inclusions. "The eutectic structure of the silicate fibers is more pronounced in this wrought iron than in present day wrought iron, indicating possible differences in chemistry and melting-casting-rolling conditions, perhaps a slower cool following forging or rolling" (Peterkin 1977, 17).

I was invited by Watts to a conference on the plate after Peterkin and Beacham completed their preliminary studies in December 1977. Held at the Naval Research Laboratory, Watts chaired the conference. Peterkin

Dr. Robert Sheridan holds a two-inch by eight-inch sample from the recovered *Monitor* hull plate that was obtained so magnetic measurements could be made. Note the corroded rivet hole.

and Beacham delivered oral and illustrated reports on their work. Peterkin also distributed his report in memo form to the conferees.

One of the purposes of the meeting was to describe where subsamples of the plate would be cut by a laser torch. Eleven samples, labeled 0400 through 0410, were identified on a handout; each subsample was a rectangular piece two inches by eight inches. Watts specified where the samples would be sent and what tests would be performed at each laboratory;

tests on corrosion, metallurgy, and strength would be performed at laboratories in the Naval Research Laboratory, at other navy locations, and at MIT.

It occurred to me that I should obtain a sample of the plate to conduct magnetization measurements, something that the other labs were not doing. Magnetic model calculations, discussed in the last chapter, relied on the assumption, based on published physical properties handbooks, that the pristine wrought iron and magnetite would have a magnetic susceptibility of 0.85 emu (Sheridan 1979, 256). With a sample of iron from the *Monitor* we could verify the hypotheses and calculations.

I wrote a letter to Watts requesting a sample for the magnetic measurements. He complied with my request and I received sample 0402 in the spring of 1978. I was impressed with the sample. The core, beneath the barnacled rust encrustation, was a pristine, silver gray wrought iron. The paper-thin nature of the remaining pristine wrought iron was just about the 0.15 inch thickness that Beacham had computed as the average thickness.

I had circular disk pieces of one inch in diameter cut from the pristine iron of the sample. I labeled these disks 0402-D through 0402-G. Three fragments of the barnacle rust encrustation had been taken previously and labeled 0402-A through 0402-C. I measured the magnetic susceptibility of the rust fragments and the pristine iron disks using a Schonstedt spinner magnetometer. Values of the susceptibilities of the rust fragments ranged from 0.014 to 0.019 emu (Sheridan 1979, 257). These values are relatively low, as would be expected from iron oxide minerals like hematite that appear in rust. The pristine wrought iron disks had susceptibilities ranging from 0.712 to 0.926 emu, which are values within the range of 0.85 emu stated in handbooks for wrought iron. This confirmed that the modeling calculations we had used were correct. The calculations indicated that only about 40 percent of the iron in the *Monitor* wreck was in the pristine wrought iron state (Sheridan 1979, 256).

Everly Keenan, a University of Delaware graduate student, did some x-ray studies of the rust fragments. Results indicated a zinc, nickel, and iron oxide [(Zn, Ni) Fe_2O_4] composition (Sheridan 1979, 257). I speculated that the zinc in this composition could have been contributed by zinc-based paints, which possibly might have been applied to the *Monitor*'s hull bottom as an antifouling, antirust preservative.

Joseph Boesenberg, another graduate student at Rutgers, studied one

Close-up photograph of sub-sample 0402, taken from the *Monitor*'s hull plate. The barnacle-encrusted rust layer on the bottom of the plate has flaked off. The pristine, silver-gray wrought iron of the sample is only about a tenth of an inch thick. Originally it was about one half inch thick.

of the pristine iron disks with an electron microprobe. He showed me images of the iron silicate inclusions in which the silicate fibers, as Beacham called them, are aligned in parallel linear bands. Some of the linear bands intersect one another at acute angles. These orientations probably originated during the crystallization of the silicate fibers under the stresses of pounding and rolling of the near-molten iron into the plates. The origin of the silicate could be in the impurities of the original magnetite ore that was the source of iron for the plates, or in impurities in the flux material used in the iron furnaces at the foundries.

The presence of the anisotropic silicate inclusions in the *Monitor*'s wrought iron has contributed to a "preferential corrosion direction," as mentioned by Beacham (Peterkin 1977, 12); this anisotropy parallels the long axis of the plate, which may be the "major wrought direction." The presence of the silicate inclusions in the *Monitor*'s wrought iron, which Beacham indicates is unlike present-day purer wrought iron (Peterkin 1977, 17), may provide an advantage. The silicate is more resistant to corrosion than the purer iron, so the silicates may have inhibited the ultimate corrosion of the plates.

I finished the magnetics measurements on the plate sample 0402 and submitted my preliminary report to Watts in October 1978. I also included the magnetic measurements of the plate sample in my submitted article to the *Journal of Field Archaeology* (Sheridan 1979, 257). I was pleased to have been able to contribute to the site testing of the *Monitor* by helping to analyze the plate. As I mentioned previously, I was impressed with the quality of the wrought iron that remained in the plate. If the wrought iron of other parts of the *Monitor* was also of such pristine quality, there is hope that many high quality artifacts may be recovered.

After the Harbor Branch Foundation debacle and the successful completion of the NOAA–Harbor Branch Foundation diving cruise, the MRRF had to rethink its position. The schism between the MRRF researchers and the federal and state agency scientists had been exacerbated. NOAA and North Carolina had taken the initiative of doing their own research on the wreck. Although Edgerton and I had participated with the 1977 efforts, we acted as individual academic scientists rather than under the MRRF permit.

The MRRF needed funds to carry out its own diving programs; equipment comparable to the Harbor Branch Foundation submersibles would have to be leased. The MRRF also needed a political constituency and power base to compete with the state and federal agencies that were doing research. Fortunately, the positive publicity that the MRRF had gained from the 1977 *Cape Henlopen* cruise, and the logical attractiveness of the recovery of the *Monitor*, drew the attention of the citizens of Norfolk, Virginia.

A delegation from Norfolk made a presentation of their interest in the *Monitor* to the MRRF board of trustees at its December 1977 meeting in Beaufort, North Carolina. Vincent Thomas, the mayor of Norfolk, was exuberant about the revitalization of the Norfolk inner harbor waterfront that was under way. He extolled the existing cultural assets of Norfolk in the harbor area, including the Chrysler Center and the MacArthur Museum. Furthermore, he reminded the MRRF board that the battle between the *Monitor* and the *Merrimac* took place within sight of the Norfolk harbor waterfront. In 1977, the battle was an attraction alluded to in the local area exhibitions of the Fortress Monroe Museum and the Newport News Mariners' Museum, as well as in the waterborne harbor tours. Thomas also noted the presence of the naval base. The large local naval population was keen on U.S. naval history. Norfolk had a ready-made constituency for the recovery of the *Monitor*. Thomas, on behalf of the city of Norfolk, proposed that the MRRF move its offices and headquarters to Norfolk to continue the efforts to recover the *Monitor*.

The MRRF board of trustees voted to accept Norfolk's offer, presuming the appropriate support could be mustered by Thomas to ensure the MRRF's viability in the new location. John Newton and I followed up with Thomas and informed him of our decision. Thomas' reply was positive:

> Thanks very much for your letter of December 20, 1977. As you may have heard from John, we held a meeting on December 21 with a broad range of representatives of our business community, and there was enthusiastic support for the project in general and the bringing of the Foundation to Norfolk in particular. I am now in the process of convening a smaller meeting to come to grips with the immediate financial problem and hope to have something definite and firm to report after that meeting.
>
> On behalf of those from Norfolk who traveled to Beaufort on December 17, I want to thank you for the warm hospitality and interest shown us by you and your fellow trustees. We enjoyed our visit with you very much (Thomas 1977, 1).

In the annals of the *Monitor*, December 1977 was noted for the beginning of the "public struggle for claims to the Monitor among North Carolina and Virginia cities" (North Carolina Department of Cultural Resources 1978, 54). Although possibly an overly dramatic statement, I believe it reflected the North Carolina bureaucracy's opinion of the pending move of the MRRF to Norfolk. The schism over the *Monitor* was deepening.

North Carolina was also reinforcing its position in fall 1977. NOAA presented to North Carolina a memorandum of agreement on 3 October in which the Division of Archives and History would be contracted "to establish and manage a distribution and evaluation system for proposals to conduct research and investigation in the Monitor Marine Sanctuary.... The Operations Coordinator of the review system shall be designated by the State Historic Preservation Officer. At the time of this agreement the Operations Coordinator is: Gordon P. Watts, Jr." (North Carolina Department of Cultural Resources 1978, 46).

The NOAA–North Carolina memorandum of agreement was modified to the mutual satisfaction of both parties and ratified on 12 December 1977, thus strengthening North Carolina's position in the control of access to the *Monitor*. Watts's position as the main officer to manage the reviews and evaluation of research proposals placed him in a blatant conflict of interest situation. He was conducting his own ongoing research on the *Monitor* and would naturally want to continue that research. Wouldn't he select reviewers friendly to him to evaluate competing proposals to his research?

Many MRRF members were frustrated by North Carolina's maneuvers. Without support from North Carolina, it was only logical that the MRRF had to seek support in another state. Therefore, by the end of 1977 the fissure among the original discoverers of the *Monitor* wreck site had widened considerably.

11

Is Recovery Feasible?

The availability of the *Monitor* artifacts—the decklight cover, the lantern, and the iron plate—gave evidence on the state of the *Monitor*'s materials. The study of artifacts had been delineated as part of the MRRF master plan's site testing phase of the *Monitor* research. The good news about the remarkably well-preserved glass and brass of the lantern bodes well for the presence of many delicate artifacts in the wreck. Although the thinness and loss of material of the hull plate evidenced extensive corrosion, this was expected for wrought iron that had been in seawater for over one hundred years. The good news was that the wrought iron of the hull plate that remained was in very good shape. Magnetic measurements indicated that the remaining iron was fairly pristine.

Thicker pieces of wrought iron would have even more volumetric preservation of pristine iron because corrosion extends inward from the outer surface at a slow rate. Over time, an originally one half inch thick hull plate can be perforated and dissolved, so that nearly the entire piece of plate is rusted away. But thicker pieces will have much more of the inner pristine iron preserved.

The bad news about the hull plate sample was the extensive corrosion of the rivet holes and the missing rivets. The contact between the plate iron and the rivet iron apparently localized corrosion at those spots. Consequently, the rivet holes were enlarged and whatever rivets were remaining had fallen out. This implies that little strength can be expected from the connection of the plates of the hull. I liken the *Monitor* to a disarticulated skeleton of a petrified dinosaur. Clearly, the wreck of the *Mon-*

itor is extremely fragile, although the long span of the port-side armor belt suspended from the turret to the bow clearly has substantial strength to support the larger hull.

With site testing information in hand, there was enough information in 1977–78 to consider different scenarios for recovery of the *Monitor.* As mentioned previously, the press coverage of the April 1977 *Cape Henlopen* cruise alluded to many ideas about techniques for the recovery. Some were better thought out than others. Some suggestions for recovery involved the relatively standard approach of clamping directly onto the hull for a single- or multiple-point lift. A standard clamp-and-lift, direct-hull-contact plan was made by the Uddeman Company, a major ocean engineering firm (Uddeman Inc. 1976, 1). The plan recognized the basic problem at the *Monitor* site: the frequent periods of bad weather. To accommodate a spell of bad surface sea state, the Uddeman plan would employ a submerged, air-filled pontoon vehicle that would be in cable contact with the lifting clamp on the main hull. In a typically bad Cape Hatteras storm, the surface salvage vessel could detach and depart the site temporarily, but the pontoon vehicle could remain at a depth below wave disturbance. If the storm occurred during mid-lift, the pontoon vehicle could be left after the *Monitor* wreck was lowered back to the sea floor. Later, after the storm abated, the surface salvage vessel could return and reattach to the pontoon vehicle with diver assistance. The recovery lift could then continue.

The MRRF researchers agreed that the site testing of the *Monitor* hull plate, and the overall photographic coverage, made it clear that the fragile hull of the *Monitor* could never be lifted by direct contact from above. One idea to modify the Uddeman plan was to have a piping system integrated with the lifting clamp. Through this piping, liquid nitrogen could be pumped to freeze the ocean water around the *Monitor* hull and in the sediments beneath the wreck. Then the lifting clamp would be attached to a large frozen block in which the wreck would be safely encased. I liken this to the frozen popsicle technique.

Although not a refrigeration expert or an engineer, I felt that such a freezing process would not work at the *Monitor* site. The bottom currents keep the water moving around the wreck. This advection will prevent any temperature changes. If the cold refrigerant started to lower the ocean temperature, convective circulation would quickly carry the heat from the surrounding water to raise the temperature again. Without confining the ocean water around the wreck, the freezing scheme could not work.

The "freezing the ocean" scheme reminds me of my experience in the Antarctic Ocean aboard the USNS *Eltanin* in 1968. Late in getting to the area, we were near Antarctica during the southern hemisphere's fall season. The ice pack would soon begin expanding northward. The ocean temperature was actually a few degrees below freezing, but the usual sea states 4 and 5 produced swell and wave motions that prevented freezing. We were always expecting a spell of calm weather that would allow a huge area of the ocean surface to freeze, possibly in as little as twenty-four hours. The *Eltanin*'s captain was fearful of getting "iced in" by such an event. Whenever he saw brash ice and "bergy bits" on the radar, he would turn the ship north and run for twenty-four hours. Even if sea water is at subfreezing temperature, movement will prevent freezing.

While there were other similar harebrained schemes to raise the *Monitor* wreck, such as filling the hull with inflatable bags, or netted bags of ping pong balls, only one idea was realistic and technically feasible. Global Marine Development Inc., one of the largest ocean technology companies, submitted a proposal to use the *Glomar Explorer* (Global Marine Development Inc. 1976, 1–7). R. Curtis Crooke, president of Global Marine Development Inc., was well qualified to speak about the capabilities of the *Glomar Explorer*; he was an authority on this extraordinary vessel (Crooke 1976, 14). In 1976–77 the *Glomar Explorer* was the most sophisticated salvage ship in the world (Editorial 1976b, 67).

During the Nixon administration, the *Glomar Explorer* had been built by the U.S. government to attempt the recovery of the Russian submarine K-129 from the Pacific Ocean's floor. Although a secret Central Intelligence Agency (CIA) operation, the cover story was that the eccentric Howard Hughes of the Hughes Tool Company was the owner of the *Glomar Explorer*. The vessel was supposedly designed to raise and lower heavy submerged vehicles for mining manganese nodules from the deep Pacific floor. Capable of actually accomplishing its reported mission, the vehicle to be lowered was the huge gripper that would grasp the K-129.

Global Marine Development, because of its vast experience with offshore drilling ships and deep sea drilling from dynamically positioned drill ships such as *Glomar Challenger*, had been chosen as the designer/operator of the *Glomar Explorer*. As we now know, after the government raised the veil of secrecy on the retrieval of the Russian submarine, the *Glomar Explorer* was partially successful in the submarine's recovery. Global Marine Development's design and operation of the *Glomar Explorer* has to be credited with much of that success. Obviously, Crooke and Global Marine Development were experienced in using the *Glomar Explorer* as a salvage ship.

Crooke described the remarkable features of the *Glomar Explorer:*

> Global Marine Development, Inc. (GMDI) is pleased to offer its services to assist in recovering *Monitor.* Using GMDI's extensive background in ocean hardware systems with the *Glomar Explorer, Monitor* may be recovered intact.
>
> The *Glomar Explorer* is a twin screw, diesel-electric powered, deep ocean working vessel with many technical features applicable directly to the *Monitor* recovery effort. The ship was especially designed by Global Marine Development Inc., to maintain its position dynamically over a work site in water as deep as 17,000 feet while lowering or raising heavy subsea equipment or operating this equipment on the bottom. The *Glomar Explorer* features:
>
> A 2,000 ton gimbaled and heave compensated stable platform in the superstructure that supports a 14 million pound capacity lift system, and effectively isolates the subsea equipment from ship motions of roll, pitch, and heave.
>
> A completely dry [or wet], weather resistant center well 199 feet long by 74 feet wide by 65 feet high, with retractable hull bottom gates that provide a secure drydock for subsea equipment.
>
> A docking leg system that minimizes the relative motions between the ship and the lift system for mating the subsea equipment with the vessel.
>
> An integrated Automatic Station Keeping System that holds the ship in extremely precise position (±40 feet in 17,000 foot water depths) (Global Marine Development Inc. 1976, 2–3).

Knowing the *Glomar Explorer*'s features well, Crooke and GMDI submitted a recovery plan to the MRRF in 1976:

Global Marine has made certain assumptions in the development of a broad recovery plan:

> To maintain the vessel's recognized historical value, it is planned to recover the vessel in one piece together with artifacts on board and in the vicinity of the vessel.
>
> Twenty-five percent of the vessel's material has corroded or eroded away due to its long submergence under water and silt. There is no remaining structural integrity to the vessel.
>
> Minimum in-water weight to be picked up is estimated at between one million and three million pounds, depending on how much sand is to be raised with the vessel.

The recovery procedure is analogous to transplanting a large tree. The area around the tree must be carefully included to preserve the root structure. For recovery of *Monitor*, the sand and silt in, around,

Drawing based on Global Marine Development Inc.'s 1976 proposal to use the *Glomar Explorer* to recover the *Monitor* wreck intact. A submerged vehicle with planes, or doors, would cut through the sediments beneath the wreck and then gently lift the sea floor and the wreck from below (Global Marine Development Inc. 1976, 6–7).

Sheridan, R. E. 1979. Site Charting and Environmental Studies of the *Monitor* Wreck, *Journal of Field Archaeology* 6:263.

> and under her would be recovered just as the root structure of a tree is "balled" during its transplant.
>
> After proceeding to the Cape Hatteras site, acoustic position reference transponders for the Automatic Station Keeping system are deployed. Well gates on the *Glomar Explorer* are opened and the recovery vehicle is lowered to the vicinity of *Monitor* and aligned for the recovery. Two large scoops open on each side of the recovery vehicle to grab *Monitor*. (One scoop is especially configured to hold *Monitor* turret in position.) A vibratory technique is used to drive the scoops through the sand and silt under *Monitor* to minimize sand disturbance.
>
> With the scoops closed about *Monitor* and locked into place, the combined recovery vehicle with enclosed *Monitor* is raised into the well of the *Glomar Explorer*. The well gates are closed. To minimize oxidation to the *Monitor* remains, the well will not be pumped dry. After appropriate preparations, the ship transits to a pre-selected location. . . . [At this location] a large, adjustably buoyant barge is lowered to the ocean floor at a depth of [fifteen to thirty feet]. The *Glomar Explorer* is then brought over the barge and *Monitor* is lowered slowly to rest. The *Glomar Explorer* is then moved clear of the barge. Preservation of *Monitor* begins in a secure, diver accessible underwater area (Global Marine Development Inc. 1976, 4–5).

Of particular note are the words "secure" and "diver accessible" in the last sentence. Despite the marine sanctuary status of the *Monitor* site, it is not "secure." Without surveillance, unauthorized entrance to the sanctuary can and has occurred. The sanctuary is not secure from the natural hazards that damage and threaten the *Monitor*. The wreck is corroded by sea water, abraded by currents, and battered by hurricane waves. Moving the *Monitor* wreck could eliminate these harmful effects on the ship itself.

While the *Monitor* wreck is "diver accessible" in the present 220 feet depths of the marine sanctuary, free diving from the surface with oxygen is unsafe and limited. Even diving from the surface with mixed gases is dangerous and limited, although it is safer and less limited than oxygen. If the *Monitor* wreck was in thirty feet of water, the diving would be much more safe and efficient. The shift in currents at the *Monitor* wreck site makes diving risky; such risks could be removed if the *Monitor* was moved to a well-selected shallow water area.

While Crooke's proposal correctly states the "in-water weight" of the *Monitor* wreck and some enclosed sediment as "between one million and three million pounds," he did not estimate the other forces involved, sea-floor sediment weight, or the weight of the "scoop" vehicle or the pipe needed for the hoist. For subsequent summaries of this proposal, the weight for these factors was conservatively estimated:

Monitor wreck	1.5 million pounds
Fifteen feet of sea floor sediment	5.0 million pounds
Pullout (frictional) forces	1.5 million pounds
Vehicle and pipes	4.0 million pounds
Total hoist	= 12.0 million pounds

Based on these weights and forces, the total lift of about twelve million pounds was within the *Glomar Explorer*'s capacity of fourteen million pounds (Sheridan 1978, 41–42; Sheridan 1979, 264).

The Global Marine Development proposal to use the *Glomar Explorer* to recover the *Monitor* included a disclaimer: "Neither Global Marine Development Inc., nor its parent Global Marine Inc., own the *Glomar Explorer* or any of her subsystems. Use in any recovery effort would be predicated on her being made available by the U.S. Government" (Global Marine Development Inc. 1976, 3). In late 1976, the status of the *Glomar Explorer* was described in an *Ocean Industry* article as "being mothballed at Hunters Point by the Maritime Administration at a cost of $2.1 million. The ship will be moved to Suisun Bay, Calif., where it will join the National Defense Reserve Fleet. The General Services Administration had requested proposals for the ship for lease from March through June, but accepted no offers. According to News reports, the GSA put a fair market value of the ship at $65 million" (Editorial 1976b, 73).

Crooke estimated the cost of his proposal would be about thirty million dollars. The cost would include taking the *Glomar Explorer* out of mothballs, mobilization, the costs of personnel and operation, and the costs of the design and construction of the scoop vehicle. While expensive, this amount in 1977–78 was not unreasonable in comparison with other high technology projects funded by the government. If private funding for the project could have been obtained, the costs would have been less to the government.

Costs of such a recovery should be put in perspective. In the 1970s the government was spending billions of dollars each year for the limited manned exploration of the moon. As in all funding of high technology research, there were major beneficial technological spin-offs from the space program. One psychological benefit was the boost to the country's prestige because the United States beat the Russians to the moon and firmly established preeminence in space research.

In a similar way, the thirty million dollar cost of the *Glomar Explorer* recovery plan would have resulted in spin-off benefits. Using the salvage ship would have created more experience with this super technology, experience that could have been applied later in other missions. For example, the same kind of vehicle scoop recovery might be used to rapidly recover sunken U.S. or allied submarines in water depths beyond diving accessibility, possibly even submarines that still had live crew members aboard.

Psychologically, using the *Glomar Explorer*'s technology would have demonstrated U.S. preeminence in ocean salvage as well as ocean technology in general. One of the reasons that the *Glomar Explorer* was partially successful in the recovery of the Russian submarine K-129, even under the watchful eyes of Russian spy trawlers, was that the Russians could not even imagine that our marine technology was capable of doing such a thing. Actually, the Russians could not even imagine the technology the United States used to first find the K-129 in such deep Pacific waters.

Also, in the 1970s the U.S. government was spending about sixty million dollars per year on historic preservation, mainly through the Office of Archaeology and Historic Preservation of the Department of Interior. After overhead expenses were paid, the balance was distributed among fifty states; each state's historic preservation offices would have its own overhead costs. The historic preservation funds, therefore, would then manifest themselves probably in just a few hundreds-of-thousand-dollar projects in various states. Federal funds were being spent on historic preservation. Temporarily diverting part of the funds to the *Monitor* recovery, which would be a project of valid national interest rather than a state-sponsored project, makes sense.

Monitor recovery fever was in full swing in 1977 and early 1978. The publicity about the "battle over the *Monitor* between the cities of North Carolina and Virginia" forced the government agencies involved with regulating the *Monitor* site to do something. A "National Conference on the *Monitor*" was convened to consider the future of this famous wreck. Held on 2–4 April 1978 in Raleigh, North Carolina, it was cosponsored by nationally based interest groups—the National Trust for Historic Preservation, NOAA, the Advisory Council on Historic Preservation, the U.S. Department of Interior, the U.S. Naval Historical Center—and two states—the State of North Carolina and the Commonwealth of Virginia. The host of the meeting was the North Carolina Division of Archives and History; its director, Dr. Larry Tise was chairman of the meeting.

The MRRF was concerned about the meeting's direction, as was evidenced by Tise's opening comments on the purpose of the meeting. "Given the fact that the USS *Monitor* is one of the most important surviving symbols of American history, what *should* [emphasis added] be its future? . . . All of the previous national meetings on the *Monitor* have occurred with the implicit assumption that the *Monitor* would be recovered, that it would be recovered as soon as technology and resources made it possible and that it would be put on display for the enjoyment of the American public" (Tise 1978a, 14). His statements imply that the "implicit assumption" about recovery may not have been valid and perhaps something else should be done with the *Monitor*. He also expressed a view, one that was perpetuated throughout the conference by many, that the *Monitor* was safe "in its relatively secure resting place" (Tise 1978a, 16). Espousing such security, despite contrary conjecture and evidence, gave a false impression that the *Monitor* can be left in the ocean indefinitely while its future is decided.

Fearing the MRRF would not get a fair hearing at the conference, the MRRF board had convened a meeting on 1 April 1978 to develop a strategy for its presentations at the conference. The board met with John Newton and Mayor Vincent Thomas at the foundation's new offices in Norfolk, just before continuing the trip to Raleigh. Earlier in 1978, the MRRF had moved from Beaufort, North Carolina, to Norfolk, Virginia, to set up headquarters in offices provided by the city of Norfolk. Ample space was provided in the Old Royster Building, a large office building on the waterfront of the Norfolk inner harbor that Thomas hoped to redevelop along with other city-owned buildings and waterfront properties. Out of the office windows, the site of the battle between the *Monitor* and the *Merrimac* could be seen.

I thought the MRRF members invited to speak at the conference were going to be the only ones to present specific recovery plans, and the only ones to advocate recovery of as much of the *Monitor* as possible as soon as possible. I knew the MRRF representatives would be walking into a lion's den of naysayers and competitors. In a zero-sum game, competitors would see any funds going to the *Monitor* as a drain on their resources to carry out their own historic preservation projects. The political competition was going to be fierce.

My fears about bias against the MRRF interests were realized when I arrived at the meeting on 2 April. The scheduled program included about thirty speakers during the three day conference. Of those speakers, I only knew six who could be considered advocates of, or leaned favorably toward, recovery of the *Monitor.* Countering these positive presentations, I knew at least ten speakers who were either biased against the MRRF or were against any recovery of the *Monitor.* Moreover, some of the remaining talks at the conference covered other potential and real recovery projects such as the USS *Tecumseh* (Friend 1978, 57), the Swedish warship *Wasa* (Barkman 1978b, 101), and the Union gunboat *Cairo* (Gibson 1979, 49). While interesting and informative, the conference time devoted to these other projects diluted the main debate on the future of the *Monitor.*

I was particularly upset by the time allotted for Newton's presentation, as well as my own; we were only allotted eighteen minutes each. This was hardly enough time to put forward our ideas and rationale on recovery of the *Monitor.* In contrast, one competitor, Ernest Peterkin was allotted one hour for his talk on the construction of the *Monitor* (Peterkin 1978, 22). While I recognize Peterkin as the "Dean" of the *Monitor* experts, and I agree that he should have had that time to talk, I felt that Newton and I should have had more time. I compiled the total time of the presentations by those speakers I considered against recovery of the *Monitor* versus the total time of those speakers for recovery. I found that those speakers against recovery were given just about twice as much time as those speaking for recovery. The bias of the conference was further evident in who was absent. R. Curtis Crooke of Global Marine Development was not a presenter of the *Glomar Explorer* plan. I had to introduce and cover that proposal in my meager eighteen minutes.

Some negative comments against early recovery of the *Monitor* came in the introductory papers of the conference. Kathleen Pepi of the Advisory Council on Historic Preservation described the council's role in the *Monitor* project. She ended her statement: "The council would like to stress that, as in all environmental issues, the best course of action may be doing nothing—an option we sometimes overlook" (Pepi 1978, 9). She was perpetuating the incorrect impression that it was perfectly safe to leave the *Monitor* where it was. Floyd Childress gave a presentation describing NOAA's plans for ocean management in general. He noted that "the effort to preserve the USS *Monitor* is a small part of a much larger national concern about managing our offshore resources" (Childress 1978a, 6). Within NOAA, the Monitor Marine Sanctuary was but one of many sanctuaries; the *Monitor*'s interests were in competition with other NOAA marine sanctuaries in other areas. This was not the best position for the *Monitor*, which would lose in this competition on occasion. Also, the administrators of the Monitor Marine Sanctuary were timid; they did not push for the federal funding, the tens of millions of dollars, that was needed to save the *Monitor*. Indeed, it would take twenty years before any significant recovery efforts were funded.

The two MRRF presentations were in a session of the conference describing recent cruises to the *Monitor* site. I had to cover the two *Eastward* cruises and the *Cape Henlopen* cruise to the *Monitor* site after the initial *Eastward* discovery cruise, as well as the proposal to use the *Glomar Explorer* to recover the *Monitor*. I did the best I could. In the same session, Newton discussed the original *Eastward* discovery cruise. He ended his talk with an impassioned plea to recover the *Monitor*: "It was apparent then in 1974 when the identification was completed, as it is now, that this vessel represents an important part of our national heritage and should not be left beneath the sea forever to completely disintegrate. This conference should conclude that the technology now exists to remove the vessel from its present environment and to preserve her for future generations" (Newton 1978, 46).

Despite our limited presentation time, Newton and I were able to focus the conference on the early recovery alternative by making comments and participating in discussions from the floor during other presentations and sessions. Also, we gave frequent interviews to the press covering the conference.

This was effective as evidenced in an objective report on the conference by J. Timberlake Gibson for the *Historic Preservation* magazine of the National Trust for Historic Preservation. Gibson correctly identified the schism of the conference:

> Two opposing points of view were evident, the wait-for-a-comprehensive-plan proponents versus the raise-her-now group, with shades of opinion between. Larry E. Tise, director of the North Carolina Division of Archives and History, thought the *Monitor* should not be raised until technology and further study provided answers to questions of safe retrieval and preservation. . . . Robert Sheridan and John N. Newton of the Monitor Research and Recovery Foundation, representing the raise-her-now faction, presented a conceptual plan using the *Glomar Explorer* to hoist the *Monitor* and the underlying seabed and for relocation in a preselected port (Gibson 1979, 48–49).

In introducing a session on the *Monitor*'s value, Larry Tise basically enumerated six negative reasons why the *Monitor* should not be recovered (Tise 1978b, 63–64), as summarized below.

1. The *Monitor* should not be touched until technology evolves to recover and preserve the wreck.
2. The *Monitor* is presently in a relatively stable and secure environment; we should not risk disturbing or destroying the wreck.
3. The *Monitor* is an essential part of the Graveyard of the Atlantic and should not be removed.
4. It will cost tens of millions of dollars to recover and preserve the *Monitor*. This will drain resources from other historic projects.
5. Why should the *Monitor* get special treatment over other historical objects?
6. Museums and historical attractions lose money. Are the United States citizens prepared to pay for the maintenance of a *Monitor* museum?

Tise said in his introduction that he personally would contribute to the *Monitor* project as a taxpayer, but he wondered about the eventual successful funding of the project by the public.

The naval historian Dr. Philip Lundeberg, a speaker during the session on the *Monitor*'s value, noted that there was real historical value in preservation of the wreck because the written record of many aspects of the *Monitor* was only partially preserved. He made a case for improving the archiving of the *Monitor*'s written records as well as recovery of the vessel's parts. "We all have much to learn, both from a comprehensive collection of documents relating to that ironclad's design and from future study of actual artifacts recovered from the vessel" (Lundeberg 1978, 67). During the same session, Lars Barkman, an official of the Wasavarwet National Maritime Museum in Stockholm, Sweden, compared the *Monitor* to the Swedish warship *Wasa,* which was recovered in 1961. The *Wasa* recovery is an exemplary success story in maritime history. Barkman stated, "In applying the *Wasa*'s success to the *Monitor*'s future, the most important consideration is the condition of the hull. If the major portion can be salvaged in one piece like the *Wasa*'s, the advantages are obvious. The interest will run high from the start. On the other hand, in those projects where the hull must be dismantled, taken up piece by piece and preserved before restoration, public interest wanes. . . . Loose finds can be of importance but are never as important as the hull itself" (Barkman 1978a, 69). Coming from Barkman, these comments had much weight, but I feared many of the conferees would paid little heed. In his summary, Barkman said, "I believe that the salvage operation might be more difficult for the *Monitor* but that it is possible. . . . The value of the *Monitor* is dependent on the outcome of the salvage, and I am optimistic that this can be done successfully" (Barkman 1978a, 70).

A contrary view on the *Monitor* was given by David Stick, the author of *Graveyard of the Atlantic.* He was emphatic in his objections:

> When the talk turns to removing the vessel from her resting place off Hatteras and placing her ashore as a tourist attraction
>
> I object because government will be expected to foot the bill from our tax dollars, and I do not consider this a proper expense of government.
>
> I object because of the estimated cost ($20 million at last report) and the awareness that a fraction of that sum could be spent to better advantage in eastern North Carolina, just locating and listing important archaeological and historical sites now threatened with destruction, or in other preservation projects.
>
> I object because of the uncertainties of such an undertaking, and

even if the project is successfully carried forward, the anticipated tourist attraction could easily turn out to be nonexistent.

And I object most of all because of my firm conviction that the *Monitor* should be left where it has been ever since it sank off Cape Hatteras on that stormy night in December 1862 (Stick 1978, 77).

Stick felt that "there is no doubt that [the *Monitor*] is [already] a national monument where it is now." In the discussion after this session, "Stick was asked if the *Monitor* in its present location is a perishable item, since ships deteriorate rapidly, and the *Monitor* cannot be expected to be in its present condition in another hundred years. The response was that the *Monitor* is indeed perishable and has already partially perished. However, it is not a concern for the immediate future" (Stick 1978, 78–79). I found his lack of immediate concern totally illogical, but this was the kind of false impression that was perpetuated during the conference.

In a session that considered underwater archaeological technology, Donald Keith of the American Institute of Nautical Archaeology stated, "The task of raising the *Monitor* with as little loss of archaeological information as possible will probably be akin more to a skillful heavy salvage operation than to a meticulous archaeological excavation. . . . For the archaeologist's purposes, more information should result if it is possible to raise the *Monitor* intact, place it on a substantial surface support platform and take it as quickly as possible to the staffed and waiting conservation facility where archaeologists and technicians can more carefully control removal of artifacts and preservation of the hull" (Keith 1978, 90). He was optimistic: "In summary, when Ericsson first proposed the *Monitor*, his detractors said it would not float. After it was built, they said it could not fight. Now that it is sunk, they say it cannot successfully be raised. The *Monitor* has proven herself a great debunker of skeptics in the past. It may be hazardous to be pessimistic about the future of the *Monitor*" (Keith 1978, 91–92).

Curtiss E. Peterson, a conservator with the Division of Archives, History and Records Management of the State of Florida, gave a realistic appraisal of the complex problems of conserving the *Monitor*. He said, "I would suggest that the sponsoring agencies plan to perform and fund conservation for at least 25 years after recovery in order to preserve the *Monitor* for the edification of the public" (Peterson 1978, 98). While

Peterson's evaluation may appear slightly negative, he was making a correct assessment.

Barkman, while discussing the management of the *Wasa* recovery project, noted that it was advantageous to conduct the conservation and reconstruction of the hull in public view. "Every procedure could be followed by the public, who evidently appreciated the opportunity to watch the work in progress. This was an important point when planning a project of this size" (Barkman 1978b, 103). Barkman also noted that in an operation of this magnitude, "sometimes it is necessary to sacrifice one piece of evidence in order to save something more valuable." Clearly, compromises must be made, especially between salvagers, engineers, and archaeologists.

Regarding the salvage approach to the recovery of the *Monitor*, noted salvage expert Capt. Willard F. Searle Jr. made a presentation (Gibson 1979, 49). He reviewed several different options for the *Monitor* recovery:

> *Plan A*—The *Monitor*... should be raised in pieces.... *Plan B*—The *Monitor*... by otherwise supplementing the hull girder strength, ...can be raised more or less intact.... *Plan C*—The *Monitor* hull and structure are sound enough to allow raising as is.... The amount of diving work will be least in scenario C... [D]iving in both A and B will be considerable but the tasks will be quite different.... In A, ... [diving] work will be slow and, doubtless, stretch over several seasons or a decade (Searle 1978, 117).

Indeed, diving operations at the *Monitor* site would be a slow affair and require great effort to keep public support for the project. The most rapid and early raising project would have the most public appeal. Searle was realistic in his evaluation of the time required for the recovery efforts using divers. The alternative of raising the *Monitor* intact would require less diving and be quicker. Searle acknowledged, "To raise the *Monitor* as a whole ship we are talking about a whale of a lot of money. But, it can probably be done" (Searle 1978, 116).

Searle criticized the *Glomar Explorer* proposal to recover the *Monitor*. He said, "The cost of such an operation would be phenomenal. The technical feasibility of using a huge lift ship in such shallow water without de-coupling from the lift system is open to serious question. . . . My intuition tells me that it will be extremely costly; feasibility is borderline at best, and damage to *Monitor* is quite likely" (Searle 1978, 121).

Perhaps it would be best to rely on Crooke's knowledge of and experience with the *Glomar Explorer* rather than rely on Searle's intuition? Apparently, Searle had not read the *Ocean Industry* article, published more than a year earlier, that described the decoupling of the lift system thoroughly:

> The *Explorer*'s gimbal system is able to provide a stable platform for all operations during adverse sea conditions.
>
> A heave of ± 7 1/2 ft, a roll of ± 8 1/2 degrees and a pitch of ± 5 degrees are the limits set for lifting operations. . . . The heave compensation system has a 15-ft stroke and is used during launch and recovery of the subsea equipment. . . . The derrick, drilling equipment, rig floor, heavy lift equipment and pipe transfer boom are supported by the inner gimbal and are independent of ship roll, pitch, and heave motions (Editorial 1976b, 68).

Crooke felt that this decoupling would work at the *Monitor* site. The parameters given above represent a fairly rough sea state. In the *Monitor* lift only a short interval of time would be needed, not like the many hours to lift the submarine K-129 from the deep Pacific. Even with the *Glomar Explorer*'s great decoupling capability, the best weather would be selected to lift the *Monitor* quickly, so the decoupling mechanisms would not have to be used under extreme conditions.

I responded to Searle's unsubstantiated statement that the *Glomar Explorer* plan would likely damage the *Monitor* in the discussion session. "Dr. Sheridan explained that in using the *Glomar Explorer* the plan is to slowly and gently fit planes under the wreck without transmitting stress or disturbance to the wreck. The remains would then be transported in the center well of the *Explorer* where they would not be subject to pressure" of currents and waves (Searle 1978, 122). Searle then criticized the use of the *Glomar Explorer*. I recall him describing it as using "a sledge hammer to drive a tack," thus implying that the *Explorer*'s hoist capacity was not needed. I replied: "Not if you are lifting the sea floor as well as the wreck!"

Dr. George Bass, president of the American Institute of Nautical Archaeology in College Station, Texas, also spoke. An archaeologist, he stated "emphatically that virtually no project instigated and directed by nonarchaeologists has been of great archaeological value" (Bass 1978, 123).

> Simply because the wreck [of the *Monitor*] has been found does not mean that it should be excavated or salvaged at this time.... Both marine scientists and professional and amateur divers have discovered many underwater sites and have been most helpful in their later excavation when working under archaeologists; when they have chosen to work alone, or with hired archaeological consultants, the results have not been significant. The only exception that comes to mind is the successful salvage and conservation of the warship *Wasa* from Stockholm harbor (Bass 1978, 124).

Bass made an astute observation that applied well to the *Monitor* project: "Underwater archaeology in the United States has been less successful than that in the Mediterranean because of the vast number of federal and state agencies, private and state institutions, foundations and individuals that seem to be involved in controlling the work. Controls and checks are valuable, but not if they consume so much time in paperwork that progress is virtually impossible" (Bass 1978, 125).

Bass's comment that archaeologists should be in charge was repeated in many discussions during the conference. I found such an argument, or lack of argument, self serving for the archaeologists making them. The desire to recover the *Monitor* intact, or to retrieve its major artifacts, appeared logical to me. If recovery was not done, remains of one of the most famous ships in American history could be lost forever. No archaeologist at the conference seemed to advocate what I considered the common sense alternative. In the absence of an archaeologist advocating recovery of the *Monitor*, Newton and I felt it was our duty to do the best we could do to convince as many people as possible.

After the presentations there was a summary discussion session, led by Tise, to wrap up the conference. Tise thus had a great influence on what was to be concluded from the conference. He began, "I would like to summarize from my perspective what seems to have been the sense of the meeting" (Tise 1978c 127). In his published summary statement, Tise recognized that the answers to the question about whether the *Monitor* should be raised included many answers: "from 'No, we should not raise it' to 'Well, maybe; yes, the *Monitor* ought to be recovered,' all the way to 'Most definitely yes, and as soon as possible.'" Tise noted that there was a consensus that "Yes, either part or all [of the *Monitor*] should be recovered" (Tise 1978c, 128). Unfortunately, Tise dwelled on the "complexities involved in doing anything with the *Monitor*" and "that too little is known at this time to make concrete and reliable plans" for the *Monitor.* This attitude conveyed a negative outlook on the future of any recovery efforts.

In the discussion session Stick stated, "It has not been said that there is any possibility in the near future of raising the *Monitor*" (Tise 1978c, 131). How untrue! In my presentation I had said technology such as the *Glomar Explorer* existed and could be used to recover the *Monitor* intact. Searle also had said that the raising of the *Monitor* was possible with existing technology, but it would cost a "whale of money."

In response to this discussion I pointed out to the group that there was some urgency to capitalize on the availability of the *Glomar Explorer.* I explained that the "National Science Foundation (NSF) has awarded a three-month contract to Global Marine Development Inc. to study the feasibility of converting and operating the *Glomar Explorer* . . . for use in the Deep Sea Drilling Project. The *Explorer* would be able to drill deeper into the seabed, operate in deeper waters" (Editorial 1976b, 71) than the *Glomar Challenger.* The plan was to replace the *Glomar Challenger* with the *Glomar Explorer* and begin this deeper drilling program in 1983. So before the *Explorer* was to be converted, there was a short time window in which it might be used on the *Monitor* recovery. I tried to tell the group at the *Monitor* conference that we might miss this opportunity if we recommended vague delays.

Unfortunately, my appeals were ignored; the naysayers carried the day. Consequently, one of the final resolutions from the meeting stated, "Americans should realize that the *Monitor* will not be raised in the near future, if it is to be treated in a scientific and technologically sound manner" (Tise 1978c, 132). What an incomplete, erroneous statement! With the existing technology in 1978, the *Monitor* could have been moved to a secure location within a five year period using just ordinary diving and crane barge salvage, not even necessarily using the *Glomar Explorer.* The scientific and technological preparations would be ongoing while preparing for the recovery.

None of the resolutions stated positively what Tise had admitted was a conference consensus: "Yes, either part or all [of the *Monitor*] should be recovered" (Tise 1978c, 128). One of the resolutions, however, endorsed the development of a master plan for the *Monitor* by the State of North Carolina.

The conference had an unfortunate effect. It was widely publicized that archaeologists had decided that the *Monitor* should not be raised. The details of the conference resolutions and the conditional statements like "the raising should be deferred until" and "the raising shall be done only if" were lost in the press headlines. The American public thought that the *Monitor* would not and could not be raised. This had a discouraging effect on the future of the MRRF, whose main purpose was to bring about the recovery, preservation, and display of the *Monitor*, either wholly intact or at least its major parts. Newton and I were frustrated by the conference results.

In 1979 the MRRF was floundering. In contrast, the North Carolina Division of Archives and History had been endorsed by the conference and was planning another summer diving cruise to the *Monitor* wreck. Momentum was with North Carolina. Newton struggled to raise funds in the Norfolk area to bolster the MRRF, hoping to generate enough resources to mount a MRRF cruise in 1979 under the authorization of the existing NOAA permit to the foundation. But this did not happen.

I resigned from the MRRF board in 1979. Not only was I feeling too frustrated and disheartened by the results of the Raleigh conference, but my other duties in research as a marine geologist and geophysicist were expanding. I was chairman of the Passive Margin Panel of the Joint Oceanographic Deep Earth Sampling (JOIDES) committee structure, which administered the scientific program of the Deep Sea Drilling Project (DSDP). The panel was heavily involved in planning the 1980 cruises around the margins of the central North Atlantic Ocean. I was to be co-chief scientist on the DSDP leg 76 on the *Glomar Challenger;* we would be drilling on the U.S. Atlantic margin in 1980. We succeeded in recovering the oldest sediments, from the Jurassic age, ever retrieved from any ocean. The success of the leg 76 drilling was important for my career, and led to my promotion to the rank of full professor in 1981.

Even though I was not directly involved with the MRRF and the *Monitor* research after 1979, I did follow the project's progress. I occasionally gave advice and made comments to the NOAA administrators of the Monitor Marine Sanctuary, and I continued to discuss the *Monitor* with my students and at public speaking events.

12

The Monitor in Crisis

The presidency of the MRRF board fell to Dr. William (Bill) N. Still Jr. after I resigned in 1979. Still remained on the board through 1983, but by then the foundation was on its last legs and about to become defunct. Even worse, John Newton, at age fifty-two, suddenly died of a heart attack on 11 September 1984. With him died the aspirations of the Monitor Research and Recovery Foundation to recover the *Monitor* intact or to recover any of its major parts. The *Monitor* lost one of its most dedicated advocates in John Newton. His dedication to and personal sacrifice for the *Monitor* were undeniable. Could his frustrations have driven him to an early grave? I personally believe he died of a broken heart.

Newton could have contributed so much if he had been allowed to be more involved in the *Monitor* research carried out under NOAA auspices. In my experience in large research projects, such as the Deep Sea Drilling Project, which required multi-investigator, multi-authored research, it is wise to have the scientist with the most interest in and passion for the subject as the leader of a particular study. Such leaders generally bring the greatest energy to the project and produce the best results. They got the job done. Newton had been such a leader for the *Monitor*'s research and recovery efforts.

After the demise of the MRRF, there was a vacuum in the advocacy for research on the *Monitor*, especially among independent academic researchers. Only the North Carolina Division of Archives and History, which was designated as NOAA's coinvestigator in 1977 (see chapter 10), and Gordon Watts, the division's underwater archaeologist, were continuing research from an archaeological perspective. In 1979 Comdr. Floyd Childress of NOAA, Roger Cook of Harbor Branch Foundation, and Watts put together a diving cruise for the summer season (National Oceanic and Atmospheric Administration 1979, 29–31). Because NOAA was an active participant in the planned cruise, as well as its sponsor, no proposal for a permit was needed. In lieu of the permit proposal, a detailed, lengthy "operations manual," specifying the plan of the cruise was created by NOAA and circulated to the members of the advisory committee (National Oceanic and Atmospheric Administration 1979, 1–73). This offered some outside review and control. The Harbor Branch Foundation's support vessel *Johnson* and submersible *Johnson-Sea-Link II* were used in 1979, just as they were used previously in 1977. The difference between the two cruises was that Watts, a professional archaeologist, would conduct a classic archaeological dig (or excavation) in one part of the *Monitor* wreck.

Watts published an article on his first dives, in part a feasibility test of the value of doing classic archaeological excavations on a site like the *Monitor*'s site, in the *Journal of Field Archaeology* in 1985 (Watts 1985, 315–32). Prior to his dives, no archaeological excavations had ever been done on wrecks so deep. Because of the depth, lockout dives were limited to less than an hour, and several hours were required for decompression in a deck decompression chamber. Launch and retrieval of the submersible was only done in daylight. Weather permitting, there were two dives a day. While the *Johnson* and *Johnson-Sea-Link II* were on the *Monitor* site from 1–26 August 1979, thirty-six lockout dives were made.

Watts reported on the most noteworthy artifacts recovered: several glass storage jars, mustard storage jars, and a dark green wine bottle (Watts 1985, 330). The excavation pit was forward on the port side near Comdr. John P. Bankhead's cabin. The concentration of the jars at the excavation pit site confirms the sinking of the *Monitor* by the stern; the "forward facing bulkheads served as collection points for small unsecured objects" (Watts 1985, 329).

Of geological interest was the evidence for the strong bottom currents. The ephemeral nature of the sand around the *Monitor* had been interpreted from the piston coring sample taken in April 1977 (Sheridan 1979, 260). Watts concluded that the "sand in the excavation is 'high energy' by finding a modern plastic garbage bag and two plastic containers at depths of up to 14 inches" (Watts 1985, 329). Beneath this high energy layer, the silt suggests that weaker currents carried the finer sediment into the hull before the bottom hull collapsed. All the glass artifacts were recovered from the silt.

After the successful NOAA–Harbor Branch Foundation dives on the *Monitor* in 1979, Watts took a teaching position at East Carolina University as director of underwater research in the maritime history program in 1982. The program received grants from NOAA to conduct research on the *Monitor*. Conflict of interest issues regarding *Monitor* projects continued to be ignored by the federal and state agencies involved. As previously mentioned, NOAA initially conducted proposal reviews through the Monitor Marine Sanctuary's technical review group (see chapter 8). By 1982 the North Carolina Division of Archives and History, through an agreement with NOAA, had established a technical advisory committee (TAC). Watts was a member of the TAC. In 1982 four of the ten members of the TAC were from North Carolina universities or agencies. TAC members, such as Edward Miller and Ernest Peterkin, had received contracts to conduct research on the *Monitor* from the North Carolina Division of Archives and History. Dr. Bruce Muga of Duke University (Muga 1983, 8), another TAC member, also received contracts to conduct research on the *Monitor* from the North Carolina Division of Archives and History. In 1983 Watts and Miller were directly involved in *Monitor* diving cruises. In 1987 Barto Arnold, an underwater archaeologist from Texas (Arnold et al. 1991, 1–366), was another TAC member who was directly involved in a diving cruise at the *Monitor* site. The North Carolina Division of Archives and History basically controlled the *Monitor* project, with review power and a TAC that included active researchers on the *Monitor* with financial support from North Carolina.

Ironically, at a 9 November 1982 meeting of the TAC, the committee passed this resolution:

> In keeping with the primary goals of protection and preservation of the *Monitor* and all its associated records, documents, and archaeological collections and to insure that the public of this and future generations have maximum access to the USS *Monitor*, including its artifacts and other data, the Monitor Technical Advisory Committee of the Monitor National Marine Sanctuary resolves and recommends to NOAA that a major goal in the management plan for the

> sanctuary be the recovery of the vessel from the wreck site and its removal to an appropriate location for study, conservation and display (Watts 1984, 1).

I was shocked when I read this. The TAC resolution called for the recovery of the *Monitor* just as the MRRF had proposed at the 1978 Raleigh conference. At Raleigh several TAC members, especially Miller, Peterkin, and Searle, were vociferously opposed to the MRRF's proposal. A resolution had even been passed at the Raleigh meeting; it stated that the *Monitor* should not be recovered! What had changed in a little over four years? The only thing that had changed was that the MRRF was nearly defunct and was no longer a competitor to the North Carolina control over the *Monitor*.

Watts, Miller, and John Broadwater planned a third NOAA–Harbor Branch Foundation diving cruise to recover the *Monitor*'s anchor in August 1983 (Watts 1984, 4–5). On the *Johnson* and *Johnson-Sea-Link I* research cruise 21–29 August, the anchor was found a distance of 450 feet south-southwest of the wreck; two of its four flukes were sticking up above the sand. A lift bag system was attached to the shank after clearing the sediment away, and the anchor was brought to the surface. Watts, Miller, and Broadwater all participated in the successful lockout dives. The anchor was delivered to the East Carolina University preservation lab where it was conserved by Curtiss Peterson (Peterson 1984, 1; Watts 1984, 5, 7).

The publicity from the August 1983 cruise to recover the *Monitor*'s anchor spurred me to voice my concern about North Carolina's management of the *Monitor* project. It was clear that the state now had an interest in recovering the *Monitor* and the conflicts of interest were worrisome. As a University of Delaware professor, I wrote a letter on 23 August 1983 on the university's letterhead to Robert White, NOAA's administrator:

> This is to register a formal complaint about the administration of the Monitor Marine Sanctuary by NOAA. I make this complaint as one of the original discoverers of the wreck of the *Monitor* and as a former president of the Monitor Research and Recovery Foundation. The basic problem stems from the relationship NOAA has with the North Carolina state agencies that, in effect, have been given control over the sanctuary. Because these agencies have been

given the roles both as planners of future activities in the sanctuary and as reviewers of proposals for permits to do work in the sanctuary, there have been abuses and blatant conflicts of interests. This is to be expected since the State of North Carolina has an obvious interest in exploiting the wreck of the *Monitor* which, by virtue of the accident of its sinking, lies off its coast, although outside state waters. . . .

Now this is more dangerous than in the past. I see where there are plans [reported in the press] to raise the turret of the wreck by 1986. Personally, I applaud this effort. I note that the Monitor Research and Recovery Foundation members first suggested this in 1975, only to be criticized by North Carolina officials that this would destroy the "integrity" of the site, whatever that is. Such unwarranted criticism succeeded in thwarting the efforts of the foundation to the point that North Carolina is now thoroughly in control without any competition.

I would like to point out that the *Monitor* wreck is a national treasure, not the property of North Carolina. Also, it was discovered by a consortium of university researchers including faculty and students from MIT and the University of Delaware, as well as those from Duke and East Carolina University. That is one reason we established the Monitor Research and Recovery Foundation, to give a more nationally-based view of the future of the *Monitor.* The Foundation included academic interests from Massachusetts, New York, New Jersey, Delaware, Pennsylvania, Virginia, and Florida as well as North Carolina. This more nationally-based group decided in 1978 that it would be more proper that the wreck of the *Monitor,* if ever recovered, be displayed near the original battle scene with the *Merrimac,* at Hampton Roads. This is the real historical site associated with *Monitor,* not North Carolina. Obviously, this upset the North Carolina state agencies and led to their consolidation of control as a defensive reaction. . . .

As one of the original discoverers of the *Monitor* wreck, I have a personal interest in seeing that the best utilization of this national treasure is made. I suspect it will not be done with North Carolina in control. I also believe that other citizens would be just as concerned if they realized what has been happening in NOAA's administration of the *Monitor* (Sheridan 1983, 1–2).

I sent a copy to my congressman, Thomas R. Carper, to begin informing the responsible governmental parties about the *Monitor* wreck developments. Carper replied, "Thank you for forwarding a copy of your letter to Mr. Robert White at the National Oceanic and Atmospheric Administration (NOAA). My staff has been in contact with Dr. Nancy Foster, head of the Sanctuary Program in CZM [Coastal Zone Management]. It is my understanding that she is aware of your concern about the management of the Monitor Project, and is looking into the problem and possible ameliorative actions. I have asked her to keep me informed" (Carper 1983, 1).

I was pleased with Carper's response, and I felt something might be done. Writing the letter allowed me to vent my anger. If the TAC members who had resolved that the *Monitor* wreck should be recovered truly felt that way, why had they not supported John Newton and the MRRF when Newton and I proposed the same thing in 1978? In addition to writing letters in 1983 and lobbying governmental concerns, I began publicly speaking about the *Monitor* to encourage the recovery of the wreck. Through the 1980s and 1990s NOAA appeared to ignore the 1982 TAC resolution to recover the wreck of the *Monitor.* Instead, NOAA seemed satisfied that the *Monitor* was being preserved within the sanctuary.

My formal complaint, however, may have prompted some action. Foster, the director of NOAA's sanctuary program, announced the beginning of a national "USS Monitor Project" on 30 January 1985 (Foster 1985, 7; Editorial 1985, 1–2). NOAA enlisted the aid of the National Trust for Historic Preservation to "provide NOAA with the means to raise private funds for the project as well as facilitate the wide-spread participation of universities, other agencies of government, and other private organizations interested in helping to preserve the Monitor" (Editorial 1985, 1). Although the words were written, action was very limited. One cruise to the *Monitor* site, on 2–11 August 1985, was cosponsored by NOAA and the National Trust for Historic Preservation, with participants from the National Trust (Arnold et al. 1991, 366). From the ocean survey vessel *Peter Anderson,* data were collected on underway sonar, sub-bottom profiles, and magnetometer measurements; I have never seen published results, however.

For years, NOAA conducted studies at the *Monitor* wreck site to document the corrosion state. Of course, the wreck was corroded when it was first discovered in August 1973 and, yes, it continues to corrode daily. What was surprising about that? An intensive corrosion study was done

25 May–9 June 1987 from aboard the navy tug USNS *Apache* while it was four point moored over the *Monitor* site (Arnold et al. 1991, 4). There was no diving on the wreck, but extensive measurements were taken from remote vehicles that retrieved photographic, video, acoustic, and electrical data. The electrical corrosion potential measurements were new and unique to this study. "An electrical field gradient measurement apparatus fixed to the ROV [remote observation vehicle]'s frame and electrode potential 'stab reader' mounted on a manipulator arm" were used to take hundreds of readings on the hull and turret of the *Monitor* (Arnold et al. 1991, 8–9). Corrosion rates were about what was expected for wrought iron. Archaeologists Barto Arnold and Gordon Watts were coauthors on the report of the *Apache* cruise, as was conservator Curtiss Peterson. These three were members of the North Carolina Division of Archives and History's TAC for the *Monitor.*

In 1986 I moved to the Department of Geological Sciences of Rutgers, the State University of New Jersey. The department at Rutgers had a growing group of active researchers.

In the late 1980s and early 1990s I was able to introduce many in the New Jersey area to the *Monitor* research project through the Rutgers speaker program and other venues. I made presentations to historical groups, high school classes (as part of admission recruitment programs), and general community groups as diverse as the American Association of Retired Persons (AARP), diving clubs, and metal detector clubs. Also, by including my research on the *Monitor* as a "case study" example in geophysics courses and in a course on the exploration of the oceans, greater exposure of the *Monitor* project was achieved. I conservatively estimate that I gave presentations, usually titled "The Discovery and Recovery of the USS *Monitor,*" to several thousand people. During each talk, I clearly stated my frustration with the lack of action on recovery of the wreck or any major parts. I emphasized that the wreck was continuing to deteriorate and was being severely threatened by its present environment. If nothing was done, the *Monitor* would eventually be lost forever.

In 1987 the Mariners' Museum in Newport News, Virginia, was designated by NOAA as the principal museum for the collection of the *Monitor* artifacts and other historical documents. I was invited to the 9 March 1987 "125th Commemoration of the Battle of the Ironclads" ceremony. Cathryn Newton, John Newton's daughter, wrote to me about the ceremony: "There was to be a ceremony next week . . . at the . . . Mariners

Museum in Newport News to celebrate the acquisition of the *Monitor* artifacts." It was her "understanding that the hatch cover and other things will be deposited there" (Newton 1987, 1). The agreement between NOAA and the Mariners' Museum resulted from an open competition among maritime museums. "The Mariners' Museum was designated as Principal Museum for the National Collection by NOAA in accordance with the request for proposals published in the *Federal Register* on Thursday, September 4, 1986" (NOAA Sanctuary and Reserves Division 1992, 27). The formal agreement between the two parties was ratified in 1989.

I was pleased with this agreement. The Mariners' Museum won the competition because of its preeminence as one of the nation's finest maritime museum. Its location near the Battle of Hampton Roads and the *Monitor*'s blockade station makes its designation even more appropriate, as I had pointed out in my 1983 letter to NOAA's administrator, Robert White (Sheridan 1983, 2). Unfortunately, I was not able to attend the ceremony at Newport News on 9 March 1987, but I was there in spirit and I gave my heartfelt blessing to the move toward a more national recognition.

Another important policy change for the management of the *Monitor* site occurred in 1990. Since its discovery, the *Monitor* wreck interested submarine photographers and amateur recreational divers. As discussed previously, the permitting process excluded research and diving on the wreck for nonscientific purposes. All proposals were supposed to be judged on their fit in a master plan to further the scientific study, as was true for the MRRF proposals that successfully received permits. Photography of and diving on the wreck merely to take pictures for commercial purposes was not permitted.

Also, there was a safety issue as far as diving was concerned. The first dives in 1977 and 1979 were submersible lockout dives, under tether with mixed gases. But sport and recreational divers, who usually would free dive on air or nitrox or heliox from the surface with mid-water decompression, had an interest in visiting the *Monitor*. Their proposals were rejected by NOAA, partly for safety reasons.

Gary Gentile, a diver from Philadelphia, persisted and eventually brought a suit against NOAA. For several years he litigated with NOAA for a permit. Gentile argued that he and other divers had successfully dived to depths equivalent to those of the *Monitor* on numerous occasions. In particular, Gentile and others had visited the wreck of the *Andrew Doria*, which had sunk to a 230 foot depth off New Jersey. On that basis he questioned NOAA's safety restrictions (Carey 1990, 8).

Gentile also objected to the permit rejections on prejudicial grounds. He noted that NOAA had granted a permit hastily to the Cousteau Society in 1979 for a set of free dives from the surface using scuba and air. The Cousteau Society wanted video footage of the *Monitor* to put in a television special on famous wrecks. The permit was granted and the dives were made. With only fifteen minutes of bottom time, and poor current and visibility conditions, the Cousteau Society attempts to videotape the *Monitor* failed (NOAA Sanctuary and Reserves Division 1992, 67). The incident, however, proved that NOAA had compromised its lofty scientific restrictions and its cautious safety concerns. Gentile used this as evidence of the arbitrariness and bias of the NOAA rejections (Carey 1990, 9).

Ruling in favor of Gentile's appeals of the NOAA rejections, John Carey, NOAA's deputy assistant administrator, wrote in January 1990: "The NOAA diving safety rules clearly state that they apply to 'all NOAA employees and NOAA sponsored personnel.' But nowhere does it say that these diving safety rules apply to non-NOAA activities or divers or that they are binding on applications to dive in the Marine Sanctuaries" (Carey 1990, 10). Gentile had presented sufficient evidence to Carey that confirmed his experience and diving methods were of "'substantially greater proficiency' than sport or novice divers" (Carey 1990, 14). Carey ruled, "A waiver and indemnification statement [must be] signed by each diver before embarking to the Sanctuary specifying in suitable language that each diver is aware that the dives proposed are characterized by NOAA as exceptional exposure and may entail substantial risk of injury or death" (Carey 1990, 15). This favorable ruling follows the basic principle that the U.S. government is not responsible to protect its citizens from risks of their own making or from stupidity.

From aboard the vessel *Quiet Waters* Gentile directed a private group of scuba divers on 30 June–11 July 1990 as they made still and video photographs of the *Monitor*. Air diving was workable at the *Monitor* site (NOAA Sanctuary and Reserves Division 1992, 69). This trip was one of the first visits of private, nonprofessional divers to the site. On 5–13 June and 18–22 June 1990, another private scuba diving group visited the *Monitor* site from the vessel *Sea Fox* under the direction of Roderick Farb (NOAA Sanctuary and Reserves Division 1992, 69).

NOAA organized summer cruises to the *Monitor* site to continue periodic scientific measurements and observations of the wreck during 1990 through 1992. The Harbor Branch Foundation again was involved, using the support vessel *Seward Johnson*, the submersibles *Johnson-Sea-Link I* and *Johnson-Sea-Link II*, and the foundation's new research vessel *Edwin Link* (NOAA Sanctuary and Reserves Division 1992, 70–71). Observations revealed increased deterioration of the wreck. Plates had fallen off the lower hull. The lower hull had collapsed in the forward area. About six feet of the stern part of the armor belt had disintegrated. The skeg and propeller had become displaced (NOAA Sanctuary and Reserves Division 1992, 71). Much of this deterioration was the result of the natural processes of corrosion, current erosion, and wave attack. Some damage was attributed to the 1991 anchoring of a fishing vessel; the anchoring possibly caused the damage and displacement of the skeg and propeller. The guilty fishing vessel was identified by the U.S. Coast Guard and fined fifteen hundred dollars (Hubinger 1997, 45).

A potentially disastrous event occurred at the *Monitor* site in early fall 1992. Two private amateur divers nearly died from the bends after overstaying their safe time at depth. Bill Geroux of the *Richmond Times-Dispatch* reported on 28 September 1992:

> All day Monday [September 20], the divers and Capt. Art Kirchner of the *Margie II* searched in vain for the *Monitor*. It showed up fine on the sonar, but finding it on the ocean bottom was another matter.
>
> On Tuesday they found it. They sank an anchor into the sand near the wreck—NOAA doesn't allow anyone to touch the *Monitor*—and ran a line from the anchor to a floating buoy. . . .
>
> Then came Tropical Storm Danielle and three days of weather so rough the dive boat couldn't leave port.
>
> So all the divers' planning and money came down to a single day of diving for photos. . . .
>
> [Peter] Hess, [Jay] Beasley, [both lawyers,] and Ed Suarez, a computer expert . . . made the first dive [on Saturday]. They took enough air to spend 15 minutes on the bottom and an equal amount of time ascending to the surface . . . [with decompression stops] every 10 feet. Hess, Beasley, and Suarez followed the line down to

the anchor. The water was green and murky. Visibility was about 30 feet. . . .

Hess and Beasley separated from Suarez [as they photographed the wreck]. Suarez decided it was time to head up. He found the anchor further from the wreck than it had been. . . .

Hess knew he was pushing his air supply . . . he signaled Beasley that it was time, but went to find the line—and couldn't.

"I knew right then we were in serious trouble," Beasley said. . . .

With their air running out, Hess and Beasley gambled. They rose as fast as they could, broke the surface of the water, and waved frantically to the boat. "We're bent," Beasley cried. . . .

Luckily, Hess and Beasley found the line close to where they surfaced. The boat sped to them. [With new oxygen tanks] they could descend to 20 feet . . . because oxygen is toxic at deeper levels.

Those on the boat readied tanks of nitrox, a mixture of nitrogen and oxygen. . . . Now Hess and Beasley could go down to 40 feet. . . .

It took three hours . . . [for decompression as] Hess and Beasley clung to the line in the cold water, the current holding them in horizontal position. . . . Suarez, the group's medical expert, pronounced them out of danger. . . .

[The dive boat *Margie II*'s skipper] Kirchner was visibly shaken. He had watched two of the last three Monitor expeditions turn into near-tragedies (Geroux 1992, A1, A6).

Hess and Beasley were lucky they rose near the dive boat and ascent-line buoy, and then had the presence of mind to dive back down to use the ocean as a decompression chamber. It saved their lives. Allowing such dives without a deck decompression chamber was reckless. NOAA used the *Margie II* to ferry me out to the *Monitor* site in 1998, and I saw no deck decompression chamber on board. When I was in charge of anchoring the current meter on the bottom from the *Cape Henlopen*, we used an approximately thousand pound concrete-filled tractor tire. I saw no winches, A-frames, or cherry picker crane on the *Margie II* to launch such a weight. A much lighter anchor weight probably was used on the 1992 near-tragic dive.

After hearing about the near-fatal diving accident on the *Monitor* wreck, I wrote to William Hooke, NOAA's deputy chief scientist, on 16 October 1992 to express my views about the mismanagement of the *Monitor*:

> I was saddened to hear that two divers were nearly killed this summer while diving on the USS *Monitor* wreck. While feeling sorry for the individuals involved, I must say that many of us involved with the *Monitor* are not surprised that this occurred. It was only a matter of time.
>
> Diving on the USS *Monitor* wreck is risky, no matter how sophisticated the procedures and how experienced the divers.... Hurricane Bob crossed the site last year and tropical storm Danielle crossed the site this summer. The USS *Monitor* wreck site is a violent and high energy oceanographic environment both at the surface and at the bottom....
>
> Many times over the past years my co-discoverers of the *Monitor* wreck, the late John Newton and the late Harold Edgerton, have pointed out that the policy of leaving the Monitor where it is and exploring it with divers is a foolish policy. Not only is it dangerous ... but it is not cost effective and scientifically inefficient.... [There was an] NOAA observer... at the scene of the near fatal diving accident. I thought the role of the observer was to disapprove any unsound activities or actions by the permit holders....
>
> I am concerned that the NOAA observer... either was ignorant of the strength of the currents at the site or ignorant of anchoring techniques of oceanographic equipment, or he was negligent in allowing inadequate anchoring of a vital support system. In either case he bears some responsibility for the incident.... In my experience with NOAA on my past cruises to the Monitor wreck, the NOAA observers, and indeed the NOAA administrators of the Monitor sanctuary were not experienced oceanographers....
>
> By way of a copy of this letter, I am informing my congressman, Richard Zimmer, of this incident. He is concerned about federally funded scientific programs. This near fatal accident at the *Monitor* wreck mars the NOAA supervised scientific programs at the site and brings into question NOAA's policy for the future of the wreck (Sheridan 1992a, 1–2).

I was surprised by Hooke's reply: "The National Oceanic and Atmospheric Administration (NOAA) is concerned about the near tragedy that occurred this past summer. Presently diving is prohibited and access to the *Monitor* is currently restricted to permitted research. . . . [The] role [of] the NOAA Observer is restricted to documenting the activities of the permittee. The observer is not present for the purpose of ensuring the safety or rescue of the permittee" (Hooke 1992, 1).

NOAA observers I know believe their role aboard ship includes being concerned about the "safety or rescue of the permittee." Anyone who has been to sea, especially if involved in possibly dangerous activities, feels that the first responsibility of every member of the personnel on a ship is the safety of all the people on the ship and the safety of the ship itself! I generally agree that it is not the government's responsibility to protect us in risks of our own choosing, but I feel it would be reprehensible for any government agent to stand by and observe a reckless undertaking without objecting. That would be gross negligence!

Hooke indicated in his reply that NOAA was "revisiting" the management issue, and all the NOAA activities at the *Monitor* site up through 1992, as well as the private diving activities, would be reviewed. He indicated there was a draft revised management plan being developed and he invited me to "review and comment" on it (NOAA Sanctuary and Reserves Division 1992, 1–90).

I received a copy of the plan and read it. A well produced document with highlighted paragraph headings and inset windows of figures and significant facts, it was a modern, slick, computer-produced document. Under the discussion of "Management Options," there was a statement on recovery: "Data generated through on-site investigations by NOAA in, 1979, 1987, 1990, and 1991 indicate that the wreck has lost much of its integrity, particularly in the area aft of the midships bulkhead. These factors, along with the exorbitant costs estimated for recovery and preservation (some estimates were in excess of $100 million), led NOAA to conclude that the recovery option was not viable" (NOAA Sanctuary and Reserves Division 1992, 37). Instead,

> *in-situ* preservation of the *Monitor* is preferred in concert with NOAA's general policy on historical and cultural resources, and the Federal Archaeological Program. . . . Thus, to further *in-situ* preservation, cathodic protection and physical stabilization of portions of the armor belt are being considered to prevent further deterioration.
>
> Other forms of *in-situ* preservation may be considered in the

> *Monitor* NMS [national marine sanctuary]. Cofferdams, freezing, and underwater domes have been suggested: however, these alternatives do not appear technologically feasible at this time (NOAA Sanctuary and Reserves Division 1992, 38).

I was dumbfounded again! How could NOAA opt for *in-situ* preservation with all the evidence of deterioration and lack of security of the sanctuary? On 5 November 1992 I wrote my review and comment on Rutgers University letterhead. I sent the information to Annie Hillary, the acting chief of the Sanctuaries and Reserves Division in NOAA's Office of Ocean and Coastal Resource Management.

> My objection is that the plan rules out the possibility of the recovery of the wreck or its major parts, such as the turret, in favor of "*in situ* preservation." The proposed *in situ* policy of conducting research at the site with divers under the supervision of NOAA observers is a questionable policy at best. . . .
>
> The proposed management plan uses the excuse that recovery options are too costly and, therefore, should not be considered. On the contrary, a statement must be made that not recovering the wreck will be very costly because of its destruction and theft. I believe a better plan would be to aggressively seek the funds for recovery from the private sector. If the U.S. Government could specify the parameters of an acceptable recovery plan, and then advertise for a commercial venture and operator who could realize a profit from the display [of the recovered wreck], the capital might be raised. I believe this is a superior alternative to the "*in situ* preservation" policy, which is really false advertising. We all know that we cannot prevent the forces of the ocean from taking the wreck. It is only a matter of time (Sheridan 1992b, 1–2).

Once again I sent a copy to Congressman Zimmer to keep him informed of what I thought was NOAA mismanagement. I have faith that letters like mine find their way, through congressional staff research, into oversight committee files on any serious matter. The term "commercial venture" in my letter to Hillary was similar to words used by a congressman in a 1997 congressional committee hearing on the *Monitor*:

Another aspect of my lobbying effort was through my public speaking about the *Monitor*. I made a presentation to Mrs. Susan Reardon's eighth grade history classes at the Readington (New Jersey) Middle School in fall 1992. I touted recovery and ridiculed NOAA's oxymoronic "*in-situ* preservation" plan. As usual, I encouraged my audiences to write their congressional representatives about this mismanagement.

Mrs. Reardon thought this would be an excellent civics lesson for her history students. She organized a letter-writing campaign to Senators William (Bill) R. Bradley and Frank R. Lautenberg and Congressman Zimmer. Mrs. Reardon set me a copy of the letter that her class sent to the legislators:

> Our eighth grade History class has been studying about the Civil War. Dr. Robert Sheridan came to visit our school and gave us a presentation on the USS *Monitor*. Dr. Sheridan is an oceanographer at Rutgers University and he helped discover the *Monitor* off the Coast of Cape Hatteras, NC in the 1970's.
>
> As you know, the *Monitor* played a significant role in the Union victory in the Civil War. Dr. Sheridan explained to us that the ship is in great danger of being destroyed by the effects of rusting, by looting, and the ocean current carrying it over a cliff in the ocean.
>
> [Congressman] Zimmer, we hope that you will help find some way to preserve the Monitor, either by finding government funds or helping a private foundation to find funding. If money is not available through these sources, would it be possible to set up a commission to raise funds similar to the commissions to restore and preserve the Statue of Liberty and Ellis Island (Letter from Mrs. Reardon's Eighth Grade History Class 1992, 1).

I was very impressed with this letter. How heartfelt, how logical, how articulate and direct, how to the point! All eighty of Mrs. Reardon's students signed the letter. I replied, "I am delighted that your classes took the initiative to inform our senators and congressman about the situation with the *Monitor* wreck. I hope the students learned an important civics lesson from this, and that their letter campaign made the history of the Civil War more real to them" (Sheridan 1993, 1).

Bradley's reply stated that he was "encouraged to learn of all your interest in the Monitor" (Bradley 1993, 1). Lautenberg said, "I have contacted the appropriate government officials regarding this matter, and as soon as I receive a reply I will be in further contact with you" (Lautenberg 1993, 1). Zimmer's reply was the most specific:

> I appreciate your bringing this matter to my attention. I share your concern about the need to preserve our national history. I applaud your desire to save this ship from destruction and am happy to assist in any way possible. I have forwarded a copy of your letter to the House Merchant Marine and Fisheries Subcommittee on Oceanography, Great Lakes, and Outer Continental Shelf so that they may be aware of this matter.
>
> I think your suggestion of a private foundation to coordinate the funding effort is a terrific one (Zimmer 1993, 1).

As will be discussed later, Congress finally did begin to get the message.

As part of NOAA's misguided *in situ* preservation program, an NOAA cruise to the *Monitor* site was completed in 1993. It was labeled the "*Monitor* Archaeological Research and Structural Surveys (MARSS) project" (NOAA Sanctuary and Reserves Division 1992, 39). "The objectives of this project include[d] completing the research necessary to detail the *Monitor*'s current condition; physically stabilizing portions of the *Monitor*'s hull; and mapping, recovering and conserving any artifacts determined to be in danger of damage or loss" (NOAA Sanctuary and Reserves Division 1992, 39). One result was the appreciation of the rapid disintegration of the *Monitor* wreck. According to a 1994 *National Geographic* report, entitled "Historic Casualty: The *Monitor* Disintegrates," "Divers from the National Oceanic and Atmospheric Administration (NOAA), using a diving bell and a four-person submersible, inspected the remains last summer. They examined a gaping hole in the stern, which had increased in size since observed by divers a year earlier.... NOAA's scientists... were dismayed by the new findings" (Geographica 1994, geog. 4). Finally, the obvious was becoming obvious to the NOAA scientists: The *Monitor* is rusting away!

During the 1995 summer, an important addition to the research on the *Monitor* wreck was made. Navy "hard hat" divers were lowered on tethers from the naval research vessel USS *Edenton* (Hubinger 1997, 44). The navy divers attempted to remove the propeller because there was a concern about the instability caused by the torque of the propeller on the engine room hull. "Bad weather and, ironically, the iron itself defeated the effort to cut through the drive shaft" (Hubinger 1997, 45).

The navy divers tried cutting the nine inch diameter propeller shaft using electric arc-welding techniques. They cut only about one quarter of the way through the shaft. Compared to cutting pure iron or steel, the silicate impurities in the wrought iron propeller shaft, the intruded salt, and the encrusting organic matter may have all contributed to the poor electrical cutting. I saw attempt results up close when the propeller was recovered in 1998.

In the 1990s in New Jersey, I began giving *Monitor* presentations to the Civil War enthusiasts, members of Civil War reenactment groups, and Civil War round tables (CWRTs). I am one of the founding members of the George W. Taylor CWRT in Clinton, New Jersey. Taylor was the only Civil War general from Hunterdon County. Mortally wounded at the Second Battle of Manassas during 28–31 August 1862, he is buried in his hometown of Clinton. Taylor began the Civil War in 1861 as the colonel of the Third New Jersey Infantry Regiment, in which my great grandfather, James Sheridan, served as a private. The Third New Jersey was part of the First New Jersey Brigade under the command of Gen. Philip Kearny. When Kearny was promoted to divisional command in 1862, Taylor became the First New Jersey Brigade commander.

In all *Monitor* talks, I appealed to the groups to contact their congressional representatives to complain about the inaction on raising the *Monitor*. CWRTs are eager to preserve as much Civil War history as possible. A typical response came from Mark Sutterley, secretary of the Camp Olden CWRT, in February 1996:

> Your presentation demonstrated your thorough knowledge of your subject. Also, you were able to clearly explain the obstacles you faced in discovery of the *Monitor* so that we novices had a real appreciation for all the effort necessary to find this ship on the bottom of the ocean's floor.
>
> I hope our government will someday recover the turret area and other parts of the Monitor. If you [would] write (or fax me) with the appropriate government agency, I'll have our members besiege

> Uncle Sam so that this piece of our Civil War heritage might be shared with our Countrymen and not just the creatures of the sea (Sutterley 1996, 1).

The cumulative effect of the public revelations of the deterioration of the *Monitor* wreck (Geographica 1994, geog. 4; Hubinger 1997, 46; NOAA Sanctuary and Reserves Division 1992, 71) and the various letter-writing campaigns pushed Congress to act. A 1997 congressional "hearing on the National Oceanic and Atmospheric Administration's report on the long-term conservation and management of the USS *Monitor*" took place. "Congress directed NOAA to undertake this report as part of last year's [1996] reauthorization of the National Marine Sanctuaries Act" (Subcommittee on Fisheries Conservation, Wildlife, and Oceans 1997, 3–4). "Congress mandated that the Secretary of Commerce produce 'a long-range, comprehensive plan for the management, stabilization, preservation, and recovery of artifacts and materials of the USS *Monitor*.' The Secretary of Commerce was also directed, 'to the extent feasible to utilize the resources of other Federal and private entities with expertise and capabilities that are helpful' and to submit a plan within twelve months of the date of enactment of the Act (October 11, 1996)" (Monitor National Marine Sanctuary 1997, v).

NOAA faithfully produced the mandated report for presentation to Congress in 1997; it was titled "Charting a New Course for the *Monitor*" (Monitor National Marine Sanctuary 1997, 1–31). The report was produced by the Monitor National Marine Sanctuary office under the leadership of John Broadwater, the sanctuary manager. The first subtitle of the report's introduction was: "Crisis: The Disintegration of the *Monitor*" (Monitor National Marine Sanctuary 1997, 3). Finally, NOAA had admitted there was a crisis. Because of the harshness of its environment, the *Monitor* wreck was in danger of terrible destruction. Loss of valuable artifacts was probable.

The report recommended a course of action in the form of a six-phased archaeology plan for recovery of the major elements of the *Monitor* wreck and shoring up of the remaining deteriorating hull:

> Phase I: Pre-Shoring Archaeological Survey, Mapping and Recovery: A NOAA-approved archaeological survey team will closely survey and map all exposed artifacts beneath the hull, from the bow to

Six Phases of the Archaeology Plan

Phase I: Pre-Shoring Archaeology

Mapping and Excavation

Phase II: Shoring Beneath Hull

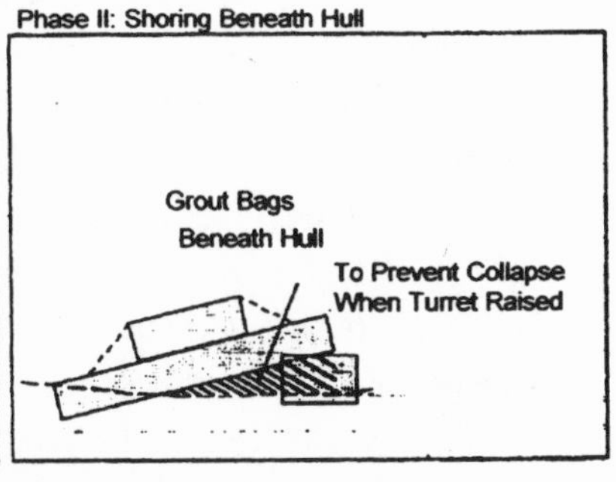

Phase III: Removal of Skeg, Propeller, Lower Hull and Engine

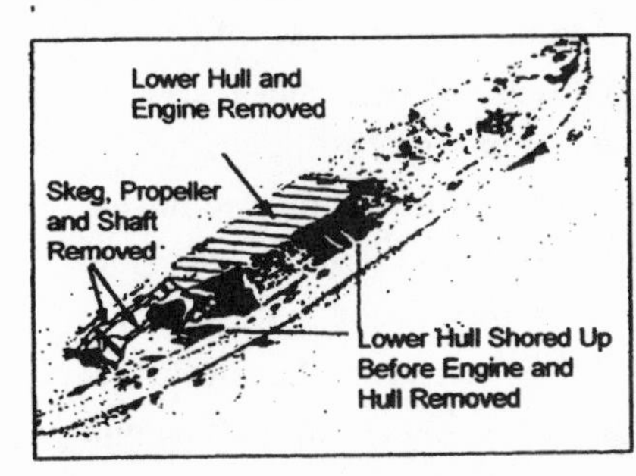

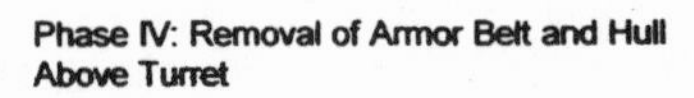

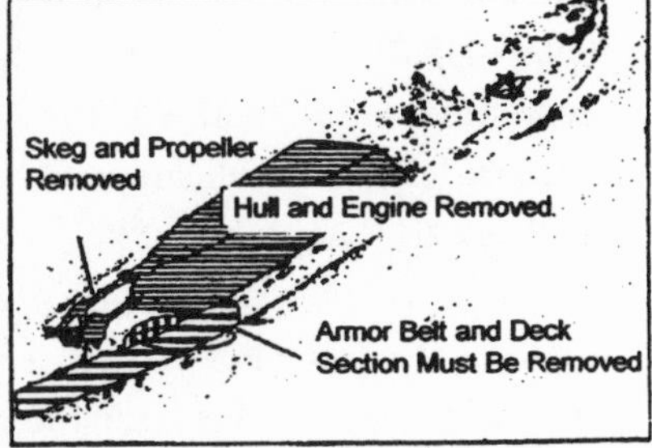

Phase V: Removal of Turret

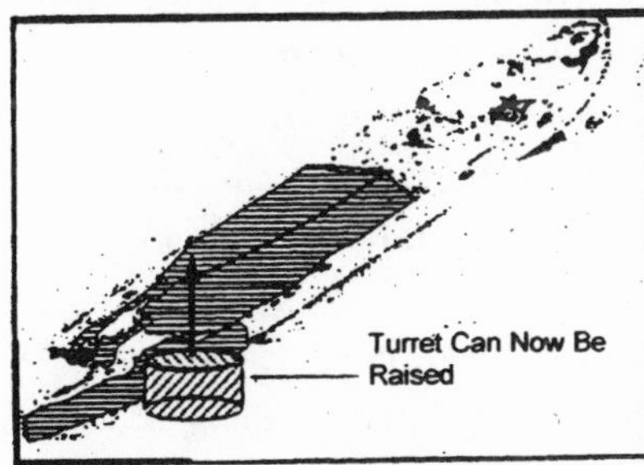

Phase VI: Post-Removal Survey and Stabilization

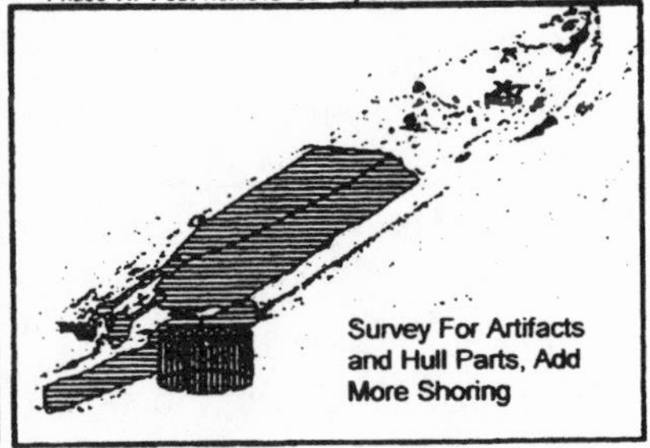

Illustrated diagram of the six-phased archaeology and recovery plan submitted by NOAA to Congress in 1997.

Monitor National Marine Sanctuary. 1997. *Charting a New Course for the Monitor, Comprehensive, Long Range Preservation Plan with Options for Management, Stabilization, Preservation, Recovery, Conservation and Exhibition of Materials and Artifacts from the Monitor National Marine Sanctuary,* Draft. Newport News, Va.: U.S. Department of Commerce, National Oceanic and Atmospheric Administration, app., 61.

> the eastern end of the stern debris field, then will conduct limited excavation, mapping and recovery in the following areas: (1) beneath the hull, in accessible areas beneath the hole in the deck just forward and to port of the midships bulkhead; (2) inside the hull between the armor belt and the lower hull; (3) in the debris field aft of the propeller; and (4) in any accessible areas beneath the hull that might be affected by the planned shoring activities. All encountered artifacts will be mapped and recovered, insofar as personnel safety permits; divers should not venture beneath the hull. An effort will be made to locate and record the rudder, which is assumed to lie in the stern debris field.
>
> Phase II: Shoring Beneath the Hull: The hull will then be shored up using pumped sand, sandbags, "grout bags" (a type of cement that will harden after being pumped into bags), mechanical jacks, or a combination of methods; the lower hull will also be shored by some method that will support the engine until it can be removed.
>
> Phase III: Removal of Skeg, Propeller, Lower Hull and Engine: The skeg will be removed and placed on the seabed to the south of the hull; the propeller and shaft will be recovered; the lower hull will be cut away and the engine recovered; lower hull plating and beams will be placed on the seabed near the skeg.
>
> Phase IV: Removal of Armor Belt and Hull Section Above the Turret: With the hull shored from beneath and the engine and other machinery components removed, the section of armor belt and hull that obstruct access to the turret can be cut away; these objects can be placed on the seabed, near the other material removed from the hull.
>
> Phase V: Removal of Turret: With the turret now clear of overhead obstructions, it can be recovered; a support cradle will be worked beneath the turret and the turret will be supported on all sides before being lifted to the surface.
>
> Phase VI: Post-Removal Survey and Stabilization: Following completion of all recovery activities, an archaeological and engineering survey must be conducted to assess the condition of the hull and contents; additional stabilization should be carried out, if necessary (Monitor National Marine Sanctuary 1997, app., 60).

On 6 November 1997 Broadwater presented the NOAA archaeology and recovery plan to a hearing on the *Monitor* before the Subcommittee on Fisheries Conservation, Wildlife and Oceans, which was part of the congressional Committee on Resources (Subcommittee on Fisheries Conservation, Wildlife, and Oceans 1997, 1). Congressman James Saxton of New Jersey chaired the hearing on the *Monitor*. At one point, Congressman Walter Jones, who is from the North Carolina district that includes Cape Hatteras, made a statement that "the USS *Monitor* is of great interest not only to the Nation, but especially to the people of eastern North Carolina." (Subcommittee of Fisheries Conservation, Wildlife, and Oceans 1997, 7). Later in the hearing, Congressman Herbert Bateman, who is from the Virginia district that includes the Newport News Mariners' Museum and the northern shore of Hampton Roads, expressed his strong interest in the recovery of the *Monitor* artifacts. He thought the NOAA plan was "well thought out" (Subcommittee on Fisheries Conservation, Wildlife, and Oceans 1997, 12). The comments of these two congressmen revealed that the rivalry between North Carolina and Virginia persisted.

Broadwater estimated the costs of the plan as "$10 to $12 million for recovery and stabilization, and the conservation costs at another $10 million" (Subcommittee on Fisheries Conservation, Wildlife, and Oceans 1997, 10). In response to this estimate, Congressman Sam Farr of California injected a rather pragmatic tone into the hearing. He said,

> I'm curious... the entire sanctuary budgets for the entire Nation is $12 million.... [H]ere you are [a] sanctuary manager having to deal with limited funds and the project that you have proposed here really has a horrific bottom line.... I think that it is more important right now that our sanctuaries protect our natural resources.... [W]e were talking about how we're having entire fisheries be destroyed and habitats be destroyed, and I guess it's a question of priorities. How do you as a sanctuary manager suggest that we as a people that have to make these tough decisions as which of our children we're going to invest in and the others that we're not, how do you suggest that we do this? Maybe is the salvage operation with a commercial bent feasible? Almost a bounty? You know, wouldn't it be easier to maybe put out a sum of money, a reward and allow the private sector to go out and do the salvage operation?... [I]n the reauthorization of the sanctuaries, we put in the ability for you to market in logos and products essentially that are consistent with the sanctuaries. And the fees for those sales can be kept with the sanctuary. It

> seems to me that you've got a commercial opportunity here. And then we ought to think boldly.... I think that this Committee would be challenged because what we're trying to do is in an era of limited budgets is think of new ways in which we can have our public/private partnership that will in the end... enhance... what we've envisioned in creating sanctuaries (Subcommittee on Fisheries Conservation, Wildlife, and Oceans 1997, 13–15).

In the ensuing discussion it was pointed out that NOAA hoped to enlist the existing assets, resources, and capabilities of the U.S. Navy to accomplish the plan. Also, the Mariners' Museum in Newport News had agreed to conserve and display the *Monitor* artifacts, using some of its own resources. This in essence is an example of the public–private partnership that is needed for success. Other private sources of support would be solicited; for example, Newport News Shipbuilding was mentioned. NOAA admitted that the cost of the *Monitor* project was beyond its own resources.

I was impressed with Farr's comments. He used the terms "commercial bent," "commercial opportunity," "fees for sales," and "public/private partnership" in his questioning. I found these words were similar to "commercial venture," "profit," and "private sector" that I had used in expressing similar interests to Hillary, an NOAA official, in 1992. NOAA now seemed convinced of the logic of raising the *Monitor*. Bateman commented that "the draft study on which I commend John Broadwater very highly shows a change in those attitudes towards the importance of the Monitor sanctuary" (Subcommittee on Fisheries Conservation, Wildlife, and Oceans 1997, 12).

I received word of Broadwater's testimony before the congressional subcommittee from William Condit, one of my former geology students. He was working as a geologist for the Department of Interior in 1997 and was the liaison with the congressional Resources Committee, of which the Subcommittee on the Oceans was a part. He attended the *Monitor* hearings.

I wrote Broadwater in December 1997:

> Today I read a good article on the recovery plan in the Science section of the NY Times [Broad 1997, F1, F6]. The plan sounds fine and I wholeheartedly endorse the project. Needless to say it should have been done twenty years ago....

> [Archaeologists] have spent years diving on the *Monitor* wreck studying what was obvious to Newton, Edgerton, and me from the beginning: the ocean floor is *not* a good place to leave such a valuable piece of our history.
>
> The costs involved in such a project, as quoted in the Times, are really minuscule when compared to many other less valuable projects that the government funds. It is about time that NOAA fights for these resources (Sheridan 1997, 1).

As usual, I sent a copy to my representatives in the Senate and Congress. Senator Robert G. Torricelli replied, "I understand your concern with recovery of the *Monitor*, and I assure you that I will keep your views in mind should the United States Senate consider this issue. Thank you for alerting me to your concerns" (Torricelli 1997, 1). Although a typical reply from a shrewd politician, such correspondence may reach a file somewhere where it can be resurrected for some future hearing.

In April 1998 NOAA made its final submission of the *Monitor* archaeology and recovery plan to Congress. Phase I of the comprehensive plan was to begin in the 1998 summer with the U.S. Navy divers of Mobile Diving Salvage and Unit Two (MDSU-2) on board the salvage vessel *Kellie Chouest.*

13

Saving the Artifacts

While NOAA awaited congressional appropriation of the twenty-two million dollars for the *Monitor* recovery plan, the personnel in the Monitor National Marine Sanctuary office in Newport News, Virginia, began executing parts of the recovery with existing resources (Subcommittee on Fisheries Conservation, Wildlife, and Oceans 1997, 18; Monitor National Marine Sanctuary 1997, app., 75). Under the leadership of John Broadwater, the *Monitor* sanctuary manager, a series of summer diving campaigns were completed. Cruises used NOAA divers in cooperation with U.S. Navy divers and divers from private nonprofit groups. The staff of the NOAA Monitor National Marine Sanctuary are salaried, and development of the *Monitor* wreck site is a rightful part of their work mission. The navy divers are always on duty, and their dives on the *Monitor* constitute part of their routine proficiency drills and training.

The navy divers are members of a mobile diving and salvage unit (MDSU); each MDSU has thirty people. An MDSU can be dispatched to any emergency site in the world. Their efficiency is well documented. MDSU divers have worked on numerous airline disasters on the east and west coasts, such as the TWA 800 crash off Long Island in 1996, the Alaska Airlines crash off California in 1999, and the John Kennedy Jr. crash off Martha's Vineyard in 1999. Within days of airplane crashes at sea, the infamous black boxes were recovered, and critical parts of the wreckage were found that conclusively determined the causes of the disasters. But, similar to firemen waiting for the next emergency call, the navy MDSU divers must train and be prepared while waiting. The *Monitor* project took advantage of the opportunity to employ these skilled professional divers.

The U.S. Navy has a great interest in the *Monitor* because it is one of the navy's most famous vessels. Since the discovery and identification of the *Monitor* wreck in 1973–74, naval officers responsible for preserving naval history have been involved in various Monitor National Marine Sanctuary committees. The navy was eager to play as big a role as possible in saving the *Monitor.* The navy contributed funds and personnel to various on-site projects, such as the photography of the wreck in the spring of 1974 (Miller 1978a, 97; Miller 1978b, 30). Naval experts at the Naval Research Laboratory in Washington, D.C., did corrosion and metallurgical analysis on a *Monitor* hull plate in 1977–78 (Peterkin 1977, 1–29). Beginning in 1995 navy divers accomplished important diving projects at the *Monitor* wreck site (Hubinger 1997, 44; Vogel 1998, D1, D8; Lane 2001, 1, 6). While the navy does not have major funds available for preserving U.S. naval history, it does fund the Naval History Museum at the historic Washington (D.C.) Navy Yard in Anacostia and the small museum at the U.S. Naval Academy in Annapolis, Maryland. The historian of the navy is usually a retired admiral who is given limited resources. Preserving naval history is not a high priority within the service, and rightly so. Given the limited defense budgets, all resources must first go to the navy's real mission of conducting naval warfare. Other activities are of much lower priority. This basic fact was discussed early in the various Monitor National Marine Sanctuary committee meetings.

The Naval Historical Center expressed an interest in preserving and displaying the *Monitor* artifacts that were recovered. It became clear that the scale of such an endeavor would require millions of dollars, much time, employment of many professional preservationists and museum curators, and, indeed, the construction of new museum facilities. Given the needed commitment, it was out of the question that the U.S. Navy should or could take on this job.

After due consideration, the NOAA management team of the Monitor National Marine Sanctuary established an agreement, under the auspices of the Department of Commerce, with the Newport News Mariners' Museum in Virginia to preserve, house, and display the *Monitor* artifacts (Monitor National Marine Sanctuary 1997, app., 43). With the museum's experience, staff, preservationists, and curators, the professional quality of the work on the *Monitor*'s artifacts is ensured. Moreover, the staff at the Mariners' Museum work well with the viewing public. Housing the *Monitor* remains there in the context of the U.S. maritime history is well justified, given its monumental role in the conversion to iron ships in the nineteenth century. Moreover, the nearness of the museum to Hampton Roads, Virginia, where the first battle between iron ships—the *Monitor* and the *Merrimac*—brings the *Monitor* back, full-circle, to the scene of its triumph. This is clearly the best repository for the *Monitor* artifacts.

Because of the necessary role of the Newport News Mariners' Museum in the preservation and display of the *Monitor* artifacts, part of the twenty-two million dollar proposal to Congress was to be used for the preservation and display effort. As much as ten million dollars was estimated for preservation, including the construction of new buildings on the Newport News Mariners' Museum campus (Monitor National Marine Sanctuary 1997, 30; Subcommittee on Fisheries Conservation, Wildlife, and Oceans 1997, 10). The facilities are needed for the enormous tanks for submergence of the larger *Monitor* artifacts, such as the propeller and shaft, the engine, the turret, and the two 11-inch Dahlgren cannons. Chemical baths and electrolytic processes are used to dissolve and remove the encrusting calcium carbonate coral and shell material, dissolve the organic material, leach out the salts from within the wrought iron, and eventually reduce the iron oxide rust phases to ferrous iron stable phases. Such processing will take decades to complete (Monitor National Marine Sanctuary 1997, app., 42; Peterson 1978, 98).

The processing and preservation needs of wrought iron artifacts are well known from experiences at the *Wasa* museum in Stockholm, Sweden (Barkman 1978b, 105). The wooden, early seventeenth century Swedish warship *Wasa* sank abruptly in Stockholm harbor. Buried in clay-rich mud in cold, fresh water conditions led to extremely good preservation of the wood. There were many iron artifacts on the *Wasa,* such as the cannons and cannon balls. The Wasa Museum preservationists used a technique of heating the iron artifacts in hydrogen gas to remove some of the oxygen and reduce the iron to the ferrous state. Once reduced, the iron artifacts are stabilized and can be displayed in normal room conditions.

The preservation of *Wasa*'s iron was well documented in an article by Olaf Arrhenius, Lars Barkman, and Erik Sjostrand (Arrhenius et al. 1973, 1–33). In extolling their technique, the authors stated, "In all work on conservation one is interested in restoring all the details to their original form. By way of example all dimensions should be equal and the degree of hardening of tools and weapons should be unchanged. By means of hydrogen gas reduction the volume of artefacts [*sic*] can be kept the same as when they were discovered. The change of an artefact [*sic*] from its original shape is entirely dependent on the type of rust, the site of the finding and the rusting medium" (Arrhenius et al. 1973, 10). The appendix to this article indicated that the rate of corrosion in sea water is about one half inch per century, which is twice as fast as the rate of corrosion in river water, and ten times as fast as the rate in tap water.

I do not advocate the use of the hydrogen gas technique for preserving the *Monitor* artifacts. Hydrogen is very flammable and extreme care must be taken for this kind of processing. Different techniques, including chemical liquid baths and electrolytic processes, have been used on the *Monitor* artifacts and will be used by the Newport News Mariners' Museum preservationists to stabilize the rusted iron (Peterson 1984, 3–4). I mention the *Wasa* article because one of the Swedish coauthors, Barkman, is a master of chemical engineering and an official of the Wasavarwet National Maritime Museum in Stockholm (Barkman 1978a, 71). During the three day NOAA conference on the *Monitor* in 1978, I was able to hear his views on artifacts and their preservation, and I received a copy of the referenced paper.

I had the pleasure and pride to see MDSU divers in action on the USS *Monitor* wreck site in 1998. This was the first diving done on the *Monitor* after Congress had made a commitment to recover the turret and other large artifacts. As discussed in the preceding chapter, Phase I of the recovery plan involves the clearing away and collection of all small artifacts and plate debris from under the overhanging, upside down deck that rests on the *Monitor*'s turret. Phase II involves the stabilization of the upside down deck with jacks and grout bags. Then, to lighten the load of the deck structure on the turret, the propeller and shaft and the engine are to be recovered in Phase III (Monitor National Marine Sanctuary 1997, app., 60). In the June 1998 cruise aboard the salvage ship *Kellie Chouest*, the navy divers were to complete some of the Phase I objectives.

John Broadwater, the manager of the Monitor National Marine Sanctuary invited me to visit the diving operation:

> I am writing to invite you to visit our forthcoming expedition to the Monitor National Marine Sanctuary. During the 1998 *Monitor*

> Expedition which will take place from May 24 through June 26, teams of NOAA and navy divers will conduct a variety of scientific activities including recovery of small artifacts from areas that may be affected by shoring the wreck, which is expected to begin next field season. The expedition is jointly sponsored by NOAA, the U.S. Navy, The Cambrian Foundation, the National Undersea Research Center/University of North Carolina at Wilmington, and The Mariners' Museum (Broadwater 1998a, 1).

There was no mention of the recovery of the *Monitor*'s propeller and shaft. In fact, the propeller recovery was not in the original cruise operations plan for the expedition. Excerpts from the cruise operational plan as it appeared on the NOAA Monitor National Marine Sanctuary website on 29 May 1998 follow:

> *Introduction*
>
> In March 1862, the Civil War ironclad USS *Monitor* survived a four-hour assault by the Confederate ironclad CSS *Virginia* at Hampton Roads, Virginia, before succumbing in December of that year to a severe storm off Cape Hatteras, North Carolina. Now the *Monitor* is facing a new crisis. Photographic evidence clearly shows that there has been a marked increase in the deterioration of the *Monitor*'s hull over the past five years, the result of both natural and human causes. All evidence suggests that collapse of the *Monitor*'s hull could occur at any time and that the result would be the loss of much of the ship's structure and many of its historic contents. To forestall the inevitable collapse and preserve the *Monitor*'s most significant components for future generations, NOAA has developed a long-range, comprehensive plan that recommends that the remains of the *Monitor* be preserved through a combination of stabilization and selective recovery options.
>
> In 1975, in recognition of the *Monitor*'s unique historical and archaeological significance, the Secretary of Commerce designated the remains of the *Monitor* as the first National Marine Sanctuary. The *Monitor* National Marine Sanctuary is administered by NOAA's Sanctuaries and Reserves Division, Office of Ocean and Coastal Resource Management, National Ocean Service. Preservation of the *Monitor* will involve considerations of technological feasibility, prob-

ability of success, review under the National Historic Preservation Act section 106 process and other applicable laws, consistency with the Division's Strategic Plan, and funding. The technological requirements for stabilization and recovery can be met by several ocean engineering firms; however, since the combined costs of stabilization, recovery and conservation are estimated to be in excess of $20 M, possibly the greatest challenge for NOAA will be to create a partnership of interested organizations that can generate the required funds.

The 1998 *Monitor* Expedition is the first phase of the recommended option of stabilization and selected recovery. The expedition will be conducted in two phases: Phase I will be conducted jointly between NOAA and the U.S. Navy, while Phase II will be a cooperative effort involving NOAA and private organizations. Expedition divers will conduct a variety of activities including observation, photography, documentation, excavation, mapping and recovery.

Expedition Goals

This expedition is designed to generate a wide range of archaeological and engineering data needed in developing a detailed plan for stabilization of the hull and for recovering selected objects from the site. Goals for the 1998 *Monitor* Expedition are divided into two categories, primary and secondary, to indicate their relative importance and to indicate the criteria applied to the development of contingency plans. The primary goals include thoroughly mapping and documenting the most unstable areas of the *Monitor*'s hull, particularly in the stern and near the turret; mapping and recovery of exposed artifacts; recovery of environmental data; and completion of a NOAA assessment of self-contained, deep-water diving methodology and equipment. All research goals are designed to obtain data necessary for ongoing site assessment and for the development of a detailed stabilization and recovery plan.

PRIMARY GOALS

GOAL 1. Document, through drawings, measurements, and photography, the following areas:

A. Overall configuration of hull

1. Obtain video imagery of the entire wreck using a digital video camera.
2. Photograph from above and from the north side.

B. Stern, particularly the propeller, shaft, skeg and aft debris field

1. Obtain video and still imagery of the stern from all angles, using scales; stern areas to include skeg, propeller, propeller shaft and coupling, stern armor belt and stern bulkheads.
2. Obtain detailed video and still imagery of the stern debris field.
3. Map and excavate debris field aft of the stern, map and recover small artifacts and attempt to locate the rudder.
4. Remove a core sample from the port side armor belt, aft of the turret, to determine the condition of the wood and iron interior structures.
5. Determine the best method of support for the propeller shaft.
6. Clear and recover all of the debris from the propeller and shaft from previous navy and NOAA expeditions.
7. Remove the Kevlar strap attached to the propeller in 1995 and remove a segment for tensile testing to see if Kevlar bags will hold up in the environment.

C. Turret and its area of contact with the inverted hull

1. Obtain video and still imagery and measurements of the turret/hull interface from all angles, using scales.
2. Obtain detailed video and still imagery and measurements of the turret/hull interface, from underneath the hull, using scales.
3. Obtain detailed video and still imagery of the inside of the turret base before disturbing the turret contents.
4. Measure and map the turret/hull interface and the angle of tilt of the turret in relation to true level and to the hull.
5. Measure and map the perimeter of the turret, measuring the distance from the upper rim of the turret to the seabed at several points.
6. Recover a core sample from the seabed in the vicinity of the turret.

D. Lower hull, machinery space, engine and boilers

1. Obtain video and still imagery, with scales, of the engine room area, with an emphasis on the following:
   Is the engine still attached to the engine bed?
   If so, how is it attached?
   Is the engine resting on the inverted deck? On the seabed?
2. Obtain video and still images, with scales, of the midships bulkhead and the areas of the turret machinery and gearing.
3. Obtain video and still images, with scales, of the galley area between the midships bulkhead and the forward end of the boilers.
4. Obtain video and still images, with scales, of the boilers, with an emphasis on the following:
   Are the boilers still attached to their beds?
   If so, how are they attached?
   Are the boilers resting on the inverted deck? On the seabed?
5. Obtain video and still images, with scales, of the auxiliary steam machinery, including the small steam engines for the blowers, pumps, etc.
6. Obtain video and still images, with scales, of the remaining sections of the coal bunker bulkheads.
7. Obtain a detailed measurement of one or more of the "bowed" deck support stanchions.

E. Hull forward of the midships bulkhead
1. Determine if the round "porthole-like" object aft-port of the midships bulkhead is actually the officer's toilet and determine the feasibility of recovery.
2. Obtain video and still images, with scales, of the entire midships bulkhead cross-section, photographed from forward, looking aft.
3. Identify and tag several key frame stations to be used as reference positions.

F. Area beneath the hull
1. Obtain measurements of the clearance between the deck and the sea bottom from bow to stern and as far under the wreck as deemed safe and practicable. Height clearances will allow

us to determine the sizes of the grout bags needed for stabilization.

2. Obtain video imagery of the area under the hull from bow to stern, with particular attention to the pilot house, smoke stacks, and ventilator boxes.

GOAL 2. Map and recover exposed artifacts that may be damaged or destroyed by the action of currents, the collapse of portions of the hull, or by the planned hull shoring activities.

A Establish a suitable reference system (grid or baseline) from which to map features and artifacts.

B Examine and extensively document the inverted deck beneath the hull from stem to stern.

C Map and recover all objects exposed on the seabed in the area of concern.

D Excavate 3 feet to 6 feet into the seabed in the area of concern, map and recover exposed artifacts.

GOAL 3. Excavate and/or probe inside and at the base of the turret in an effort to locate the guns and other contents and to identify obstructions at the base of the turret.

A. Excavate a test pit (approximately 1/2 meter square and 1 meter deep) inside the turret, using a dredge device, in order to determine the turret contents and condition.

1. Map and recover small objects encountered in the test pit.
2. Probe gently into the bottom of the test pit to determine what lies below.
3. Excavate a test pit (approximately 1 meter square and 1 to 1 1/2 meters deep) at the outside base of the turret, using a dredge or DPV [diving program vehicle] propwash device, in order to confirm the presence of the rifle shield and stanchions and to determine their condition and orientation; map and recover small objects encountered.

GOAL 4. Excavate and map the stern debris field and attempt to locate the rudder; move all material to a safe area to the northeast of the wreck; recover the rudder, if practicable.

A. Recover the current meter placed on the stern anchor in 1997.

1. Download the data to a computer file and back up the file.
2. Replace the meter's batteries and service as necessary.
3. Re-deploy the current meter.

GOAL 5. Recover data from the current meter placed at the site in 1997, and reposition the current meter for additional data collection.

SECONDARY GOALS

GOAL 6. Inspect the permanent mapping datums installed in 1997, replace as necessary, and measure the distances between those datums; and

GOAL 7. Document and assess the untethered, mixed-gas method of conducting research dives at the Monitor National Marine Sanctuary.

Additional Objectives and Tasks

A. Document on film and video, to the extent possible, both surface and subsurface expedition operations and activities.

B. Locate coal supply and recover samples for education and research purposes.

C. Recover a 5-gallon bucket of sand for education and research purposes.

D. Provide opportunities for the press and other visitors to be briefed on the status of the expedition and observe surface and subsurface operations.

E. Examine and, when necessary, replace datum markers placed on the site in 1997, and install additional datum markers as appropriate.

F. Inspect subsurface moorings and repair/strengthen if necessary...

Phase I: U.S. Navy Expedition

The Navy dive team will be completely responsible for the conduct of its own dive operations. However, the Navy will coordinate all dive activities with the NOAA Chief Scientist in order to ensure that the expedition goals are met and that there are no adverse effects to the *Monitor* and its contents.

During Phase I, NOAA dives will be conducted from the *Kellie Chouest,* employing a small team of NOAA and Cambrian Foundation divers. NOAA dives will be conducted completely independently of the Navy dives; however, dive schedules and work tasks will be coordinated in order to maximize effectiveness and to permit NOAA supervision of work activities. All NOAA dives will follow procedures and protocols established by NOAA, NURC [National Undersea Research Center], and the Cambrian Foundation, and approved by the NOAA Diving Safety Board for assessment of self-contained mixed-gas diving techniques. All NOAA dives will follow NOAA-approved decompression schedules; and all dives will be supported by a Navy deck decompression chamber (DDC) and diving medical technician on board the *Kellie Chouest.* The use of mixed gas will greatly improve the divers' effectiveness and ability to deal with possible emergencies due to the minimization of nitrogen narcosis and oxygen toxicity, potential hazards when breathing compressed air at the *Monitor*'s depth.

NOAA Trimix I, or "*Monitor* Mix," used on the NOAA 1993 and 1995 expeditions and approved by the NOAA Diving Program, will be used. *Monitor* Mix Tables were developed in 1993 for NOAA by Hamilton Research Institute and used successfully on the 1993 and 1995 expeditions. Gas mixing and testing will be conducted by NOAA and Cambrian Foundation personnel, and testing will be conducted for every dive by the diver and verified by a dive supervisor.

Once the *Kellie Chouest* is moored over the *Monitor,* two options will be available: A diver downline can be established from a 3000-pound anchor near the turret to the *Kellie Chouest* or to a surface buoy floating near the *Chouest.* NOAA divers can then choose to ascend directly up the line to the side of the support vessel for recovery or, in the case of strong currents during decompression, can elect to use the breakaway decompression line for drift decompression.

Weather and other conditions permitting, at least two dives will be made each day. Each dive will consist of a team of two to four divers and a minimum of two surface support personnel, two support divers and a safety diver to respond to contingencies. A small inflatable boat will be available if needed to respond to a diving emergency or other emergency situation.

The divers will descend to the bottom on a down-line attached to one of the NOAA moorings. The divers will then follow a guide line along the bottom from the mooring to the work area. Well before the planned bottom time has elapsed, the divers will return to the down line, where they will begin their ascent on or before the end of the planned bottom time. Decompression will be completed in the water column. No additional dives will be made until the first divers have completed their decompression and have been found to be asymptomatic. The Expedition Diving Supervisor, or designee, will observe and record all activities.

Phase II: NOAA Expedition

During Phase II, NOAA will conduct dives from the R/V [research vessel] *Cape Fear*, with support from the NOAA Ship *Ferrel*, which will be moored near by. The *Ferrel* will be equipped with a deck decompression chamber, with qualified operators and medical personnel provided by NURC/UNCW [University of North Carolina at Wilmington]. The Navy will not participate in Phase II.

The breathing gas, decompression schedules and other dive procedures and equipment will be the same as described for NOAA dives in Phase I, above. Prior to each operational dive all key personnel will assemble for a briefing, to include a discussion of the dive profile, objectives, personnel assignments and other pertinent information. Weather and other conditions permitting, at least two dives will be made each day. Each dive will consist of a team of two to four divers and a minimum of two surface support personnel, two support divers, and a safety diver to respond to contingencies. A small inflatable boat and a boat from the *Ferrel* will both be available if needed to respond to a diving emergency or other emergency situation (Monitor National Marine Sanctuary 1998, 1–8).

This cruise plan is exemplary in the length and detail required of all cruises to the *Monitor*. Again, I point out that the recovery of the propeller and shaft was not mentioned anywhere. In fact, under Goal 1, part B, sections 5–7 of the cruise plan, stabilizing and clearing the propeller and shaft were discussed. Instead, as discussed below, the navy divers retrieved the *Monitor*'s propeller and shaft on the 1998 cruise. Why? Success requires flexibility and opportunism. When an opportunity presents itself, decisions should be made and appropriate action taken. The old admonition "strike while the iron is hot" works well in oceanographic research. This is what happened on the 1998 *Kellie Chouest* cruise, just as it had been done on all *Monitor* cruises in which I participated when we took quick action to find the wreck and dredge the first identifiable artifact.

I timed my visit to the *Monitor* site for the first week of June 1998 during the Phase I part, which was the complete responsibility of the U.S. Navy under the coordination of Broadwater of NOAA. The *Kellie Chouest* was under contract to the U.S. Navy for use of the Mobile Diving and Salvage Unit Two (MDSU-2). A remarkable salvage ship, I was happy to see the *Kellie Chouest*'s capabilities when I came on board. The *Kellie Chouest* had been the "star" in a made-for-television movie about navy divers in 1999, and it had also played a major role in the Alaska Airlines crash recovery that same year. *Kellie Chouest*'s bright orange hull is a world famous picture seen many times on TV.

On 6 June 1998 my wife Karen and I drove to the Outer Banks to join the Monitor National Marine Sanctuary officials at their operations center at the Sea Gull Motel in Hatteras Village. Although I had taken many cruises off Cape Hatteras, this was the first time I had a chance to stay on the Outer Banks for a few days vacation before my visit to the *Monitor* site. We visited Kitty Hawk Museum and the Cape Hatteras Lighthouse. The Outer Banks National Seashore is a low-key, quiet area with few crowds; it has more people fishing than sunbathing. Karen and I watched sunsets over Pamlico Sound from quaint seafood restaurants. The weather was so clear that the "Carolina Moon" rays danced across the small waves of the Atlantic while we sat on the beach. A few tourists, strolling the beach in the moonlight, extended casual hellos and passed by.

Early Monday morning, 8 June, we met Dina Hill, NOAA's Monitor National Marine Sanctuary coordinator, for breakfast. She briefed us on the operations aboard the *Kellie Chouest* in the last few days. Because of the unusually good weather the diving was ahead of schedule and several cruise goals and objectives had been accomplished. As discussed previously, the poor weather and frequent storms off Cape Hatteras make it difficult to perform diving operations at the *Monitor* wreck. Often re-

The salvage ship *Kellie Chouest*, on the *Monitor* wreck site in June 1998, was the diving platform for the U.S. Navy's Mobile Diving and Salvage Unit Two (MDSU-2). The divers recovered the *Monitor*'s propeller and shaft.

search vessels can occupy the site for thirty days yet only accomplish thirteen days of diving. However, in these last few days in early June 1998, fair weather conditions moved slowly across the Hatteras area with mild breezes out of the northwest and west. I had commented to Karen the evening before, as we enjoyed the view over Pamlico Sound, that the westerly breeze boded well for the work at the *Monitor* site. Offshore breezes offered less fetch to build strong waves at the site, and the westerlies sometimes pushed the stronger Gulf Stream current to the southeast off the wreck. Milder waves and currents are always better when working out at the *Monitor* site. The current remained slack for days under these good weather conditions.

As Hill discussed at breakfast, blessed with these ideal diving conditions at the *Monitor*, the work at the site was ahead of schedule. The divers had swept the area under the overturned deck and recovered small artifacts and several pieces of corroded, thin deck plates. They had effectively completed the first two goals of the mission.

Then Hill shocked us with the news that the MDSU-2 divers had cut the propeller shaft and recovered the Ericsson propeller that past Friday night. This was great news and a surprise, given that this recovery was not mentioned in the Monitor National Marine Sanctuary plans for the cruise. Somehow a change in plans had occurred. Whatever the mechanism for the change in plans, I was delighted that the lengthy ideal weather conditions at the *Monitor* wreck had provided such an excellent opportunity. Often at the *Monitor* site divers should not even enter the water.

With eager anticipation I was escorted by Hill to the shuttle vessel *Margie II* for the 7:00 A.M. departure from Teach's Lair Mariner. Not only would I be able to examine the Ericsson propeller, but I would hear first-hand about how it came to be recovered!

Aboard the *Margie II*, I met Steve Vogel, a *Washington Post* reporter who later wrote an admirable story about the *Kellie Chouest* cruise and recovery of the propeller and shaft (Vogel 1998, D1, D8). There were also television crews from the Norfolk NBC news station and from the Swedish National Television. The Swedes reminded me that they had an interest in the *Monitor* because John Ericsson is their Swedish-born national hero. I was also surprised that their filming was not so much for the audience at home in Sweden, but that the Swedish National News has a U.S. cable channel for Swedish nationals in this country. Apparently there are quite a few Swedes in the United States, working in various Swedish and American companies, and they want to keep informed about home.

When our group boarded the *Kellie Chouest* we were greeted by Comdr. Chris Murray, commanding officer of the navy MDSU-2. He guided us to the ship's lounge and gave us a briefing on their operations on this cruise to the *Monitor* site as well as the organization of MDSU-2. All the equipment, including numerous tanks of helium-oxygen mixed gas, diving suits and helmets, umbilical cables, diving stage, control panels, television and radio, decompression chambers, winches and cranes, can be mobilized via military or commercial air transport to anywhere in the world in twenty-four hours. The thirty men and women divers can maintain almost continuous diving on a target by rotating three divers for each lowering. Two of the divers are lowered on a diving stage platform to the sea floor. The two divers, each with a separate umbilical, colored green and red, can carry out work on the target. For safe and clear communication, the divers are called "red" diver and "green" diver to avoid any confusion. Meanwhile, the third diver is completely suited up on deck; this

Two MDSU-2 divers are being readied for lowering on the diving stage platform. The navy divers completed more dives on the *Monitor* wreck site than had occurred during all previous cruises combined. Comdr. Chris Murray checks out the "green" diver on the left and Lt. Chuck Hulsizer checks out the "red" diver on the right.

diver is the "yellow" diver and has a yellow umbilical. The yellow diver is on standby for emergency situations. If needed to rescue the other divers he or she can quickly enter the water. The two divers on the bottom can dive for about twenty to thirty minutes before returning to the *Kellie Chouest* for about two hours' stay in a decompression chamber. As soon as two divers are back on deck, another team of three divers is suited up and two are lowered to the bottom again. Using this procedure, MDSU-2 logged more diving hours on the *Monitor* site during this one cruise than all divers on previous cruises.

Murray mentioned with pride that MDSU-2 divers had succeeded in cutting the propeller shaft and recovering the famous four-bladed *Monitor* propeller. He seemed well aware of the importance of this accomplishment. The propeller is a major artifact of the *Monitor* and it should have been recovered as soon as possible. I noticed that the propeller and shaft were already wrapped for transport back to port. I asked Murray, "Can we unwrap the propeller and examine it?" To forestall any reluctance on the

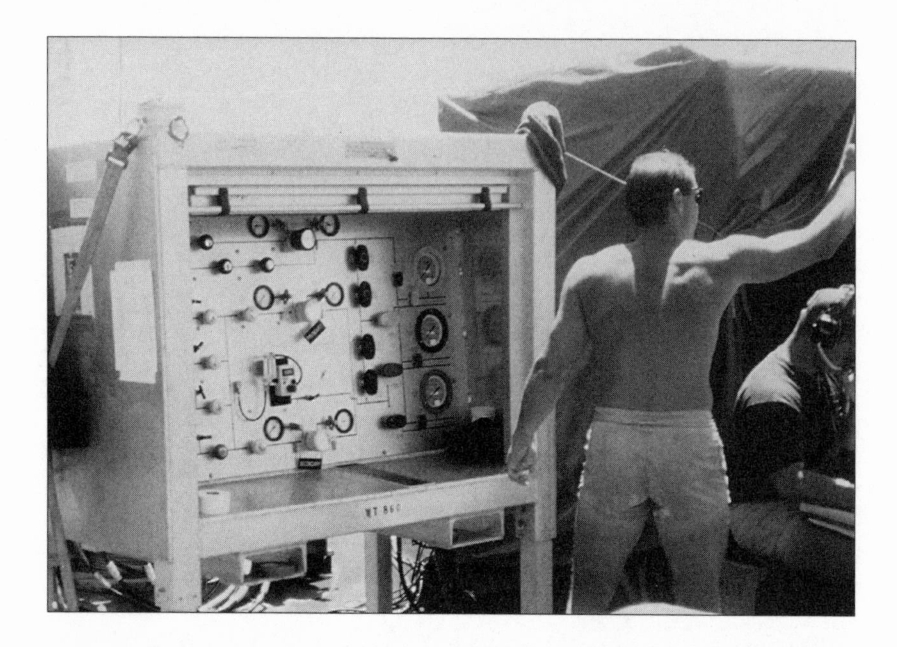

MDSU-2 divers at the pressure and mixture control panels and the voice communications center. The "red" and "green" dials are for the divers on the "red" and "green" umbilicals.

part of any officials at the briefing, I said, "You know these Swedish TV newsmen have come all the way from Stockholm to shoot it, I hope we can oblige them." Murray assured us that the propeller would be unwrapped.

We proceeded to a small laboratory space, which was used for dive preparations, to view a detailed three-dimensional model of the *Monitor* wreck. Murray showed us in detail how the shaft was cut, and how it was raised to the *Kellie Chouest.* For twenty-one hours the MDSU-2 divers worked on sawing the nine inch diameter wrought iron shaft. The divers used a hydraulically driven, carbide-blade guillotine saw. Changing worn-out blades, defeated by the strength of the *Monitor*'s iron, required the sawing process to continue for eight dive lowerings. Murray himself was the diver that operated the saw when the shaft parted. Murray proclaimed, "Hey, topside, she's free—bring her up" (Vogel 1998, D1). The propeller arrived on deck at 11:00 P.M.

Murray noted that the sawing operation was complicated by the close proximity of the five suspended lines at the point of operation: two um-

Comdr. Chris Murray in command of the MDSU-2 divers aboard the *Kellie Chouest* points to a scale model to explain how he sawed off the propeller shaft to recover the propeller from the *Monitor.*

bilicals for the divers, one hoisting cable attached to a bridle on the shaft, the hoist cable for the diving stage platform, and the hydraulic connection for the guillotine saw. At the 220 foot depth, these are long connecting lines. It would be an extremely dangerous situation if any current arose and tangled the lines. The remarkable condition at the *Monitor* wreck over these days in early June 1998, when the current was slack for days, provided a unique opportunity to recover the propeller. Murray took advantage of this situation and successfully cut the propeller shaft. So, rather than wait for a later cruise to recover the propeller, as originally planned (Monitor National Marine Sanctuary 1997, app., 60), the decision was made to grasp this opportunity to accomplish something very important for the preservation of the *Monitor.* Flexibility of this type is needed and should be encouraged.

While waiting for the propeller to be unwrapped, Murray took us to talk to John Broadwater, who was just returning from a dive to the *Monitor*. From the aft elevator platform of the *Kellie Chouest*, the NOAA personnel were using the platform to recover their untethered divers with a small zodiac boat. Goal 7 of the cruise plan was to assess these kinds of dives. Broadwater described the untethered technique.

The NOAA divers were using self-contained tanks of helium-oxygen gas mix, thus allowing them to freely swim around the wreck site. For safety, the divers descend and ascend to the *Monitor* wreck on buoyed lines attached to three thousand pound anchor weights. The ascent/descent lines are critical to prevent divers from being blown off course by abrupt current accelerations. Two ascent/descent lines on anchors weighing thousands of pounds had been permanently installed by NOAA at the *Monitor* wreck site.

Upon ascending, the untethered free divers must attach to the line to be able to stop at prescribed depths for the prescribed times for decompression. Without the line, it would be difficult to stay in the correct position. This is especially true if the current shifts or strengthens. If a diver cannot hold onto the ascent line in a strong current, the diver can attach to a floating buoy, a large blaze orange ball, and release the ascent line to float off in the current. Then, it is essential for the pickup crew in the zodiac boat to sight and follow the buoy and wait for the diver to decompress and rise. This procedure can take more than an hour in certain situations, and the zodiac chase can cover miles. During this time, other divers cannot enter the water until the zodiac is available. Also, such dives cannot be made after dark because the orange buoy must remain visible. Consequently, the untethered diving technique proved less safe and less efficient than the navy's tethered technique.

Broadwater asked me to examine some sediment cores that the navy divers had recovered. He mentioned that my past publication (Sheridan 1979) on the sediments at the *Monitor* site is referred to by NOAA. I was directed to Lt. Chuck Hulsizer, who was in charge of the coring attempts. He was very knowledgeable about testing of physical properties of marine sediments using shear vanes and penetrometers.

Hulsizer showed me two short cores less than three feet in length. They were both unconsolidated coarse sand of speckled black and tan color. Coal and rust fragments in the quartz sand are very common. As found in the twenty foot long core collected in April 1977, the surficial sand is only a thin cover on older Pleistocene sediments that include stiff clays and gravels (Sheridan 1978, 39; Sheridan 1979, 260). The Gulf Stream current is strong enough to carry and transport the sand to the northeast, while the Labrador current to the southwest is weaker, so the sand is not permanent at the *Monitor* site. It does accumulate temporally on the south side of the wreck, however, and buries the southern part of the overturned deck.

Wanting to recover longer cores, Hulsizer asked my advice about the coring device they were using. It was a four foot length of plastic tubing with a steel cutting edge and a sliding weight to hammer the core into the sea floor. Problems were identified for coring loose unconsolidated sediments with this device. There was no piston to create a pressure to keep the sediment up in the tube. There was no core catcher to prevent the loose sand from washing back out the mouth of the tube when pulling out and raising the corer. Also, the sliding weight was approximately ten pounds and did not provide the force needed for deep penetration. In contrast, we had used a two thousand pound weight to drive a twenty foot long piston corer into the *Monitor* site sediments. Hulsizer seemed to appreciate my advice.

We watched while two divers were launched on the diving stage platform. Orders were shouted across deck to controllers on the panels regulating gas pressures and mixtures. Checks were shouted for all hose connections and helmets, much like the check-off procedure before a plane takes off. The tether umbilical cables were tended by divers who would dive on a later shift. The tethers were several hundred feet long and flaked on the deck; they had to be carefully led to the ship's side as the divers were lowered on the diving stage. In strong currents it requires several hands to control these long tether umbilicals. The deck communications by voice and video with the divers was constant through the umbilicals.

After the dive, the divers were brought up on the diving stage. Stripping off their helmets and diving suits, down to their bathing suits, they moved quickly across the deck to the decompression chamber. They had twenty seconds to do this and a lieutenant counted down the seconds aloud with a stopwatch. The gases that the divers had breathed under pressure would cause potentially deadly ill effects when they reached the deck if decompression did not commence quickly.

Finally the propeller and shaft were unwrapped and available for our inspection. The encrustation, consisting of rust, sand, shells of clams and

Dr. Robert Sheridan stands before the *Monitor* propeller and shaft on board the salvage ship *Kellie Chouest*. Note the extensive encrustation.

barnacles, and calcium carbonate cement, was complete. About three quarters of an inch thick, the encrustation is about what is expected for corrosion in sea water, approximately one half inch per century. One of the large blades of the four-bladed propeller was broken, with a corner missing. The cut cross section of the shaft showed the saw marks. The rust stain on the cut surface was just a coating from the water flowing from the crust. I wiped away the rust stain, and pristine silver-gray wrought iron showed through. Where not corroded, the *Monitor*'s iron is in good shape. The toughness of the iron was evident to Murray when it took so long to saw through the nine inch diameter shaft. This bodes well for eventual preservation of the *Monitor*'s iron artifacts.

After seeing the propeller, my enthusiasm was evident and was documented during onboard television interviews with the Norfolk NBC news station and the Swedish National Television reporters. As usual, I stressed the need to get as much of the *Monitor* up as soon as possible. I reiterated that the longer the artifacts stay in the ocean, the worse the corrosion and disintegration. The *Monitor* is in a crisis situation.

Close-up view of the sawn cross section of the *Monitor* propeller shaft. The encrustation of the corroded and calcium carbonate–cemented rind is about three quarters of an inch thick. The near-pristine wrought iron shows the saw marks. The skull-and-cross-bones flag is the MDSU-2's symbol when they recover "treasure from the deep."

I congratulated Murray on his success in recovering the propeller. I bid my farewells to Broadwater and Murray, and then boarded the *Margie II* to shuttle back to Hatteras Village.

I was impressed by the Norfolk NBC news group. Upon the arrival of the *Margie II* at Hatteras Village, they had their mobile truck and satellite feed at the dock of Teach's Lair Mariner. The NBC reporters immediately did their on-site statements. By 6:00 P.M. in our room at the Sea Gull Motel, Karen and I watched my interview aboard the *Kellie Chouest* as it played on the local television news. Our ability to have near-instant communication and news in this country is outstanding.

The *Kellie Chouest* operations at the *Monitor* site ended on 10 June 1998. The treasure of the *Monitor*'s propeller and shaft was delivered to the Mariners' Museum at Newport News on 12 June (Vogel 1998, D8). This was one of the most important *Monitor* artifacts to be added to the museum's collections.

As fate would have it, the weather deteriorated shortly after the *Kellie Chouest* left the *Monitor* site. The planned NOAA phase of the 1998 operation at the *Monitor* site was abandoned after the bad weather persisted. No further diving could be accomplished. More often than not, successful cruises will not be achieved. Murray struck while the iron was hot, and another successful step in the recovery of the *Monitor* was accomplished.

14

The Engine Is Recovered

After returning from the *Kellie Chouest,* I was elated to see that recovery of the *Monitor*'s major artifacts was beginning. The 1998 *Kellie Chouest* operation was relatively simple in terms of the salvage operation. The propeller was on the upper part of the overturned wreck and exposed outside the remaining lower hull. The salvage procedure of attaching Kevlar straps to the propeller shaft, sawing through the shaft, and lifting was straightforward. The next recovery operations would not be so simple.

John Broadwater contacted me in July 1998 for more consultation on the core samples taken by the navy divers aboard the *Kellie Chouest:*

> We were delighted that you were able to visit the *Monitor* Sanctuary during the 1998 expedition. It was a pleasure to see you again and we appreciate your guidance in recovering core samples from the Sanctuary. In view of your expertise and your previous experience in analyzing core samples from the vicinity of the *Monitor* Sanctuary, we were wondering if you would be willing to analyze the samples recovered in 1998. Information on the sediment types may be crucial in planning for recovery of major components of the wreck (Broadwater 1998b, 1).

I quickly replied:

> Thank you for inviting me to visit the USS *Monitor* wreck site aboard the Salvage Vessel *Kellie Chouest* in June. I was very impressed with

> the navy diving operation and the leadership of Commander Chris Murray. . . .
>
> In spite of the difficulties of diving at the site, I am happy to see that at long last some action is being taken. The potential prize of recovering the turret is worth the effort. I want to encourage you in this effort and wish you success in the future. As one of the co-discoverers of the *Monitor* wreck I endorse the plans to recover the turret as proposed to Congress. I hope your office will lead the way in securing the funding for the project.
>
> Regarding the attempts to recover sediment cores by divers from the *Kellie Chouest,* I was disappointed to see the coring device being used. It was deficient in the amount of weight used to hammer the core barrel into the sediment and in the lack of a cutting edge and core catcher. The core tubes apparently were unable to penetrate more than a few feet beneath the sand and the lack of a core catcher allowed the sand to wash out on retrieval of the core. This is most unfortunate, especially in light of the other equipment available on the *Kellie Chouest.*
>
> For example, the hydraulic power used to run the saw that cut off the propeller shaft could also have been used to run a hydraulic vibrator on a diver-held vibracore with a cutting edge and core catcher. The tuggers used to lift the propeller are quite adequate to pull out a vibracore that might have penetrated ten feet of sediment. For excavations around the turret it would be useful to know what the sediment is like to about ten feet. This is especially true if there is some complication with an imbedded rifle shield. At those depths below the sea floor, there is a potential of encountering stiff clays, sands, gravels, and shell layers of Pleistocene age (Sheridan 1998, 1–2).

It appeared to me that the few feet of medium to coarse sand with the black specks (rust and coal fragments) recovered in the *Kellie Chouest* cores was the ephemeral layer of sand carried past the wreck by the Gulf Stream current. The Pleistocene sediments beneath the ephemeral sand layer are firm because they had been previously buried, dewatered, and slightly compacted. The flimsy coring device used in 1998 would not penetrate the Pleistocene sediments. These older firmer sediments will have to be excavated from around the overturned turret.

In summer 1999 Phase I, the preshoring archaeology, of NOAA's archaeology and recovery plan progressed. Loose artifacts were cleared from beneath the overhanging main deck and armor belt. In summer 2000 Phase II, the shoring beneath the hull, was completed, as well as the beginnings of Phase III, the removal of the lower hull and engine. I kept track of operations by checking the NOAA and Mariners' Museum websites.

A large salvage barge, with the deck area about as large as a football field, was used in the 2000 operations. Container trailers were mounted on the barge to provide the berthing, mess, laboratory, and office space for about sixty people. More important, the barge held a crane with a 350 ton hoist capacity. This was the size of crane that was going to be needed for hoisting the engine and its attached lower hull, a weight of more than thirty tons. The lift would include the engine and hull as well as an especially designed and constructed engine recovery structure (ERS) that weighs about ninety tons. The barge deck space also had to have sufficient room for the four legs of the large ERS. The barge's large deck area made it convenient to have the machinery aboard for the mixing and pumping of the cement to fill the grout bags for stabilization of the hull.

With about a month of time for the work with the barge and crane in 2000, there were the usual problems with the weather off Cape Hatteras. As previously discussed, the lift of the propeller by the *Kellie Chouest* was simple compared to what was needed for the engine recovery. When hoisting such large weights with cranes, the surface motion of the barge was critical. Lifts can only be done in the mildest sea states with only one to two foot waves and swells. Such mild sea states are rare off Cape Hatteras.

Good planning for the 2000 program allowed for "waiting on weather" time for the hoists. Meanwhile, the navy divers worked rapidly in relatively rough sea states to complete the shoring of the hull with grout bags. The individual Kevlar grout bags were installed in rows of increasing height from the bow area toward the turret. The rows ranged from two feet high nearer the bow to six feet high nearer the turret. The empty bags were put in place by the navy divers; they attached the bags to preemplaced metal anchor brackets. The bags then were pumped full of the grout cement until the different elevations were achieved and the rows of bags fit snugly under the inclined hull.

There was a feeling of desperation at times during the work in 2000.

The seas were rough and the lease time on the barge was being consumed. It was possible that the seas would never be calm enough to hoist the ERS with the crane and lower it to be installed over the *Monitor.* It would be too dangerous to attempt such an operation in rough seas. The seventy ton ERS bridge structure might swing when leaving the large deck and smash into the trailers and personnel. The heavy ERS might swing near the bottom and smash the *Monitor* wreck. It could happen that the barge lease would run out and the ERS would never leave the barge. What a loss of money that would be!

Fortunately, there was a short window of calm seas and the ERS bridge was lifted off the barge, lowered to the sea floor, and installed over the engine room area of the *Monitor* hull. In summer 2001, Capt. Chris Murray, the U.S. Navy supervisor of diving, explained to me the workings of the ERS using a scale model. The ERS was designed and built by the Office of the Supervisor of Salvage and Diving, Naval Sea Systems Command (SUPSAL/NAVSEA). The largest part of the ERS was a rectangular steel "bridge" about thirty feet high, sixty feet long, and twenty-five feet wide. With four support legs, it would straddle above the engine room hull. Another rectangular piece of steel grating called a "trolley" was attached to the upper part of the bridge. The trolley allowed horizontal movements and adjustment of positions of the engine lifting frame, which would be suspended from the trolley. Straps would be used to attach the engine and hull to the lifting frame.

The weather was not calm enough long enough to complete the engine lift during the 2000 operations. In the last few calm days, the trolley was lowered and divers attached it to the bridge. Then some smaller pieces of the *Monitor*—the skeg, the remaining propeller shaft, and some small engine room artifacts—were recovered by the divers. The ERS would remain installed over the stern area of the *Monitor* wreck until summer 2001 when the engine was finally recovered.

Broadwater wrote to me in May 2001, inviting me to visit the operation that summer at the *Monitor* site. "It's a rare opportunity during a year in which NOAA's goals are to recover the engine that has rested on the ocean's floor for over 140 years.... One of the most complex underwater artifact recovery efforts ever attempted.... I hope you'll be able to visit us this year—it's going to be much more complex than 1998!" (Broadwater 2001, 1).

I contacted Carol Myers, NOAA's liaison person at Hatteras Village. I told her I could come down to the *Monitor* operation on 25 July. By following the progress of operations to raise the engine, I knew how complex the operation would be. Knowing the weather and seas off Cape Hatteras, I thought the raising of the engine would happen later in the operation, which was planned to span more than a month, from 25 June through 31 July. Carol, however, felt I should come as early as possible in June. She thought the navy divers would be recovering the engine very early in the cruise and thought I should like to visit the operation before the engine was raised.

I was able to rearrange my schedule so I could get to the site on 12 July. Ron Steinwehr, an old high school buddy of mine and the best man at my wedding in 1966, accompanied me on the trip. A high school history and social studies teacher before retirement, he had a keen interest in the Civil War and the *Monitor*. He had a special research interest in General Steinwehr, who fought with the Union Army at Gettysburg.

Myers called me before my trip to advise me that she had contacted my local newspaper, the *Newark Star Ledger*, the largest paper in New Jersey. She advised the paper of my visit to the recovery operation, and suggested that a story be done on my visit and the recovery project in general. Organizing press visits and generating publicity for the project was part of Myers's job. Alexander (Alex) Lane, a *Star Ledger* reporter, called and said he would be making the trip; he interviewed me briefly over the phone.

On 12 July 2001, I met Myers in the lobby of the Hatteras Village Holiday Inn, where the NOAA and navy people were staying. They were using the hotel as a shore base of operations. I met Lane and Joe Epstein, a *Star Ledger* photographer. Accompanying us on the crew boat were several navy personnel as well as a television producer and an editor from NOVA, a television production company.

The two hour ride out to the *Monitor* site was rough. The wind was out of the northeast at ten to fifteen knots with five foot swells and breaking white caps. With the waves so high, jumping from the crew boat had to be well timed to get aboard the large salvage barge. The barge *Wotan* was owned by the Mason Gulf company and had been bare chartered by the navy for the recovery operation.

The *Wotan* was loaded with what looked like a small city of container trailers, stacked three stories high on one end of the barge. The container trailers provided the space for mess, berthing, laboratories, and offices for

The salvage barge *Wotan*, owned by the Mason Gulf Company, was chartered by the U.S. Navy for on-site work during the 2001 summer. The large five-hundred-ton crane on the *Wotan* successfully lifted the *Monitor*'s engine and attached lower hull on 16 July.

about one hundred personnel. Three stories of the container trailers and a smaller one hundred ton capacity crane on treaded tracks counterbalanced the weight of the five hundred ton capacity hoisting crane on the other end of the barge.

We met with Murray in the main control center office next to the base of the huge crane. Two television monitors showed the diving operation taking place. One monitor was from the helmet of one of the divers lowered from the *Wotan* on the diving stage. The tethered divers from the deck of the *Wotan*, lowered two at a time as a team, spent about thirty minutes on the bottom, and several hours in a deck decompression chamber.

The other television monitor showed the view from the helmet of a saturation diver. He came out of a diving bell that was lowered to a few feet above the wreck. The saturation divers each stayed on the bottom and worked for about four hours. The two-diver team stayed down in the bell for eight hours. Upon raising the bell, which was kept under pressure equal to that at the depth of the *Monitor*, the saturation divers stayed under pressure in a deck pressure chamber on the *Wotan*. Here they ate and slept under pressure. They continued this operation for up to two weeks, before finally decompressing at the end of the job. The saturation diving procedure allowed essentially an eight hour day of diving work on the *Monitor* wreck with far fewer divers than the tethered operation from the deck of the *Wotan*. This was a tremendous increase in efficiency and effectiveness.

Murray explained that the divers had spent many hours clearing the calcareous concretion that cemented the coal and other debris below the overturned engine to the engine itself. This concretion was removed by hammer and chisel and by a high pressure (two thousand pounds per square inch) jet hose. Once the area beneath the engine was cleared, flat chain-mail steel straps were threaded through the space beneath the engine. The straps were then shackled to turn-buckles and tightened. The turn-buckles were connected to Kevlar straps that were attached to the lifting frame. Six or seven straps were in place. After being secured to the lifting frame, hydraulic jacks supported the engine and hull while the lower hull braces and stanchions were cut free with saws. Murray said that the chain-mail straps would not be frayed by the *Monitor*'s jagged iron, as Kevlar straps might have been, and the flat steel straps would not cut into the *Monitor*'s iron, as steel cables might do.

Using a scale model of the *Monitor* wreck and the ERS bridge, Murray explained the use of the ERS. Its purpose was to permit hydraulic lifting of the engine with the lifting frame and trolley in order to first secure the engine and hull to the bridge. The bridge's four feet were securely set in the stiff Pleistocene clay beneath the *Monitor*. Any engine motion would be disconnected from the motion of the surface barge and crane, which were rolling in the swell. Despite eight anchors, the *Wotan* rolled badly in five foot swells. The cranes and the three-story container building, however, did make the *Wotan* top heavy.

The engine and hull next would be moved clear of the *Monitor* wreck and suspended beneath the bridge of the ERS. On a very calm day the bridge could be lifted without banging into the *Monitor* wreck. Because *Wotan*'s deck was totally occupied with containers, cranes, and diving equipment, the ERS bridge holding the engine could not be landed on the *Wotan*. A second bare-decked barge would be brought to the site to carry the ERS and engine back to the SUPSAL/NASEA base in Little Creek, Virginia. The large deck area on another barge would provide maneuvering room for the landing of the bulky ninety ton ESR and its cargo—the thirty ton engine and hull.

Broadwater joined the briefing in the control center. He showed us a scale model of the hull and engine. The famous side-lever engine, invented by Ericsson to fit in the low-overhead space of the shallow draft *Monitor,* was a unique artifact of great importance. Previous steam engines on larger ships had vertical cylinders and top levers, because space was not a constraint.

I visited the diver launch area on the midships area of the *Wotan.* Chief Machinist Mate Russ Mallet, a MDSU-2 master diver, showed me his name on the "Wall of Shame"; he was involved in a situation that required the launching of a "yellow" diver on this cruise. Just as he was coming up through the cut hole in the hull bottom, Murray had jumped off the diving stage and landed on him.

Over Mallet's shoulder I watched the television monitors. I was impressed with how quickly the tethered divers dismantled pipes and copper tubing from the engine. Pipes as long as three to four feet were being removed and placed in a metal cage basket, which the smaller crane then lifted to the deck of the *Wotan.*

Myers next introduced me to Comdr. Barbara Scholley, the commanding officer of MDSU-2. I complimented her on the diving operation. It was the most complex diving operation I had ever witnessed. I told her there were so many television monitors all over the *Wotan* at various stations, and in color, that I was reminded of our staring at a single black-and-white monitor when we saw the first video pictures of the *Monitor* from aboard the *Eastward* in 1973. The color images were so clear compared to our first lined and grainy images. It was beautiful!

Scholley informed me that as many as seventy to one hundred divers had gone down to the *Monitor* wreck during this cruise. This was not merely a job for the thirty divers of MDSU-2, but included divers from Pearl Harbor–based MDSU-1, SEAL (Sea, Air, Land) units, and several other navy units.

I was able to view some artifacts recovered by the divers as they cleared the spaces beneath the engine. Jeff Johnston, an NOAA historian, was in charge of the artifacts that were carefully stored in water-bath containers. I saw a hardened-rubber hair comb. Numerous glass oil lamp chimneys were found intact. A fancy, decoratively molded, brass wall holder for an oil lamp was recovered. The details of the brass decorations

On board the salvage barge *Wotan*, Dr. Robert Sheridan views and examines a well-preserved engine room thermometer recovered by U.S. Navy divers. The mercury is still in the glass tube and correctly measures the temperature on the deck of the *Wotan*.

were still evident; the gimbaled mount still moved relative to the wall bracket. The most remarkable artifact recovered was an engine room thermometer, encased in a calibrated and marked holder of brass and copper. Liquid mercury was still in the intact glass tube. Amazingly, the thermometer still worked, accurately registering 82°F on the deck of the *Wotan*.

The good preservation of these delicate artifacts bodes well for the recovery of more artifacts in the future. The intact glass items, such as the thermometer and the oil lamp chimneys, are environmentally significant. As mentioned in previous chapters, there had been suggestions that the most extensive damage to the *Monitor* was man-made, caused by a World War II depth charging. An explosion would have shattered these artifacts. This depth charging myth had also reduced the appreciation of the extensive damage that can be caused by nature. It led to the false impression that the *Monitor* would be "safe" and "secure" at its seafloor location if further human damage could be prevented.

Taking a phone call in the control center office, I heard the weather forecast. That evening the seas and winds would get worse. Small craft warnings were being issued. The weather would abate by the following Monday or Tuesday to one to three foot seas. Waiting on the weather would continue over the weekend. Maybe the lift of the engine could occur on Monday.

I had to leave the *Wotan* on Sunday to begin a family vacation trip. I would not see the raising of the engine. I bid my farewells to Murray and Broadwater and wished them luck with the raising of the engine on Monday. The increasingly stormy seas made the jump from the *Wotan* to the crew boat deck a challenge. On my first attempt I miscoordinated my jump with the peak height of the crew boat. The *Wotan* deck hands caught me before I had leapt down to the crew boat. The second opportunity was better and I landed on my feet thanks to the helping hands of the crew boat people. No matter how many times I have jumped to pickup boats from large vessels, it is always scary.

I returned home, and, as planned, began our family trip to Kentucky. We heard the radio and television reports about the raising of the engine on 16 July 2001. When we returned home the following week, we eagerly perused our *Newark Star Ledger* newspapers. Alex Lane's front page story, along with color photographs of me and the *Wotan* taken by Joe Epstein, gave a good account of the raising of the *Monitor* engine (Lane 2001, 1, 6).

The engine and lower hull portion were lifted while attached by Kevlar straps to the lifting frame, which was attached by chains to the trolley and bridge of the ERS. The entire ERS was secured to an empty barge, and towed to Newport News Shipbuilding's facilities. The engine, hull, and lifting frame were then removed from the ERS and transferred to an especially built steel cradle for transport by barge and truck to the Newport News Mariners' Museum. Lane stopped by the Mariners' Museum to interview Curtiss Peterson, now the curator to oversee conservation of the *Monitor* artifacts. "The engine will be stored behind the Mariner's Museum in Newport News, Va., where it will soak for 10 years on public display as chemicals eat away barnacles, oysters, and other hangers-on" (Lane 2001, 6). Actually, by passing electrical currents through the metal, electrolysis removes salts from within the iron over many years and thus stabilizes the iron against further corrosion.

While on board the *Wotan,* I asked Broadwater how the recovery was being funded. Had Congress appropriated the twenty two million dollars that had been estimated in his testimony before the Oceans Subcommittee? Broadwater said no. As discussed in previous chapters, much of the costs of the NOAA and navy personnel came from existing operating budgets; their time spent on the various aspects of the *Monitor* project has been considered part of their normal duties. The costs of leasing the lift barges and cranes, as well as outfitting the barges with the necessary equipment, has required separately budgeted expenditures. Broadwater said that Congress had increased funding in an existing navy program to cover these expenditures. "Most of the funding of the retrieval—$2 million last year [2000] and $4.9 million this year [2001] is coming from the Navy Legacy Resource Management Program" (Lane 2001, 6). This program funds natural and cultural resource projects within the Department of Defense. The training in underwater salvage that the navy is gaining, especially in such a challenging environment, is well worth the expenditure.

15

Recent Achievements and the Monitor's Future

The next phases of NOAA's archaeology and recovery plan, Phase IV, the removal of the armor belt section over the turret, and Phase V, the recovery of the turret, were planned to be executed in 2002–3. According to Bill Geroux, who interviewed John Broadwater in 1998, "A proposed timetable in the plan suggests the project could be completed by 2003. But that's not much more than a guess at this point, Broadwater acknowledged" (Geroux 1998, 4). I expected the turret recovery to be perhaps ten times more complex than recovering the engine and therefore Phases IV and V would extend beyond 2003.

First, a decision had to be made about whether to cut the guns free of the turret and raise them separately. It may be more efficient, however, to keep the cannons in the turret and recover both guns and turret together. Then removal of the guns from the turret might be possible from a shore-based water tank. New tank facilities must be built on the Newport News Mariners' Museum campus to hold the turret and guns. There was ample space there, so no new land had to be purchased. There was sufficient time for such construction before the guns and turret would reach the surface. Broadwater told me on the *Wotan* in 2001 that the Mariners' Museum would be funding the construction, the processing of the artifacts, and the hiring of Curtiss Peterson as a conservator from its own resources. Eventually, the preserved and restored artifacts would be displayed in a new Mariners' Museum "Monitor Center," which would be a complete "interpretive exhibit" (Monitor National Marine Sanctuary 1997, app., 71).

I was happily surprised my pessimistic prediction about the length of time required for the turret's recovery was proven wrong. In a cruise during July and early August 2002, the enormous efficiency of the navy divers completed Phase IV, the removal of the overlying deck, and Phase V, the recovery of the turret. The joint NOAA–U.S. Navy six and a half million dollar effort to recover the turret and guns of the *Monitor* using the barge *Wotan* was a success.

The navy increased the diving hours by using four saturation divers instead of two, and did six hour saturation dives instead of four hour dives for each diver each day. Working a twelve hour on–twelve hour off schedule greatly improved the efficiency. In this continuous saturation diver mode, the number of saturation diving hours increased threefold over the previous cruise's hours.

Principal participants were Chief Scientist John Broadwater, Historian Jeff Johnston, Capt. Chris Murray, and Capt.-Select Barbara Scholley. In addition to the MDSU-2 divers, other navy divers brought the total diving contingent to more than 150.

The recovery of the turret and guns was a major engineering feat. For the salvage, a specially designed eight-armed "spider" claw device was pried under the lower edge of the overturned turret. The sediment in the 150-ton turret was suctioned out, and the two Dahlgren 16-ton cannons were strapped to the upper part of the spider's lifting frame. The lifting frame with the turret was then lifted a few feet and positioned over a base platform; turnbuckles on each of the eight legs were connected by divers and tightened to bind the spider lifting frame to the base platform. The total weight of the turret, guns, and lifting apparatus was over two hundred tons.

During the operation, divers uncovered human skeletons beneath one of the cannons. Some of the skeleton bones were recovered for possible identification and proper military burial. Some bones were cemented to the guns and will have to be removed later. Some of the *Monitor*'s sailors had been trapped in the turret when the *Monitor* sank.

I was privileged to witness the raising of the turret from aboard the research vessel *Cape Fear*, which was positioned within about fifty yards of the *Wotan*. The *Cape Fear*'s captain skillfully maneuvered the ship to place us in the best light, with the sinking sun over our shoulders, for taking photographs of the turret.

The "spider" claw lifting frame and base platform, holding the *Monitor*'s turret along with the two Dahlgren cannons inside, were lifted by the barge *Wotan*'s five hundred ton crane. The raising of the turret was completed on 5 August 2002.

The rigging of the turret lifting frame was a "sling," or bridle, that included spreaders. Shackling the sling to the frame required several hours of work by the saturation divers. After the divers completed their work and were recovered to the *Wotan*, the slow lift began. Removing parts of the sling as the lift progressed took about an hour. At about 5:55 P.M. on 5 August 2002 the turret of the *Monitor* broke the surface of the ocean to see the light of day for the first time in nearly 140 years! Everyone cheered, and I said a silent prayer in the memory of John Newton to thank him for his gift to the American people. Landing the turret on the deck of the *Wotan* a few minutes later was the most important step so far in the recovery of the *Monitor*'s iron from the deep.

While waiting for current and wind conditions to improve the day before the successful lift of the turret, I had been lucky to have lunch ashore with John Hightower and his wife. Hightower is the chief executive officer and director of the Newport News Mariners' Museum. As I was, he also was considered a *Monitor* VIP that was going out on the *Cape Fear* to see the raising of the turret. Hightower had informed me that the tank for holding the turret had already been constructed at the museum, and that they were expecting to receive the turret on 9 August 2002. There are portholes through the tank walls so visitors can view the turret close up. Hightower also discussed the plans to open a complete interpretive Monitor Center at the museum in 2007. He had already begun a fund raising campaign to raise thirty million dollars for the center. The conservation and display of the *Monitor*'s artifacts are his responsibility.

The final phase of NOAA's archaeology and recovery plan, Phase VI, the post-removal survey and stabilization, is currently under way. Broadwater says that some smaller objects, such as the engine that turned the turret, would be searched for and might be recovered. Smaller debris and artifacts would also be removed. Only smaller vessels will be needed as opposed to the large barges and cranes that were necessary to recover the turret and guns.

The conservation of the large *Monitor* artifacts will proceed in tanks over the next two to three decades. During this time, visitors to the Mariners' Museum will be able to view these artifacts in their tanks, and see the "behind the scenes" work of the conservator. This will provide a valuable educational experience. Broadwater said that the Mariners' Museum expected to recoup its investment in the *Monitor* artifacts and exhibits from the visiting public. "During 1996, The Mariners' Museum had over 100,000 paying visitors from all fifty states and eleven foreign countries" (Monitor National Marine Sanctuary 1997, app., 69). The museum excellently serves patrons interested in maritime history. Broadwater stated that the museum administrators hope to increase the number of visitors with the newly added attraction of the *Monitor* artifacts.

Criticisms by archaeologists have arisen, based on the expense of the entire endeavor versus the value of the *Monitor* artifacts. The pure archaeological value of the *Monitor* artifacts can be validly questioned. The value of an artifact to an archaeologist is measured by how much new knowledge is gained from that piece. This standard works well for prehistoric artifacts where the physical piece is all that might be known about some subject, in the absence of a written record. Most prehistoric artifacts, therefore, have immense value to an archaeologist. In the archaeological sense, the first *Monitor* artifact recovered in the exploration stage, the decklight cover, produced new knowledge because it provided "ironclad proof" of identification (Newton 1975, 60; Sheridan 1977, 10; Sheridan 1979, 256).

The other recovered *Monitor* artifacts, on the other hand, are described in the written record, albeit with some small uncertainties in details. Not only is there a written record, but there exist artistic, engineering drawing, and photographic records as well. An archaeologist rightfully can ask, "What new knowledge will be gained by the recovery and display of the *Monitor* artifacts?" Are the artifacts really of any archaeological significance?

As discussed in previous chapters, another value of an artifact is its inspirational value. Artifacts are a physical record of some historical event; the artifacts make history real to the viewer. History can become more than mere words on pages in some musty history book. The artifacts evoke a "tactile response" from the viewer that enhances an appreciation of history (Monitor National Marine Sanctuary 1997, app., 70).

The value of an artifact has to be gauged by the significance of the history it represents. I do not think anyone disputes the significance of the *Monitor* as a seminal point in the evolution of naval architecture and naval warfare. The *Monitor*'s victory over the *Merrimac* will equally remain historically significant. The *Monitor* also helped maintain the Northern blockade at Hampton Roads.

The *Monitor*'s artifacts provide the physical evidence that prove that marine geophysicists have the skills and technology to locate wrecks. The future Monitor Center display will pay honor to these abilities. John Newton's legacy will be affirmed.

The tremendous effort being put forward by the navy divers to salvage "one of their own," and the risks inherent in those efforts, will be honored by the display of the *Monitor* artifacts. The ocean engineering skills being utilized display our preeminence in marine and offshore technology. This preeminence will be honored in the future Monitor Center.

The *Monitor* display will honor John Ericsson, the genius inventor of this extraordinary vessel. There are many statues of Ericsson already in the United States, but when viewers see the major artifacts, and realize what was involved in saving them, then they will realize how much our nation appreciates and treasures innovative thinking skills.

The exposure of the *Monitor* artifacts to hundreds of thousands of visitors each year will give the sailors and officers who served and died on the *Monitor* the remembrances they deserve. The sacrifice and courage of the men helped save the Union. Our nation was preserved. The *Monitor*'s crew deserves this memorial.

I always have viewed the *Monitor* recovery more as a salvage project rather than an archaeological project. However, attempts to deal with the *Monitor* wreck as an archaeological site, following the rigors of precisely locating fragments and objects, may provide new and as yet unknown information. The artifacts' positions are the result of the processes of the sinking and the subsequent action of waves and currents. Their location fits the scenario of capsizement, rolling to starboard, and sinking by the stern, but just the orientation of the wreck and logic tell us that much. At this point it is hard to tell what benefits will be derived from knowing the precise location of the glass jars or a wine bottle or the glass oil-lamp chimneys.

Another important aspect of creating a Monitor Center for display of the artifacts is the expression of appreciation for our country's role as a maritime nation. I was impressed with the respect for maritime heritage displayed by the Norwegians when I visited the Viking Ship Museum in Oslo. The Vikings were present in a huge part of the world in their time, from what is now Newfoundland and New Brunswick, Canada, to the eastern European plains. The Swedes have the *Wasa* Museum in Stockholm, and the United Kingdom has the recovered *Mary Rose* displayed in a museum. These wooden warships exemplify the navies of their time, and reflect those nations' glory as maritime powers.

Saving and displaying the *Monitor*'s most important artifacts would be a statement that the United States has also played a significant role in maritime history. The *Monitor* spawned a new ironclad U.S. Navy that became the most powerful in the world at the end of the Civil War. The great international races for iron and steel dreadnaughts and battleships began. The U.S. Navy kept pace and proved that it was a world-class fighting force of global reach during the Spanish-American War. The modern U.S. Navy has maintained dominance ever since for the benefit of the security of its grateful citizens.

I appreciate the restoration work that is under way and look forward to the future presentation of the *Monitor* artifacts in the Monitor Center at Newport News Mariners' Museum.

References

Arnold, J. B. III, G. M. Fleshman, D. B. Hill, C. E. Peterson, W. K. Stewart, S. R. Gegg, G. P. Watts Jr., and C. Weldon. 1991. *The 1987 Expedition to the Monitor National Marine Sanctuary: Data Analysis and Final Report.* Washington, D.C.: Sanctuaries and Reserves Division, NOAA.

Arrhenius, O., L. Barkman, and E. Sjostrand. 1973. *Conservation of Old Rusty Iron Objects, Reduction of Rust with Hydrogen Gas.* Bulletin No. 61E. Stockholm: Swedish Corrosion Institute, 1–40.

Barkman, L. 1978a. The *Monitor:* Her Value in American and International Minds, in *The* Monitor, *Its Meaning and Future,* ed. L. E. Tise. Washington, D.C.: Preservation Press, National Trust for Historic Preservation in the United States, 68–71.

———. 1978b. The Management of Historic Shipwreck Recovery and Conservation as Experienced from the Wasa, in *The* Monitor, *Its Meaning and Future,* ed. L. E. Tise. Washington, D.C.: Preservation Press, National Trust for Historic Preservation in the United States, 101–11.

Bass, G. F. 1978. The *Monitor:* An Archaeological Venture, in *The* Monitor, *Its Meaning and Future,* ed. L. E. Tise. Washington, D.C.: Preservation Press, National Trust for Historic Preservation in the United States, 123–25.

Berent, I. M. 1985. (April) The Crewmen of the U.S.S. *Monitor:* A Biographical Directory, *Monitor National Marine Sanctuary Historical Report Series* 2, no. 1.

Bradley, Sen. B. 1993. (11 January) Letter to Mrs. Reardon's Eighth Grade History Class, Readington, N.J. (copy in author's possession).

Brennan, W. 1975. (April) The Monitor Marine Sanctuary: An Historic Ship Launches an Important Marine Program. *NOAA magazine,* 12–15.

Broad, W. J. 1997. (2 December) Saving the Ship That Revolutionized War at Sea. *New York Times,* F1, F6.

Broadwater, J. D. 1996. Applications of Technology in the Monitor National Marine Sanctuary: The Coastal Ocean-Prospects for the 21st Century, *Proceedings from the Oceans 96 MTS/IEEE Conference,* Houston, Tex., 1269–73.

———. 1997a. Rescuing the *Monitor:* Stabilization and Recovery Efforts at the Monitor National Marine Sanctuary, in *Underwater Archaeology,* ed. D. C. Lacey. Tucson, Ariz.: Society of Historical Archaeology, 54–61.

———. 1997b. (4 December) Letter to Robert Sheridan Requesting Review of Long Range Plan for U.S.S. *Monitor* (original in author's possession).

———. 1998a. (6 May) Letter to Robert Sheridan Inviting Participation in 1998 Summer Expedition (original in author's possession).

———. 1998b. (27 July) Letter to Robert Sheridan Regarding Core Samples at *Monitor* Site (original in author's possession).

———. 2001. (25 May) Letter to Robert Sheridan Inviting Participation in 2001 Summer Expedition (original in author's possession).

Butts, F. B. 1885. (December) The Loss of the *Monitor,* by a Survivor, *Century Magazine* 31:299–302.

Carey, J. J. 1990. (4 January) *Acceptance of Appeal in the Matter of Gary Gentile for Permit Applications for the Monitor National Marine Sanctuary.* Washington, D.C.: U.S. Department of Commerce, Deputy Assistant Administrator, NOAA (copy in author's possession).

Carper, Congressman T. 1983. (6 October) Letter to Robert Sheridan Regarding North Carolina Involvement in the Management of the *Monitor* (original in author's possession).

Childress, Lt. Comdr. F. 1977. (October) The Lantern, *NOAA magazine.*

———. 1978a. Seeking a New Approach to Ocean Management, in *The* Monitor, *Its Meaning and Future,* ed. L. E. Tise. Washington, D.C.: Preservation Press, National Trust for Historic Preservation in the United States, 6–8.

———. 1978b. NOAA/Harbor Branch Foundation, Inc. Expedition for Stereo Photography and Artifact Retrieval, in *The* Monitor, *Its Meaning and Future,* ed. L. E. Tise. Washington, D.C.: Preservation Press, National Trust for Historic Preservation in the United States, 42–44.

Childress, Lt. Comdr. F., G. P. Watts, R. W. Cook, and C. C. Slama. 1977. *Preliminary Report: Stereo Photography and Artifact Retrieval, 16 July–2 August 1977 Monitor Marine Sanctuary.* Washington, D.C.: NOAA, Department of Commerce.

Crooke, R. C. 1976. *Glomar Explorer: Innovative Engineering Features.* Houston, Tex.: Global Marine Development Inc.

Davis, W. C. 1975. *Duel between the First Ironclads.* New York: Doubleday and Company, Inc.

deKay, J. T. 1997. *Monitor.* New York: Walker and Company.

Edgerton, H. E. 1977. (22 April) Letter to Mr. Edwin Link Inviting Him to Use His Diving Submersibles on the *Monitor* (copy in author's possession).

Editorial. 1976a. (January–February) How They Found the *Monitor, Army Reserve Magazine.* Washington, D.C.: Chief Army Reserve, Pentagon, 15–18.

———. 1976b. (December) Glomar Explorer's Many Technical Innovations, *Ocean Industry,* 67–73.

———. 1985. National Trust for Historic Preservation Joins Effort to Preserve *Monitor* on Tenth Anniversary of Sanctuary, *Cheesebox* 4, no. 1, 1–2.

Ericsson, J. 1885. (December) The Monitors, *Century Magazine* 31: 280–99.

Ewing, M., J. L. Worzel, and A. C. Vine. 1967. Early Development of Ocean-Bottom Photography at Woods Hole Oceanographic Institution and Lamont Geological Observatory, in *Deep Sea Photography*, ed. J. B. Hersey. Baltimore, Md.: Johns Hopkins Press, 13–39.

Farr, A. 1997. (June) The Real Genius Behind the *Monitor*, *Civil War Times*, 34–36.

Foster, N. 1985. Remarks on Tenth Anniversary of the Monitor National Marine Sanctuary, *Cheesebox* 4, no. 1, 5–8.

Friend, J. H., Jr. 1978. U.S.S. *Tecumseh:* Child of the *Monitor*, in *The* Monitor, *Its Meaning and Future*, ed. L. E. Tise. Washington, D.C.: Preservation Press, National Trust for Historic Preservation in the United States, 57–59.

Geer, G. S., W. Marvel, W. C. Davis, and the Mariner's Museum. 2000. *The* Monitor *Chronicles, One Sailor's Account: Today's Campaign to Recover the Civil War Wreck*. New York: Simon and Schuster.

Gentile, G. 1993. *Ironclad Legacy: Battle of the U.S.S.* Monitor. Philadelphia, Pa.: Gentile Productions.

Geographica. 1994. (June) Historic Casualty: The *Monitor* Disintegrates, *National Geographic* 185, no. 6, geog. 4.

Geroux, B. 1992. (28 September) Divers Nearly Die Exploring *Monitor*. *Richmond Times-Dispatch*, A1, A6.

———. 1998. (15 January) Time to Do More Than Monitor the Ironclad, *Richmond Times-Dispatch*, 4 pp.

Gibson, J. T. 1979. The *Monitor:* Anchored to the Deep? *Historic Preservation* 31, no. 2, 45–49.

Global Marine Development Inc. 1976. *The Recovery of the U.S.S.* Monitor, *A Bicentennial Program*, A Proposal. Houston, Tex.: Global Marine Development Inc.

Gorman, B. 1980. (January/February) U.S.S. *Monitor:* The First . . . , *NOAA magazine*, 1–3.

Greene, S. D. 1956. In the "Monitor" Turret, in *Battles and Leaders of the Civil War* (selections from original 1887–88 edition of R. U. Johnson and C. C. Buel), ed. N. Bradford. New York: New American Library, 111–18.

Guernsey, A. H., and H. M. Alden. 1866. *Harper's Pictorial History of the Civil War*. New York: Fairfax Press.

Harper's Weekly. 1863. *Reports on the* Monitor *and* Merrimac, vols. 6 and 7, 15 February 1862–24 January 1863. New York: Harper and Brothers.

Hayes, J. D. 1969. *Samuel Francis Dupont: A Selection from His Civil War Letters*, vol. 3. Ithaca, N.Y.: Cornell University Press.

Hoehling, A. A. 1976. *Thunder at Hampton Roads*. Englewood Cliffs, N.J.: Prentice Hall, Inc.

Hooke, W. H. 1992. (5 November) Letter to Robert Sheridan from NOAA Acting Chief Scientist. Washington, D.C.: U.S. Department of Commerce (original in author's possession).

Hubinger, B. 1997. (June) Can We Ever Raise the *Monitor? Civil War Times,* 38–48.

Keeler, W. F. 1964. Aboard the USS *Monitor;* 1862: The Letters of Acting Paymaster William Frederick Keeler, U.S. Navy, to His Wife, Anna, in *Naval Letters Series,* vol. 1., ed. R. W. Daly. Annapolis, Md.: U.S. Naval Institute.

Keith, D. H. 1978. An Evaluation of Underwater Archaeological Systems Which May Be Applicable to the Excavation of the U.S.S. *Monitor,* in *The* Monitor, *Its Meaning and Future,* ed. L. E. Tise. Washington, D.C.: Preservation Press, National Trust for Historic Preservation in the United States, 89–92.

Knecht, R. W. 1976. (27 May) Letter to John Newton of Monitor Research and Recovery Foundation Granting NOAA Permit for Magnetic Profiling Survey (copy in author's possession).

Lane, A. 2001. (17 July) History Resurfaces: Recovery of *Monitor* Gratifies Rutgers Prof, *Newark Star Ledger,* 1, 6.

Lautenberg, Sen. F. R. 1993. (6 January) Letter to Mrs. Reardon's Eighth Grade History Class, Readington, N.J. (copy in author's possession).

Lundeberg, P. K. 1978. The *Monitor:* Fragile Survivor, in *The* Monitor, *Its Meaning and Future,* ed. L. E. Tise. Washington, D.C.: Preservation Press, National Trust for Historic Preservation in the United States, 65–68.

———. 1984. Remarks on Tenth Anniversary of the Monitor National Marine Sanctuary, *Cheesebox* 4, no. 2, 4–5.

Marston, J. 1862. (13 March) The Naval Action in Hampton Roads (Captain's Report to Gideon Welles on the Battle between *Monitor* and *Merrimac* from U.S. Steamer *Roanoke*), *Hunterdon County Democrat Newspaper* (Flemington, N.J.).

Marx, R. F. 1967. *Always Another Adventure.* New York: World Publishing Company.

McCauley, Sgt. J. J. 1869. *"Got Martching [sic] Orders," A Memorandum By James Joseph McCauley, Co. H, 177 Reg. of Pennsylvania Drafted Militia 1862, As recounted in 1869,* transcribed by Karen McCauley Sheridan, 2001, 43 pp. (original in author's possession).

Midshipmen, Class of 1974. 1974. *Project Cheesebox: A Journey into History,* Research Manuscript. Annapolis, Md.: United States Naval Academy 2:357–745.

Miller, Lt. E. M. 1978a. *U.S.S.* Monitor*: The Ship That Launched a Modern Navy.* Annapolis, Md.: Leeward Press.

———. 1978b. The Use of the Alcoa Sea Probe to Verify the *Monitor* Wreck Site, in *The* Monitor, *Its Meaning and Future,* ed. L. E. Tise. Washington, D.C.: Preservation Press, National Trust for Historic Preservation in the United States, 29–33.

———. 1981. Bound for Hampton Roads, *Civil War Times* 20, no. 4, 22–31.
Millholland, J. A. 1978. The Legal Framework of the Monitor Marine Sanctuary, in *The* Monitor, *Its Meaning and Future,* ed. L. E. Tise. Washington, D.C.: Preservation Press, National Trust for Historic Preservation in the United States, 19–22, 31.
Mindell, D. A. 2000. *War, Technology, and Experience Aboard the U.S.S.* Monitor. Baltimore, Md.: Johns Hopkins University Press.
Monitor National Marine Sanctuary. 1997. *Charting a New Course for the Monitor, Comprehensive, Long Range Preservation Plan with Options for Management, Stabilization, Preservation, Recovery, Conservation and Exhibition of Materials and Artifacts from the Monitor National Marine Sanctuary,* Draft. Newport News, Va.: U.S. Department of Commerce, National Oceanic and Atmospheric Administration, 125 pp.
———. 1998. Monitor*'s Distress Signal Heard: NOAA Plans First Phase of Stabilization Study, 1998* Monitor *Expedition,* http://www.nos.gov/nmsp/monitor/education/Whats New.html.
Mrs. Reardon's Eighth Grade History Classes. 1992. (17 December) Letter to New Jersey Congressman and Senators Asking for Help to Save the *Monitor,* Readington, N.J. (copy in author's possession).
Muga, B. J. 1983. An Engineer Looks at the *Monitor, Cheesebox* 2 no. 1, 5–8.
National Geographic Society. 1970. Ghost Fleet of the Outer Banks (map), *National Geographic Magazine.*
National Oceanic and Atmospheric Administration (NOAA). 1979. *Operations Manual, Monitor Marine Sanctuary, an Archaeological and Engineering Assessment.* Rockville, Md.: Office of Coastal Zone Management, NOAA.
Newton, C. R. 1987. (26 February) Letter to Robert Sheridan Indicating That "Hatch Cover" Will Be Deposited in Newport News Mariner's Museum (original in author's possession).
Newton, J. 1973. (11 May) Memo to H. E. Edgerton, R. E. Sheridan, and G. P. Watts on Cruise Planning (copy in author's possession).
Newton, J. G. 1975. (January) How We Found the *Monitor, National Geographic Magazine,* 48–61.
———. 1978. U.S.S. *Monitor* Found: The Beginning of an Epic Quest, in *The* Monitor, *Its Meaning and Future,* ed. L. E. Tise. Washington, D.C.: Preservation Press, National Trust for Historic Preservation in the United States, 45–46.
Newton, J. G., H. E. Edgerton, R. E. Sheridan, and C. P. Watts. 1974. *Final Expedition Report: Cruise E-12-73.* Beaufort, N.C.: Duke University Marine Laboratory.
Newton, J. G., R. E. Sheridan, H. E. Edgerton, W. N. Still, and C. J. Clausen. 1976a. *Request for a Research Permit for a Baseline Magnetic Profiling of the Monitor Marine Sanctuary.* Beaufort, N.C.: Monitor Research and Recovery Foundation.
———. 1976b. *A Proposal for Environmental Engineering Studies and Site Chart-*

ing at the Monitor Marine Sanctuary. Beaufort, N.C.: Monitor Research and Recovery Foundation, 86 pp.

NOAA Sanctuary and Reserves Division. 1992. *The Monitor National Marine Sanctuary Draft Revised Management Plan.* Washington, D.C.: National Ocean Survey, NOAA, Department of Commerce, 90 pp.

North Carolina Department of Cultural Resources. 1978. *The Monitor Marine Sanctuary Research and Development Concept.* Raleigh, N.C.: Division of Archives and History, Department of Cultural Resources, 56 pp.

Office of Coastal Zone Management. 1977. *Draft Permit to Conduct Scientific Research in the Monitor Marine Sanctuary* (in response to MRRF proposal for environmental engineering studies and site charting). Washington, D.C.: NOAA, Department of Commerce.

Pepi, K. F. 1978. Historic Preservation of the *Monitor*, in *The* Monitor, *Its Meaning and Future.* Washington, D.C.: Preservation Press, National Trust for Historic Preservation in the United States, 8–9.

Peterkin, E. W. 1977. *Memo on U.S.S.* Monitor *Hull Plate Status, Plate Treatment by R. N. Bolster, Photography and Interpretation by E. W. Peterkin, Microchemical Analysis by C. D. Beacham.* Washington, D.C.: Naval Research Laboratory.

———. 1978. The Construction, Contents, and Condition of the Wreck of the U.S.S. *Monitor*, in *The* Monitor, *Its Meaning and Future,* ed. L. E. Tise. Washington, D.C.: Preservation Press, National Trust for Historic Preservation in the United States, 22–28.

———. 1981a. Building a Behemoth, *Civil War Times* 20, no. 4, 12–21.

———. 1981b. To Raise Her, *Civil War Times* 20, no. 4, 42–43.

———. 1981c. Stereo Postscript, *Civil War Times* 20, no. 4, 46–49.

Peterson, C. E. 1978. Conservation Systems, in *The* Monitor, *Its Meaning and Future,* ed. L. E. Tise. Washington, D.C.: Preservation Press, National Trust of Historic Preservation in the United States, 92–99.

———. 1984. Conservation of the Anchor and Chain (Recovered from the Wreck of the USS *Monitor*, August 1983), *Cheesebox* 2, no. 2, 1, 3–4.

Rossler, R. N. 1995. (October) Treasure of the Depths, *Diver Training Magazine,* 40–47.

Schneider, K. A. 1975. (2 September) Letter to Robert Sheridan Confirming Membership in the Technical Review Group for the Monitor Marine Sanctuary (original in author's possession).

Searle, Capt. W. F., Jr. 1978. Saving the *Monitor*, in *The* Monitor, *Its Meaning and Future,* ed. L. E. Tise. Washington, D.C.: Preservation Press, National Trust for Historic Preservation in the United States, 112–22.

Sheridan, R. E. 1976. Comment on Finding the Ironclad *Monitor* after 111 Years, *Marine Technology Society Journal* 10:41–42.

———. 1977. (fall) "Quite a Curiosity": The Project to Recover the U.S.S. *Monitor*, *Sea History, Journal of National Maritime Historical Society,* 10–12.

———. 1978. Site Charting and Environmental Studies of the *Monitor* Wreck, in *The* Monitor, *Its Meaning and Future,* ed. L. E. Tise. Washington, D.C.:

Preservation Press, National Trust for Historic Preservation in the United States, 33–44.

———. 1979. Site Charting and Environmental Studies of the *Monitor* Wreck, *Journal of Field Archaeology* 6:253–64.

———. 1983. (23 August) Letter to Robert White, Administrator of NOAA, Formal Complaint about North Carolina Personnel Conflicts of Interest, Being on the Review Board for Permits and Receiving NOAA Contracts (copy in author's possession).

———. 1992a. (16 October) Letter to William H. Hooke, NOAA Deputy Chief Scientist, U.S. Department of Commerce, Washington, D.C. (copy in author's possession).

———. 1992b. (5 November) Letter to Annie Hillary, Acting Chief, Sanctuaries and Reserves Division, NOAA, Washington, D.C. (copy in author's possession).

———. 1993. (10 February) Letter to Mrs. Reardon's Eighth Grade History Classes, Readington Middle School, Readington, N.J. (copy in author's possession).

———. 1997. (4 December) Letter to John Broadwater on the Plans to Recover the *Monitor* Turret (copy in author's possession).

———. 1998. (11 September), Letter to John Broadwater, Manager, Monitor National Marine Sanctuary (copy in author's possession).

Smith, G. R. 1993. (26 December) Last Chapter of the Ironclad, *Western Broome Penny Saver Plus* (Binghamton, N.Y.), 1, 6.

Stick, D. 1978. The Value of the *Monitor:* Above and Below Sea Level, in *The* Monitor, *Its Meaning and Future,* ed. L. E. Tise. Washington, D.C.: Preservation Press, National Trust for Historic Preservation in the United States, 75–79.

Still, W. N. 1961. Confederate Naval Strategy: The Ironclad, *Journal of Southern History* 27:330–43.

———. 1981. The Most Cowardly Exhibition, *Civil War Times* 20, no. 4, 32–37.

———. 1985. *Iron Afloat, The Story of Confederate Ironclads.* Columbia: University of South Carolina Press.

———. 1988. *The Historical Importance of the USS* Monitor, Naval History, Seventh Symposium of the U.S. Naval Academy, Scholarly Resources, Wilmington, Del.

Stimers, A. C. 1936. *The Monitor and Alban C. Stimers.* Orlando, Fl.: Julia Stimers, publisher, Durbrow, Ferris Printing.

Subcommittee on Fisheries Conservation, Wildlife, and Oceans. 1997. *Hearing on the U.S.S. Monitor National Marine Sanctuary,* Honorable James Saxton, New Jersey, Presiding, U.S. Congress, Washington, D.C.

Sutterley, M. C. 1996. (12 February) Letter to Robert Sheridan from Secretary of Camp Olden Civil War Roundtable, Hamilton, N.J. (original in author's possession).

Thomas, Mayor V. J. 1977. (27 December), Letter to Robert Sheridan about

Bringing the Monitor Research and Recovery Foundation to Norfolk, Virginia (original in author's possession).

Tise, L. E. 1978a. The *Monitor:* Its Meaning, in *The* Monitor, *Its Meaning and Future,* ed. L. E. Tise. Washington, D.C.: Preservation Press, National Trust for Historic Preservation in the United States, 13–17.

———. 1978b. The *Monitor,* An American Artifact, in *The* Monitor, *Its Meaning and Future,* ed. L. E. Tise. Washington, D.C.: Preservation Press, National Trust for Historic Preservation in the United States, 63–65.

———. 1978c. The *Monitor:* Its Meaning and Future, in *The* Monitor, *Its Meaning and Future,* ed. L. E. Tise. Washington, D.C.: Preservation Press, National Trust for Historic Preservation in the United States, 127–32.

———. 1981. Off Carolina Searching for the *Monitor, Civil War Times* 20, no. 4, 38–41, 44–45.

Torricelli, Sen. R. G. 1997. (10 December) Letter to Robert Sheridan Regarding Recovery of the *Monitor* (original in author's possession).

Uddemann Inc. 1976. *Plan to Raise the* Monitor *Hull,* Eight Step Diagram. Stockholm: Uddemann Inc.

Vogel, S. 1998. (11 June) The Monitor's Last Fight, *Washington Post,* Metro Section, D1, D8.

Watts, G. P. 1975. The Location and Identification of the Ironclad USS *Monitor, International Journal of Nautical Archaeology and Underwater Exploration* 4:301–29.

———. 1982. The Monitor Is No More, *Cheesebox* 1, no. 1, 4–5.

———. 1984. Monitor '83, *Cheesebox* 2, no. 2, 1–7.

———. 1985. Deep-Water Archaeological Investigation and Site Testing in the Monitor National Marine Sanctuary, *Journal Field Archaeology* 12, no. 3, 315–32.

Weeks, G. M. 1863. (March) The Last Cruise of the *Monitor, Atlantic Monthly* 11:366–72.

Welles, G. 1996. The First Iron-Clad *Monitor,* in *Annals of the War Written by Leading Participants North and South* (originally published by *Philadelphia Weekly Times,* 1879), ed. A. K. McClure. Edison, N.J.: Blue and Gray Press, 17–31.

Wood, J. T. 1956. The First Fight of Iron-Clads, in *Battles and Leaders of the Civil War* (selections from original 1887–1888 edition by R. U. Johnson and C. C. Buel), ed. N. Bradford. New York: New American Library, 97–109.

Zimmer, Congressman D. 1993. (21 January) Letter to Mrs. Reardon's Eighth Grade History Class, Readington, N.J. (copy in author's possession).

Index

About the Author

Robert E. Sheridan is a marine geophysicist and a marine geologist who studied the North American Atlantic continental margin for forty years. A descendant of a Union army veteran, his work on the discovery and recovery of the USS *Monitor* allowed him to combine his vocation with his avocation as a Civil War history enthusiast. Robert Sheridan has a bachelor's degree in geology from Rutgers University and master's and Ph.D. degrees in marine geophysics from Columbia University. He was an associate professor at the University of Delaware in 1973 when he was part of the team that discovered the *Monitor* wreck off Cape Hatteras. Sheridan moved to Rutgers University as a full professor in 1986 and retired in 2003. Sheridan lives with his wife Karen in New Jersey.

The Naval Institute Press is the book-publishing arm of the U.S. Naval Institute, a private, nonprofit, membership society for sea service professionals and others who share an interest in naval and maritime affairs. Established in 1873 at the U.S. Naval Academy in Annapolis, Maryland, where its offices remain today, the Naval Institute has members worldwide.

Members of the Naval Institute support the education programs of the society and receive the influential monthly magazine *Proceedings* and discounts on fine nautical prints and on ship and aircraft photos. They also have access to the transcripts of the Institute's Oral History Program and get discounted admission to any of the Institute-sponsored seminars offered around the country.

The Naval Institute also publishes *Naval History* magazine. This colorful bimonthly is filled with entertaining and thought-provoking articles, first-person reminiscences, and dramatic art and photography. Members receive a discount on *Naval History* subscriptions.

The Naval Institute's book-publishing program, begun in 1898 with basic guides to naval practices, has broadened its scope to include books of more general interest. Now the Naval Institute Press publishes about one hundred titles each year, ranging from how-to books on boating and navigation to battle histories, biographies, ship and aircraft guides, and novels. Institute members receive significant discounts on the Press's more than eight hundred books in print.

Full-time students are eligible for special half-price membership rates. Life memberships are also available.

For a free catalog describing Naval Institute Press books currently available, and for further information about subscribing to *Naval History* magazine or about joining the U.S. Naval Institute, please write to:

Membership Department
U.S. Naval Institute
291 Wood Road
Annapolis, MD 21402-5034
Telephone: (800) 233-8764
Fax: (410) 269-7940
Web address: www.navalinstitute.org